ROOMS

To Donna —
Blessings.
Becky

ROOMS

an AUTOBIOGRAPHY

by REBECCA WILSON

Scriptures taken from the Holy Bible, New International Version®, NIV®. Copyright © 1973, 1978, 1984, 2011 by Biblica, Inc.™ Used by permission of Zondervan.

Most of the photographs in this book are by the author. Those by John Johnson are used by permission.

Published by Artist Publishing, Goshen, Indiana
HarrietLM@comcast.net

ISBN 979-8-218-25392-9

PREFACE

I have always visualized life as a house. Each room in that house represents a portion, location, or experience in life. People frequently tell me my life has been unusual and interesting—that I should write a book. So, here you are—this is my "house" and the rooms I've experienced. I hope it blesses you as God has blessed me.

When I set out to write the story of my life, I knew there would be three "difficult" topics I must either completely omit or honestly include—my dad, my sister, Cheri, and my daughter, Amanda. Ultimately, after much prayer and consideration, I chose to include the pertinent information about those three painful topics—to "air" my dirty laundry, so to speak. Just reliving them, through writing, caused me renewed cathartic pain, but this book wouldn't be a true representation of my life if I left them out. Through both devastatingly painful and incredibly wonderful experiences, God has developed my character. Knowing that this book will never be distributed to the general public and will only be read by carefully selected individuals, who in some way might benefit by having the whole story, I hereby present all the public and private, bare bones of my life.

Rebecca Wilson, 74 years old, 2023

INTRODUCTION

As I age, I am increasingly reminded just how valuable and important a "safe" childhood is for producing a well-balanced, morally rich, and productive adult. A solid foundation lays a firm beginning in attitudes, morals and motivation. While I am calling it a "foundation" or "basement," in no way do I want to downplay the importance of that "room." It is really the most critical of all the rooms in a house. A weak, cracked, or broken foundation can produce an adult riddled with problems and issues. That "baggage" can haunt one for life. For the most part (there are always exceptions), a child who experiences a solid foundation in life is usually fortunate to avoid mental, social and emotional turmoil in adulthood and to have a better chance at a "normal," happy life.

Let me define what I think a "solid" foundation includes. It is loving, supportive and kind. It teaches good morals and sound decision-making. It provides a child with the freedom to explore life choices with confidence. The child is nurtured, valued and prepared for life. His/her self-confidence grows through positive experiences. Through lessons learned from failures, the child learns to say, "I have failed," rather than "I am a failure." Self-motivation and the confidence to try again is strongly developed. The framework for life decisions is based on sound principles.

TABLE OF CONTENTS

Chapter   **page**

CHAPTER ONE
BASEMENT • FOUNDATION
CHILDHOOD
(Wabash, Indiana)
1949-1962

I was born July 8, 1949, in Wabash, Indiana (the first electrically lighted city in the world!). I am the product of a safe, happy and idyllic childhood. My "foundation" was solid. I thank God for that blessing every day. That one fact alone made a huge difference in my life.

At the time, my childhood just seemed "normal," but I now realize how rare it really was and how fortunate I was to experience such an upbringing. It wasn't perfect, but it was physically and emotionally safe, and morally rich. My parents were kind, middle-class, hard-working, self-motived, dedicated Christians. They both came from a "country" life and knew each other all their lives. They even played together when they were babies. Dad had three siblings, but Mom was an only child. They both attended Bachelor Creek Church of Christ and even though they went to different high schools, their families knew each other, so their social circles were similar.

DAD'S PARENTS

Dad's parents, Allen and Charlotte Wilson, were married in 1918. Grpa Allen served as a baker in France during W.W.I. For many years, until it broke, I had the shovel he used to dig trenches in France. Dad (DeVon) lost his father (a mail carrier) to cancer at age 45, when Dad was a junior in high school. With four children to care for (three boys and a girl) and no education beyond high school to rely on, his mother, Charlotte, had

Allen Wilson 1918

Allen and Charlotte Wilson 1918

Allen and Charlotte Wilson circa 1924

  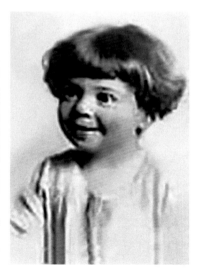

Dale, Eileen, DeVon (Dad) (Dean had not yet been born.)

a difficult struggle to support her family. She had never worked outside the home before, but found a job working as a clerk at J.C. Penney's. Charlotte died in 1989.

MOM'S PARENTS

Mom's parents, Faye and Ora Haupert were married in 1919. Grma Faye attended Manchester College for one year, then taught all the elementary grades in a one-room schoolhouse for a year until she got married, when she had to resign. In 1919, women teachers were not allowed to be married. Decades later, she still talked about her students fondly. I know she would not have recognized teaching as I experienced it.

Grpa Ora dropped out of school in the eighth grade to support himself. For reasons unknown to us, he had been raised by a family acquaintance and didn't ever really feel loved or accepted. He had a hard life. Grpa Ora was in the army, but was never posted overseas. Marrying Faye was the best thing he ever did. She brought love, stability, and God into his life. They were married for 62 years before Ora died in 1981. Faye died in 1999 at age 98.

Marcellus and Rebecca Hubbard circa 1925 (Faye Haupert's parents) I was named after Great Grma Rebecca.

A rare photo of Ora Haupert 1896

**Faye and Ora Haupert
circa 1916**

She had been a sickly baby and no one thought she would live long.

My grandparent's generation saw more changes than any other in the history of mankind. They went from horse and buggies to a man on the moon, from the beginnings of the telephone to computers. They lived through W.W. I, W.W. II, the Korean War and the Vietnam War.

One interesting tidbit about both sets of grandparents. Brothers married sisters on both sides of my family, so we had double cousins! On Mom's side, Ora and his brother, Ross, married sisters, Faye and Ada. On Dad's side, Allen and Bryon, married sisters Charlotte and Enola.

I always loved Dad's baby picture—the devilish twinkle in his eye and that kicking foot that showed he wanted to get a kick out

Faye and Ora Haupert circa 1975

MY PARENTS

DeVon Wilson, born 3-9-1923 **Marcella Haupert, born 1-8-1924**

of life! Grma Charlotte always said he was an active and curious little stinker. That continued throughout his life.

One Sunday, as a youngster, he misbehaved in church. His dad picked him up and carried him out, while Dad cried out loudly, "Don't spank me, daddy!" It disrupted the whole church service.

Eileen, Dad's sister, was the favored child and her parents doted on her, to the exclusion of the three boys. Dad felt ignored and undervalued. Even Grpa Allen's obituary supported that bias: "Allen is survived by his wife, Charlotte, his daughter, Eileen and three sons." No mention of their names at all! I always suspected that because Dad felt ignored and undervalued as a child, he did whatever he could to get attention and prove himself his whole life.

Money was extremely tight. To help makes ends meet, his parents raised a garden and the kids wore hand-me-down clothes. Dad was a self-starter and a hard-worker and wanted to go to college. He knew he would have to find a way to make that happen without any financial support from his mother. "Lazy" is not a word anyone would ever use to describe Dad! He was never still. He worked odd jobs and was the church janitor. He hitch-hiked to and from Fort Wayne Institute of Technology (an hour away) every weekend so he could come home to see Mom. He earned his bachelor's degree in chemical engineering in three years by going year-round, to temporarily avoid the draft, and so he could finish his education without interruption.

After graduating, he enlisted and served as a radio gunner in the Army Air Corps until the end of W.W. II. The war ended just as he was about to be sent overseas. He and Mom were married when he got a furlough in

DeVon Wilson
Chippewa High School, 1941

Marcella Haupert
Urbana High School, 1942

1945. After the military, Dad worked at General Tire and Rubber Company in Wabash until he retired 40 years later. One of the rubber compounds he wrote was used on a NASA space capsule. Dad was never idle outside of work, either. He served as Sunday school superintendent, Sunday school teacher, youth group leader, church treasurer, choir member, deacon and then elder, a Toastmaster, a Mason, and was president of the PTA. He also bowled on a league, played on the church baseball and volleyball teams and spent two years building Mom a house with his own two hands (1958-60). He could fix anything and loved helping people, so his handyman skills were a real blessing.

Dad was pleasant, jovial, appealing, charming, fun-loving, quite handsome, and very teasable. He went out of his way to open doors for

people, assist women with heavy loads, etc. People always raved about his gorgeous curly hair (which only Cheri inherited). Even in his 90's, his hair still brought him much admiration and attention. He was a good father (when he was around). But he was busy and away from home in the evenings, so Mom carried the burden of family life.

Mom (Marcella Haupert) was an attractive farm girl with a gentle soul. Her parents, Faye and Ora, farmed about 100 acres and struggled financially all their lives, but they were rich in other ways. Mom raised the grand champion calf one year in 4-H and that income paid for her first year of college.

FAMILY LIFE

DeVon and Marcella Wilson married June 12, 1945

Mom graduated with a bachelor's degree in Home Economics from Manchester College in 1945. She was a talented seamstress, played the piano and organ at church for decades, and was an excellent cook. After they married, Mom stayed home to take care of three kids. I remember she baked every day and we always got to "lick the pan." She was an excellent mother. When I was just a few months old, I got whooping cough. She held me and walked me for weeks. Fortunately, penicillin had just been discovered and it literally saved my life.

Mom and Dad started their married life living with Grma Faye and Grpa Ora for two years. Then they bought a duplex in Wabash, living in half of it while, Dad's sister, Eileen, and her husband, Paul, lived in the other half. I do have one memory of that old house in Wabash. I got my head caught between the banister railings one day and Mom couldn't get me out. She had to call Dad home from work to rescue me

Brent (1)	Becky (3)	Cheri (5)
Born 1-14-1951	Born 7-8-1949	Born 3-19-1947

When I was three or four, they bought a small house on five acres out in the country, north of Wabash on State Road 15. I learned later they paid $8,000 for that house—an incredible sum at the time. Our new little house was closer to both sets of grandparents and just a quarter mile from Bachelor Creek Church (and Grma Charlotte and Grpa Ford, who lived next to the church), which was their social life. In our new house, Cheri and I shared a bedroom with a flat roof. My favorite memory of that house was listening to the rain beat on that roof while snuggled securely in bed. We had a chalk board in the small hallway and I constantly played "teacher" with my siblings.

The whole house was heated by one huge register in the living room. We loved to straddle the grate till we got overheated. There was a telephone in the front entry, and we shared a party line with the neighbors. We had to listen for our special ring before we answered the phone. Each house

Cheri 3, me 8 months, 1950

Circa 1959

on the party line had a different ring. It was very tempting to eavesdrop on our neighbors' calls, but we weren't allowed to do that.

I adored my Dad. He used to put his hands on our shoulders, with fingers under our armpits and lift and twirl us till we were magically sitting on his shoulders. He was always fun and cheerful. He never got angry. One time, when I was three or four, we were swimming in a pool somewhere. I was scared and did not want to put my head under the water. Dad was holding me and knew how scared I was. But he decided it would be funny to dunk me under. He howled with laughter at my fright. Even at that tender age, I was devastated that someone I trusted completely would betray me

Age 6 1955

Right: 1957

and laugh at my fear. It was the first time I had encountered what I now consider to be a tiny "mean" streak in Dad. A tiny seed of doubt about Dad was planted, and there was a slight dent in my adoration for him.

I later learned to swim and got over some of my fear, but have never been completely comfortable in water. Many years later, at the lake, when everyone else was learning to water ski, and pressuring me to try it, I made myself learn, too, even though I didn't really want to. I managed to get up as the speed boat pulled me along behind. I struggled until I stayed upright for a while, then I purposely let go of the rope. I'd had enough. All that mattered to me was that I had proven to myself that I could do it. I never skied again.

We had a fenced in back yard (with a swing set), but no fancy playground toys—no playhouse, no jungle gym, no pool. In fact, when it got really hot (it had to be 80 degrees) we filled out little red wagon with water and that was our "pool." We didn't always have the latest toys, but we did get a hula hoop when they came out. We spent hours playing with it.

Mom was a stay-at-home mom until my younger brother, Brent, started first grade at Chippewa in 1957 (our county school had no kindergarten). Then Mom began teaching Home Ec., English, and P.E. at Roann High

School. One time, mom was so tired, she stayed home from church on Sunday morning to rest. Grma Faye "spoke" to her about that, and it never happened again. Poor Mom. She must have been exhausted most of the time. I vividly remember her sleeping on the living room couch while we watched TV in the other room. She always said she was "resting."

After the county schools consolidated in 1962, Mom moved to Southwood High School. She purposely avoided teaching at Northfield, where we kids attended, because she thought that might be awkward for us. She taught for 18 years and never cashed one paycheck. Her salary always went straight to the bank into her children's college fund.

We rode the school bus to Chippewa Elementary School. Dad had attended Chippewa when it was a high school. He played basketball there and Mom was cheerleader at Urbana High School. By the time we attended, Chippewa was an elementary school with only one class for each grade—first through eighth grades. I have fond memories of Chippewa and only had one teacher I didn't like—Mrs. Duker (fourth grade). Most of the teachers were kind and caring. I loved my first-grade teacher, Mrs. McKinley and absolutely adored my fifth-grade teacher, Mrs. Rife. She also happened to be the mother of Mom's friend, Georgia Bush. I vividly remember having a carton of milk each morning during our daily break. We sat in long rows of desks attached to each other front to back. We never packed our lunches. Mom gave us each $1.25 every Monday for that week's lunches (25 cents a day!), so we could eat in the lunchroom. I loved recess, and I know I played well with others, but I also remember sitting alone sometimes singing songs to myself, like "Around the World in Eighty Days," and "Somewhere Over the Rainbow." I dreamed of seeing the world. I had an insatiable curiosity to know how the rest of the world lived and to see all the wonders of the world. I wasn't shy. My report card frequently said I talked too much!

I remember every Friday, we went to a small cabin just off the school property for a Bible class. Schools would never allow that now, but I loved it especially since it was taught by Jean Wilson, a relative.

My older sister, Cheri, was feminine, attractive, strong-willed, popular, musically-talented, and a leader, but rather "haughty." She was the first (and Brent and I sensed "the favored") grandchild when we were young. Cheri and Grma Faye had a special musical bond and they frequently played piano-organ duets at church. My younger brother, Brent, was handsome, quiet, laid back, kind, gentle and easy-going—traits they said he inherited from Grma Faye's father, Grpa Marcellus. He was left-handed and they made him switch to using his right hand. I felt so sorry for him. Educators don't do that today, knowing it can create other issues. I often wonder if that hindered Brent in any way.

Brent and I were very close in age (just 18 months apart) and had a good relationship. We spent long hours playing together. I was a tomboy—I hated the thought of washing my hair all the time! I wanted to run and go on adventures. I frequently sat on Brent and pinned him down when we wrestled. When he finally got big enough that I could no longer do that, Dad warned him he couldn't get even by sitting on me, since I was a girl. Brent always resented that! It wasn't until my teen years that my feminine side began emerging.

I was the middle child and, as proves to be true so much of the time, I was the peace-maker between siblings (a great percentage of ambassadors are middle children). Cheri and Brent never really spent much time together, but I played with both ends of the threesome. Studies report that middle children frequently feel ignored, and that may have been true in our family. I wasn't exactly ignored, but I was left to my own devices while Mom and Dad were busy dealing with Cheri's stubbornness, attitude, and treatment of others, and Brent's laid-back lack of motivation. But in the long-term, being left to my own devices was a blessing, as I learned how to solve my own problems and be independent. I was also the most adventurous of the three kids. As a child, Mom always said she never knew where I was. I could be in Timbuktu, for all she knew! Of course, none of us knew where Timbuktu was, but it certainly made me curious. My adventuresome spirit continued into my adulthood, when Mom literally never knew what country I was in. I never made it to Timbuktu, in Mali, but I wish I had! What fun it would have been to call her from there! My curiosity knew no bounds—a trait I inherited from Dad?

Sometimes we met up with Sally, a neighbor down the road, who had a pet raccoon. Her family owned the local gas station/bait and tackle/mini grocery store at the intersection of 15 and 115, called Poorman's Corner. Mom would sometimes send us there to buy a loaf of bread or lunch meat. One time we held a small circus for customers and charged ten cents. We collected a few dollars and donated it to missions at church.

Since Cheri and Sally were the same age, they were in the same grade at school, but I don't think Cheri socialized with Sally there. She played with Sally at home, but it was like she didn't want to associate with Sally in public. I often wondered about that.

Sometimes we ran up and down the lane to the back highway, built forts in the woods, went exploring, played baseball, wrestled, and NEVER played inside. We didn't have bikes at that age. After every meal Mom said, "Go out and play." We never checked in, and because we lived in the country, there were no streetlights to alert us to the time, but we knew when it was time to come home for supper. Dad built us a sandbox inside a huge old tractor tire. Mostly, I remember us burying dead mice there after we took them away from the cat.

One time, Sally, Cheri and I formed a "club" of some kind. They got to be president and vice president. I was assigned the job of being the treasurer. We each paid five cents in dues. Since I had no idea what a treasurer was supposed to do, I felt rich and spent that 15 cents on candy!

Before Coke and Pepsi were well-known, Grma Faye bought "Fizzies" at the store. They were colored tablets (purple was grape, pink was cherry, etc.) that you could drop into a glass of water to make it carbonated. We thought that was great! Then Coke/Pepsi became popular, and we decided to try it, so we bought a bottle down at Sally's store. We tasted it lukewarm and weren't impressed. No one told us it was supposed to be ice cold!

We got a black and white TV (a fairly new thing!) when I was about six years old (1955?). It was on a rotating stand so we could turn it to watch TV while eating in the kitchen, but Mom would not allow that. Dinner time was for family. We had three channels (ABC, NBC and CBS) and no remote control! I loved watching Mighty Mouse ("Here he comes to save the day!"), The Lone Ranger ("Hi-Ho Silver!"), Howdy Doody, Captain Kangaroo (and Mr. Green Jeans) Roy Rogers and Dale Evans ("Happy Trails to You"), Red Skelton, Ed Sullivan, and The Lawrence Welk Show (we loved the Lennon sisters). But I couldn't make myself watch scary shows like Sea Hunt, and Twilight Zone. I didn't like being scared. We didn't watch a lot of TV. We were a game-playing family and spent many happy hours together playing board games (and tetherball, croquet, baseball), laughing, mushroom hunting, wrestling, and teasing each other.

My funniest memory of our back lane happened the summer I was about six years old. I ran fast and took off flying. I told mom I could fly! That became the joke of the summer. It hurt my feelings that everyone thought I was lying because with my vivid imagination, I really thought I was flying. It seemed so real to me—I wasn't purposely lying. When they insisted I show them, and I told them I couldn't fly while anyone was watching, I meant it. My imagination wouldn't work when others were around. My imagination served me well in life. But that was the only time I recall that it embarrassed me.

I never intentionally misbehaved, but I know I caused Mom and Dad some trouble. One year, in early December, I convinced Brent to climb up into the storage space in the top of the garage. There were loose boards laying across the beams so there was no secure "floor" in the attic. Up there we found boxes of gifts, which we figured out were to be our Christmas presents! We agreed not to tell anyone what we had found. But that night at dinner, I proudly announced I had found a toy saxophone for Cheri and a new basketball for Brent. Mom and Dad didn't say much, but those are the gifts we got that year! They certainly didn't go out and buy different gifts just because I had been nosy and couldn't keep my mouth shut! Today, I have a sign in my office that says, "God, please walk beside me, put your arm around me, and put your hand over my mouth." I still struggle with keeping my mouth shut!

Another time, I had coaxed Brent up to the garage attic space when Mom called for me. I told Brent to sit still in the middle of the boards so he wouldn't fall. But while I was climbing down to see what Mom wanted, he sat on the end of a board, fell to the garage floor and broke his foot. I don't recall ever being punished for that. I think Mom and Dad knew my terrible guilt was enough punishment. I was too nosy and curious for my own good—a trait I inherited from Dad, who was the biggest snoop of all.

One day, I had been especially good all day, and Mom rewarded me by letting me stay up a half an hour later than Cheri and Brent. She "let" me iron Dad's hankies. I hated that job and decided right then and there, that it didn't pay to be good!

Dad had the strangest expressions. "Dad gum it." "What in tarnation?" "Crout a mile!" "What in the Sam Hill?" "Gee for socks" and "Fang Bang Bang." But I suppose those were better than cussing!

Dad was an eternal optimist. He believed and trusted everyone, thus making him susceptible to being taken advantage of—and he was! Mom, on the other hand, was a pessimist in private. She was a worrier and doubted things would turn out well, cautioning us about everything, always questioning outcomes and quietly making discouraging comments. But in the public eye, she was cheerful and positive, an encourager.

Mom was an excellent cook, so we always loved what she fixed. But one day she fixed liver and onions. I hate liver. It makes me gag. To this day, it is the one food I cannot eat and that is saying a lot because I've been to 57 countries and have eaten things you would not believe. But Mom was from the old school of thought—we weren't spoiled. She was not about to fix something different just because I didn't like what was on my plate. We were expected to clean our plates before we left the table, not matter what. So, whenever she served liver, I sat there for several hours, unable to eat. Leftovers were a constant at our house. We didn't waste anything.

Dresses by Grma Faye, Easter, 1955

My parents grew up during the Depression, so things were repaired or reused, never thrown away!

Saturdays were for piano lessons and getting ready for church on Sundays. We took baths, washed our hair, ironed our clothes, tended to our nails, studied our Sunday school lessons, etc. And going to church meant wearing our best clothes—hats and gloves for the gals, suits and ties for the guys. There was no children's church in those days, so we had to sit still through the sermon. But I loved the hymns and the message found in those verses. I taught myself to sing alto (and sometimes tenor) by watching the notes in the hymn book. Easter was the biggest Sunday of the year. We always got new Easter outfits (new dresses Grma Faye made for us).

As I searched for childhood photos for this book, I noticed that almost every picture had me wearing a dress Grma Faye made for me!

We all three took piano lessons. Cheri was masterful at it and sight read and played classical music beautifully. I was just average and, as an adult, play for my own amazement. Brent didn't thrive with piano lessons. We first took lessons from a lady (Mrs. Hipskind) that lived across from the courthouse in Wabash. While Cheri and Brent had their lessons, I walked a few blocks down to the library. What a wonderful world I discovered there! I loved to read—it helped me experience new things and fed my desire to experience the rest of the world. Later we took piano lessons from Mrs. Lavengood. We hated recitals. I think I took lessons for about eight years.

We all learned to play an instrument, too—Cheri a flute, me a clarinet, and Brent a trombone. Again, Cheri outdid us all. Her musical abilities were wonderful. Mine were just average. I vividly remember all of us gathered around the piano. Cheri played hymns and we sang in four-part harmony (I sang soprano). Sometimes we even sang specials in church. I joined the church choir in high school and continued doing so wherever I lived.

During the school year, we went to Grma Faye's house for dinner after church every Sunday. I suppose Grma was trying to give Mom a break from cooking since she worked full-time and had little time to relax. Every Sunday, Grma got up early, beheaded a chicken, started dinner, picked and arranged flowers for church, played the organ for church, taught Sunday school and then cooked a fabulous meal for all five of us! Now, I realize how tired she must have been every Sunday, but what wonderful times we had. The afternoon ended after we watched Marlin Perkins'

"Wild Kingdom" on TV. Then we went home and got ready for evening youth group at church. Following that, we had popcorn and Coke while we watched Bonanza. We weren't allowed to drink pop any other time of the week so that was a special treat.

Mom was very wise. She knew when to press an issue with us (and Dad!) and when not to. She used psychology! Once, when Cheri decided she was going to run away from home, Mom didn't try to talk her out of it. She helped her pack! Of course, Cheri came back a few hours later—after playing the organ for a while at a neighbor's house. Other times, if Mom knew one of us was lying, she sometimes waited till we got caught in our own lie, rather than lecture us about it. In other words, we came to the realization "naturally" that lying would come back to bite us. It was my precious mother who taught me to do something nice for someone every day and not let them know who did it.

Mom modeled how to honor her husband. She always saved the biggest piece of meat for him, never argued with him in public (or in front of us) and tidied up the house before he got home every afternoon. Sometimes, she even laid a chair across the living room doorway so at least one room stayed neat till he got home.

I am now amazed that Mom worked a full-time, stressful job and managed her second full-time job (running the home) with such grace and dignity. Our house was always clean, our homemade meals nutritious, and our clothes clean and neat. Since Dad was involved in so many outside activities, that meant Mom was frequently left to deal with the lion's share of parenting. She never said, "Wait till your father gets home!" No, sir! She dealt with our misbehavior then and there!

Dad was gone most evenings—church board meetings, elders' meetings, choir practice, barbershop quartet, Toastmasters, PTO, baseball, bowling, etc. He was a busy, active guy. But I vividly remember one time Dad was home for the evening and he showed us how to make popcorn holders out of newspaper. We were very impressed and loved his attention. Mom praised him for spending time with us. I remember wondering, "Why did she praise him for that? Was that unusual?" I didn't realize he hadn't been spending much time with us. His being gone most evenings just seemed normal to me.

Dad was very "old school." He couldn't break out of that "male domination" thinking. Brent was allowed privileges that Cheri and I weren't. He made sure Brent had a car in college, while I wasn't allowed one. As an adult, if we went out to eat, he always had to pay the bill because I was a woman. If I wanted to pay, I had to secretly consult the waitress before Mom and Dad arrived. Some of that was gallantry and some "male dominance" thinking. When I bought my first house, he expressed doubt that I would be able to take care of it (but I've done fine!). After they moved to a senior living community in N. Manchester, he voiced outrage that a woman was head of maintenance. After all, "What does a woman know about fixing things?" And when Abbi was going to be married, he was dumbfounded when he found out that I would be walking her down the aisle and giving her away . I figured I deserved that privilege since I was the one who raised her. He thought he should be the one to do that since he was the only male in her life.

Dad considered hugging his son to be unmanly, so even after Brent became an adult, Dad shook his hand when greeting him. Finally, Mom convinced him to show a little more affection and he began hugging Brent.

We knew we could never play one parent against the other. Mom and Dad had their disagreements behind closed doors but presented a unified front to us kids. We were not spoiled. They were strict, but we knew we were loved. Yes, my parents spanked us when we needed it, but it was never in anger, not prolonged, and not frequent. I remember the last time I was spanked. I was in eighth grade and had slammed a door because I was mad at Dad for something.

Yes, Mom worked two full-time jobs, but I'm sure Dad didn't "get" that. It was in the days before being a housewife and mother was considered a "job." So, he figured she only had one job—teaching. Men never helped out around the house in those days. Dad didn't know how to boil water and certainly never lifted a finger to help around the house. But he took care of all the yard work and cars and was a masterful repairman. There were times, however, when getting things fixed around the house didn't happen in a timely manner. I remember when we lived in the new house and our shower quit working. Mom waited patiently for dad to fix it. She walked through the living room to the other bathroom whenever she wanted to shower. She did that for several years before he "got around to fixing it." After he retired, he realized that he should do more to help Mom, so he took over making the bed each morning and helped around the house more.

When we were young, we started out with 25 cents for an allowance every Saturday. By the time I was in high school it was one dollar each week. We all had our chores to do and were expected to comply and obey. We made our beds, changed our sheets every Saturday (nothing smells better than cuddling under clean sheets fresh off the clothesline!), mowed yard, took out the trash, swept the kitchen daily, and Cheri and I had to wash dishes after every meal. Cheri always insisted that she wash the dishes, so I always had to dry. Cheri always got her way in things.

One thing that drove me crazy was that Mom saved, washed and reused plastic bags. Grocery stores were still using paper bags then, so these were like zip-lock bags, but not as fancy. I hated drying those things! What a pain. I decided that when I grew up, I was never going to reuse plastic bags. To this day, I don't!

Mom was a stickler about punctuality. She considered being late—especially to church—very rude! She preferred that we arrive places a few minutes early—a habit I still maintain today! She even went so far as to set all the house clocks ahead five minutes to help us leave the house on time. However, we soon caught on to her scheme. Dad had been raised

ALWAYS with a cat! 1956 and 1964

1958

Age 12   **Becky, Cheri, Brent 1966**

in a family that always ran late, so she had to retrain him when they got married, and she was successful! He became more punctual.

Since Mom was a home-economics teacher, besides teaching us to cook and sew, she made sure we knew and used proper table manners. She was also a stickler for grammar and spelling. To this day, I owe her much in that area. It eventually played into my career as a teacher—especially when teaching the language arts to future teachers and writing books.

Mom valued education. She made sure we understood that we would be going to college. I always sensed this value came from Grma Faye, who attended one year of college, which was unusual for a young woman in the 1910's. Mom's philosophy was that your husband may not always be around to take care of you, so you'd better have a degree to support yourself. She was also opposed to the husband being the only one who took care of the finances. She figured any sensible woman should know how to manage money. Not only did all three of her children earn college degrees, but I earned a master's and a doctorate and her daughter-in-law, Nore, earned a master's. All six of her grandchildren earned degrees, Kara and Jason earned master's degrees and Chad earned two doctorates! Mom was so proud of all of us.

We had the best of two worlds growing up—farm life up at Grma Faye's and Grpa Ora's (Mom's parents), and lake life at Grma Charlotte's (Dad's mom) and Grpa Ford's lake cottage. We spent a week at the lake cottage every summer. We didn't take many "trips" as a family because of the expense. However, just after my junior year in high school, Dad bought a pop-up trailer to pull behind our car and we drove out west. We had no air-conditioning in the car and with three teenagers crowded into the back seat, it got pretty hot. Once we got the beds pulled out in the trailer, there was no floor space, so things were tight. Mom cooked on a gas stove Dad rigged up. We loved Mt. Rushmore and all the prairie dogs in their holes. We didn't manage to get up Pike's Peak due to car troubles, but we saw Yellowstone, the St. Louis Arch, the dinosaur museum, and visited relatives in Oklahoma.

Grma Charlotte, a widow for many years, married Ford when Cheri was just a baby. Ford was the only grandfather we knew on that side of the family. Grpa Ford used to sing me silly songs (although he had a terrible voice) and called me "Jo Becky." He always said if he had to be a cat, he would want to belong to me because he knew how much I loved and spoiled cats.

We always had cats—outside cats with litters of kittens every spring. Between practically growing up on a farm and having litters of cats, we learned a natural education about birth and death. We did have a dog or two, but cats were our favorite. The idea of an "inside" cat was foreign to us, though. Cats lived outside and only came inside on occasion. I loved them, dressed them up in doll clothes, and smothered them with attention. That was the beginning of my life-long love of cats. One time, Brent, Cheri and I each had our own cat. Cheri named her cat "Inky", mine was "Chocolate" and Brent named his "Minerva!" Tibby was the cat we had the longest and she certainly produced the most kittens—year after year. We kept a box just outside the back door, where she birthed the kittens, and we kept an eye on them.

But I also noticed that sometimes a cat would just disappear. Living in the country, outside cats came and went as they pleased and sometimes didn't come back at all. But when I was an adult, Dad admitted that sometimes he had shot a cat (or dog) if he thought it was sick. Going to the vet was an unacceptable expense. Long after they retired, Mom wanted an "inside" house cat to cuddle. So I got her a sweet male tuxedo cat and named him "Oreo." I had him "fixed" and purchased a litter box and all the paraphernalia they needed. But I noticed that after they had had him for a while, he changed. Dad thought it was funny to tease him and provoke him to the point that Oreo turned "mean." Dad's hidden mean streak had emerged again. I took possession of the cat two years later, after Mom's and Dad's health declined. Oreo seemed relieved to be in a home where he was treated kindly. One time as an adult, when Mom and Dad came to visit me for a couple of days, I had been temporarily feeding and caring for a stray cat. It suddenly "disappeared." I always wondered if Dad had "taken care of it," so I wouldn't adopt any more cats.

We rarely ate out at restaurants. It was too expensive. There were no drive through "fast food" restaurants in Wabash. We were excited there was a Penguin Point south of town, and an A&W's, but we rarely went there. I can only remember going to the movies about three times in my younger years. It was an extravagance that was not part of our thinking. The only movies I can remember seeing as a child were Bambi and Perry (about a squirrel).

Grma Faye was the grandparent that had the biggest influence on my life. In the summer, each of us kids got to spend a whole week by ourselves up at Grma Faye's and Grpa Ora's on the farm. It was wonderful to have their undivided attention. Grma Faye fixed all our favorite foods and we got to go with Grpa Ora when he worked out in the barn or the field. I remember standing under the combine chute as the wheat poured down on us in the wagon. We were filthy, but happy kids. And if we were ever sick and couldn't go to school, we spent the day up at Grma Faye's!

We used to swing on the rope in the hayloft. The rope went through a pulley, so we had to hang onto both ends of the rope as we swung way out over the edge of the hayloft and over the farm implements below. If we didn't hang onto both ends, it would come out of the pulley, and we'd fall onto the dangerous implements below. Mom found us doing that one day and had a fit that Grpa would let us do that. But he would let us do anything! He let us ride to Roann (about two miles away) while standing on the side running boards and hanging onto the sides of his truck. There were no child safety laws then! Grpa taught me how to drive his tractor when I was six or seven. I drove round and round the circular driveway. Again, Mom wasn't too thrilled! We collected eggs in the hen house, frequently got our hands pecked by angry hens and then sat in the spooky basement to buff the eggs clean every day. The egg man came once a week to collect the large boxes of eggs. That egg money was valuable income for Grma Faye. She used to count her "egg money" to see if she had enough to buy groceries. They went to town to buy groceries every Friday morning. She sorted through her coupons, and they went to at least three stores to get the best deal on things.

I memorized the names of all the books of the Bible at night while in bed with Grma Faye. She always slept with us in the guest room till we fell asleep. Then she'd slip upstairs to sleep with Grpa. We didn't like to sleep with Grpa because his breath was so bad. He loved eating raw onions at every meal.

I got my love of birds from Grma Faye, too. She got me a coloring book about birds, and I learned all their names. She was an avid gardener, so I learned flower names when I helped her pull weeds. And she was very artistic. She arranged beautiful flower bouquets for church every Sunday, wrapped the most beautiful presents, created gorgeous quilts, and taught herself how to macrame in her 70's. But my favorite activity was helping her make homemade noodles. Even into adulthood, I still made noodles the way she did—all thinly sliced and spread out on the countertops to dry. Her potato soup with noodles was always my favorite, but I could never figure out why she served it on flat plates instead of in a bowl. When I asked her about it, she didn't know either. It was just the way she had always done it. After I became a mother, I made sure my girls got to visit Grma Faye to experience her potato soup! A few times, I even hand carried her homemade noodles back to Korea with me after my summer visits!

Grma Faye was a spectacular cook. Most of my valued recipes today came from her. She was famous at church potlucks. Everyone went for her cream pie. I've still never found a cream pie recipe as good as hers and that includes the Amish cream pies where I live now! While we visited for our individual weeks, she spoiled us with her cooking. I remember once Brent wanted homemade doughnuts, so she made them for him. He ate so many he got sick. When pizza first came to the U.S. (in the 50's or 60's?), she made her own rather than buy one, which they couldn't afford. They were great! And her homemade French fries were fabulous. She cut them paper thin, so they were crispy sticks. I didn't value "soft in the center" French fries till I went to college!

She was also an excellent seamstress. She constantly made Cheri and I dresses and vests for Brent including Easter outfits every year. She hand stitched beautiful quilts. She made stuffed animals to sell at the church bazaar. What a talented woman she was!

Grma Faye reinforced my love of reading. She had only one year of college before she began teaching in 1919, but she loved knowledge. She didn't like talking about people (that was gossip) but about ideas. When I was in college, I knew that during visits home I'd better be ready to discuss things I was reading and learning in college. From the Outer Hebrides to philosophy, she knew more than most people and I was always impressed that she was just a simple farm wife. There was a radio quiz show on at noon that we listened to while we ate in her kitchen. She always knew the answers before the contestants did. Grma Faye was a multi-talented woman—a woman before her time—highly intelligent, artistic, musical, an excellent cook, wise and kind-hearted. Her flower beds were fabulous and colorful. She weeded for hours in a dress (she would never wear slacks, even though Mom tried to get her to) and she took her gorgeous flower arrangements to church every Sunday. She had boxes full of ribbons she won at the county fair. She would have gone far in life had she been blessed with the opportunities and education I've had. As it was, she made her mark on us and that impact has stayed with me throughout the decades. Her love of reading was contagious. She would sit on the couch with all three of us grandkids by her side and read to us till she fell asleep. We nudged her till she woke up and read again. To this day, I consider the day wasted if I don't have time to read. I was fortunate to teach Children's Literature during my 25 years teaching college and I always thank her mentally for instilling that love of reading in my soul. I always quoted this last stanza of a poem by Strickland Gillilan to my college students:

"You may have tangible wealth untold…
Caskets of jewels and coffers of gold…
Richer than I you can never be …
I had a mother who read to me!" (or Grma!)

In the 1940's, during W.W. II Grma began writing letters to a young girl in Germany named Astrid. They corresponded for many years and Grma sent her gifts, including dolls and clothes she had made. In the mid-1960's, Astrid, now an adult, came to visit for three weeks! She was a modern woman and found farm life boring and difficult, I think. All she wanted to do was sit and watch American TV all day. It was difficult for Grma and Grpa and I think they were glad when the visit ended. I don't remember hearing anymore about her after that visit, so I don't know if they continued to correspond or not.

Brent and I "adopted" one of Grpa Ora's cows and named him Measles. He was fairly tame and we loved to sit on the fence to pet him. One Sunday, during our weekly family dinners up at Grma Faye's, we discovered we were eating Measles for dinner that day. Brent and I were heartbroken. I don't think Grpa even knew we had developed a special bond with poor Measles! He felt so bad.

We loved it when Grpa Ora got new pullets (baby chickens). They were so yellow, soft and adorable scrabbling around under those heat lamps. We weren't allowed to hold them much but loved watching them. Brent and I loved playing out in an old spare shed. It was crammed full of unwanted junk, so we tried to clean out a small space for us to play in. The adults nixed that because of all the dust, dirt, germs and mice in there. However, we did play out in the corn crib where the rats were, and in the water wagon Grpa used to haul water back the lane to his cows.

Ora was such a gentle soul. He loved animals and a neighbor's dog, named "Blackie" kept running away from his country home down the road and showing up to see Grpa. Grpa would return him to the family, but Blackie just kept coming back. Finally, the family realized they were beaten and gave the dog to Grpa. That dog went everywhere with Grpa. He rode in the truck, on the tractor, back to the fields, etc. Blackie became a true farm dog and was happiest when he was with Grpa. We rarely saw one without the other.

Grma Faye admitted that Grpa Ora was a real softie. He never disciplined Mom when she was growing up. Grma Faye did that. But she never got angry or raised her voice. The strongest language I ever heard her use was, "oh, pshaw!" Once, when Mom was having surgery, the three of us kids stayed at Grma's and Grpa's house. Of course, we started arguing about something. Grma stepped into the room, put her hands on her hips and calmly said, "Now see here!" That was all it took. We knew she meant business.

On Dad's side of the family, we had the wonderful lake experience. In the 1950's, Grma Charlotte and her sister, Enola, bought a terrible, run-down, old lakefront cottage on Winona Lake. They fixed it up somewhat by installing running water and an inside toilet. During the summers, our family went up to the lake every Sunday after church, where we played with our cousins. We spent a whole week there every summer. We learned to swim, row, boat, fish, and water ski. The cottage was in such poor shape that the floor was literally higher in the center than on the two sides of the cabin. But it worked perfectly for us. It didn't matter if we sat on the couch in our wet bathing suits or tracked water in from the outside. We certainly weren't worried about ruining anything! When I was in high school, the shower stopped working altogether. After that, during our week-long family vacations at the lake, we knew we would all be smelly by the end of the week from lack of showers, but who cared? Swimming was enough to keep us decent. After I began teaching (in 1972), Dad and

Family fun at our terrible, old, wonderful cottage on Winona Lake (Warsaw)

my Uncle Paul inherited the lot and cabin together. They had to either buy half from the other or sell it. The city condemned the cottage, and it was torn down. Dad and Uncle Paul sold the lot. I now regret I wasn't earning enough money to buy the lot. What wonderful memories I have of that old place. I wish we could have built a new cabin on that lot for the next generation to enjoy.

During the summers, we always spent a week at the old Pearson's Mill Church Camp, which I loved. I was very young the first time I went, and I got so homesick, Mom had to come get me. Thereafter, I loved it. It was later flooded when they built the new Mississinewa Dam, so they built a new church camp to replace it, but Rainbow Camp just wasn't the same. I also attended 4-H camp one summer, but it wasn't as fun as church camp.

In 1960, after two long years of Dad working on it every night and every weekend, we moved into our new 2000 square-foot house Dad had built just across the field from our old house. It cost $30,000. Brent had been slightly too young to help Dad work on the house. Cheri and I still shared a bedroom, but now there were two bathrooms! We had a separate family room, an office, and a huge living room. What luxury! I was ten and so impressed with how modern and up to date we were. And I vividly remember when Dad bought Mom a garage door opener so she wouldn't have to climb in and out of the car to open the door all the time. Such luxury! Mom and Dad lived in that house until 2013, when they moved to a retirement home in N. Manchester.

I remember when Alan Shepard was scheduled to be the first American in space in May, 1961. I was in sixth grade, and wanted desperately to watch that broadcast, but there was no television in our school. So I lied and acted sick so I could go to Grma Faye's for the day and watch the event. I felt terrible lying, but just had to watch that piece of history.

Dad needed a truck while he built the house. For a few years, Mom and Dad took turns driving the car and the old truck to work. Mom hated the week she had to drive it, because it had no heat. They never had a "new" car—always used.

Brent and I spent hours riding our bikes around the countryside and exploring places down country lanes. We rode to "the store" every day at Poorman's Corner to collect the newspaper for Dad. That was cheaper than paying to have it delivered to our house. Dad put a basketball hoop on the front of the garage. We had frequent croquet tournaments and Dad and Brent bonded over ping-pong in the garage. We were always barefoot—even on the gravel driveway. To this day, I don't like to wear shoes!

During the summers, we were busy with 4-H projects. During my ten years in 4-H, I always took cooking and sewing and had to produce a project to take to the fair every August. I usually earned blue ribbons. But poor Mom gave up her summer rest to patiently teach us everything she knew about cooking and sewing. I hate to think how many butter cakes and yeast rolls the family ate while I experimented. One time, well after my 4-H years were over, I was mending a white blouse with black thread just because I was too lazy to change the spool of thread on the sewing machine. Mom just shook her head and said, "Where did I go wrong?" But sewing skills came in quite handy for me over the years. I made my own dresses, bathing suits, slips, and robes. One year, as a teacher, I vividly remember making myself a new dress the night before school started as a treat to myself. Who doesn't feel better in new clothes? Being able to sew was a blessing. While Cheri excelled in cooking and my cooking skills were just o.k., I excelled in sewing, while her sewing skills were just o.k.

One Sunday evening, in 1962 (I was in eighth grade), while Mom was at home, the rest of us were involved in a semi-truck accident while trying to pick up a friend for youth group. We tried to turn left into our friend's driveway, just as the semi-truck behind us decided to pass us on the left. He

Sept., 1962, our car was crushed by a semi-truck.

hit us, went up a steep embankment and fell over onto our station wagon, grinding it into the ground. The car roof caved in and pinned us half-way down, but one back door sprang open so we could exit the station-wagon. The truck was carrying 17 tons of apple cider in glass jars, but not one jug was broken, and Cheri's broken nose was the only injury (other than sore shoulders and muscles). Mom remembered that as the day she almost lost her entire family. We found out later that our left turn signal didn't work. That wreck was traumatic for me and to this day, I still feel myself tense up somewhat when encountering large semi-trucks on the road.

What I remember most about our family life was the strong church influence, the solid family relationships (both sets of grandparents lived within five miles of us), family holidays, country life and innocence. I thrived under secure parenting and a great home life. I know now that what we experienced was good parenting.

While the environment I grew up in was carefree and wonderful, I didn't realize until adulthood the values that were instilled in me. Those values became part of my thinking. My parents taught me to work hard, to be honest, responsible and trustworthy, to dress modestly, abstain from drinking, smoking and drugs, to always do my best, to refrain from sex outside of marriage, to see and value people for their character, not for their outer appearance (like the world does), and to honor Christ above all else. I was taught not to give adults a reason to dislike me for my youth by being insolent or rude to them. I learned to "delay gratification," to work hard now for a future payoff. I learned respect and dignity, not to "show off" and to avoid being the center of attention. To this day, I don't like to be the center of attention (don't you dare throw me a surprise party—I'll

I seem a bit confused, holding my picture of Jesus and my toy gun! 1954

hate it!). I learned to be interested in others, to learn from all experiences, even if they were painful, because there is always something you can learn from hard times. In other words, I learned that living on the "straight and narrow" would help me avoid a plethora of pain and heartache in life. I wanted no part of the problems that can result from bad decisions (addictions/recovery, sexual promiscuity, unwanted pregnancy, drunk driving, abuse, divorce, financial hardships, prison, etc.). Now I would call those consequences paying "stupid tax" (a Dave Ramsey phrase!), but then I just knew I would have a much better chance for a rewarding life if I avoided all those bad choices. What a great foundation that was!

ELEMENTARY SCHOOL PICTURES

First grade, Chippewa Elementary School 1955-56 Mrs. McKinley

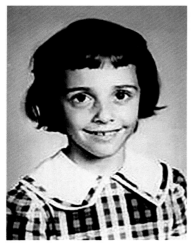
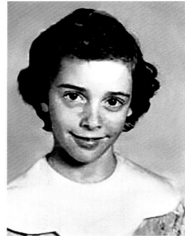

Second grade?   **Third grade**   **Fifth grade**

CHAPTER TWO
LAUNDRY ROOM
NORTHFIELD HIGH SCHOOL
(Wabash, Indiana)
1962-1967

I relate my high school years to being in the "laundry room" because here I washed out some old childish behaviors and ironed in new ones. I paid attention in church and youth group and put a little "starch" into my values and morals. I accepted Christ as my personal Savior and was baptized when I was 15. I matured past my tomboy days, became more feminine, and grew up some, even if my maturity didn't fully "come out in the wash" (blossom) until college.

I was miserable in eighth grade (aren't most middle schoolers?). Mom made me wear bobby pins (pin curls) at night and my hair always looked ugly. I got ugly braces and my teeth hurt all the time. But I was glad to have braces because my teeth were so crooked, I was embarrassed to smile. We drove to Fort Wayne once a month to see Dr. Berkey, the orthodontist. There were no orthodontists in Wabash. Dr. Berkey was over 80 years old when we started going to him and was still practicing when I got those dreaded braces off five years later. He was nice to us (Brent had to get braces, too), but during those five years, he had a new assistant every time we went because he was nasty to his staff! I suppose my parents couldn't afford a more expensive, younger dentist. Going to Fort Wayne was a new and daring experience for us. We were introduced to Azar's Big Boy hamburgers. I felt so brave walking down the streets of a busy city (if Mom dropped us off to park somewhere) or learning to shop in the mall. We certainly never had those experiences in Wabash! It made me feel quite brave. Having nice straight teeth changed my personality and I opened up and smiled a lot more.

I went to Chippewa through seventh grade (junior high school) and in eighth grade, moved on to Northfield when the newly consolidated junior high/high school opened in 1962. The feeder elementary schools were Roann, Urbana, Lagro and Chippewa. The bigger school was so different and modern, and classes were much larger than we were used to, but

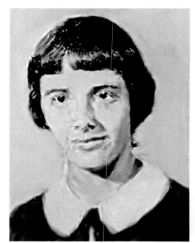  

Eighth grade   **Freshman 1963 (in the**   **Junior 1966**
                        dress I made for 4-H)

I don't remember having a very hard time adjusting. I met a wonderful new group of friends that I am still friends with today! Jenny, Sally, Sue, Becky and Linda came from Urbana and Roann Elementary Schools and had known each other before, but they welcomed me into their group. I don't recall having had any close friends at Chippewa, so it was wonderful having these new friends with similar Christian values and backgrounds. We were all innocent and naïve together. We had frequent slumber parties and laughed a lot!

The seventh and eighth grades were in one wing of the new building and the high school in the other three wings of the square. Our men teachers wore suits and ties, while the women wore dresses and high heels every day. Girls wore skirts or dresses every day. I was assigned to 8B, which indicated my aptitude, I suppose. 8A and 8B students were destined for college while 8C and 8D students were routed into the trades. In general, we had a very nice class of about 120 students. I don't remember even one class bully and we had wonderful class clowns.

I played clarinet in the concert and marching bands, sang in the choir, was involved with cheer block, French Club, and Future Teachers of America. I was honored to be inducted into the National Honor Society (along with my friends) and served as the president of Tri-Hi-Y during my junior and senior years, but I was certainly not in the highly popular group or one of the leaders of our class. I was very introverted

Senior Picture 1966-1967

and was content being in the background! Being a leader brought me too much attention. I didn't "bloom" until college.

In high school, I loved art class, with the sarcastic Mrs. Hamilton, took French I and II with Mrs. Deck, struggled through chemistry with Mr. Graham (Dad didn't understand why I couldn't "get" chemistry), hated algebra, but loved geometry (the art in geometry really appealed to me). However, I dreaded English class with Mr. Jones. He was really the only bully I can remember in high school. He was a retired army colonel who stood on the raised platform in our class and never made eye contact with us as he gazed over our heads. He was extremely stern, loved embarrassing students, and we were scared to death of him. We had a one-page theme due every Friday. I always got mine back on Monday with a big, fat, red "F", with absolutely no help or instructions about how to write better. That man convinced me I could not write. It wasn't until many years later that I discovered I could write! In fact, I learned to love writing. He just hadn't taught me how. His philosophy seemed to be that constant negativity and criticism was the best method of producing good writing.

By far, the most valuable class I had in high school was typing. Just knowing my way around a keyboard has helped me tremendously in life. I am amazed that with today's technology, students aren't taught to keyboard first! To me, it seems like we have the cart before the horse!

I always used the library period and bus rides home to do most of my homework. While other kids goofed off, I studied so my evenings were free. I may not have been the brightest, but I was diligent.

For some reason I couldn't explain, I didn't want to be like other teenagers. I never took summer school to be with my friends, or driver's education class. Dad taught me how to drive. I never had my own car, so I only got a little driving experience by going to town on errands for Mom, driving to youth group, or back and forth from marching band practice. But that never bothered me. I never rebelled. I wasn't a teenager who wanted to be out and about with the gang. I was an introvert and didn't care to be overly social. I was content to stay home, read (I LOVED to read!), sew, and have slumber parties with my friends. Many years later, when people insisted I was an extrovert, I still disagreed. "But you are a teacher," they said. "You have to be extroverted to get up in front of students all the time." But it was different with children. And, as I learned when I moved to the college level, even teaching in front of adults was O.K., because the focus was on the content, not on me. I was a facilitator!

I think even back then, I knew I wanted to be different than what the world said a teenage should be. My sister, Cheri, got a transistor radio as a gift one year and literally carried it around the house so she could constantly listen to rock and roll. That never appealed to me. Mom and Dad then got me a portable radio one year, but I barely used it. The Beatles were quite popular then, as was Elvis Presley, but I wasn't interested in rock and roll. Mom constantly played classical records on the stereo, so I grew up loving classical music. I still do. Van Cliburn, an internationally known classical pianist was my idol. I was beyond thrilled to hear him play in person when he came to the Honeywell Center in Wabash and then later to Taylor.

One day, I was walking down the hall in high school and I realized I was smiling. Then it dawned on me that I usually did! I decided I was basically a happy person or I wouldn't do that.

I didn't really date much in high school. Sue set me up with her cousin one time. I was a late bloomer and just wasn't interested in dating or dancing. I did sit with Bobby on the school bus, but we rarely talked. He was a friend from church. I worked on the Prom Committee but didn't attend the dance. Several of us gals dressed up in prom dresses and went out together and had our own innocent fun. But one year, Niles, who sat beside me in French, slipped me a note asking me to go to the prom with him. I wrote him back that I didn't dance but could attend the banquet (I was the chairman of the Banquet Committee). He didn't respond and I

**Junior year as president
of Tri-Hi-Y**

**Senior year as president of Tri-Hi-Y
(Becky, Sue, Jenny—fellow officers)**

was very disappointed, but I felt I had to abide by my values and morals. My youth group sponsors had cautioned us against dancing and I felt I needed to listen to their words of advice. I also opted out of the dancing segment of P.E. class one year and as punishment, the teacher made me write a paper about dancing.

When I was in junior high, a year or so after we moved into our new house, Mom and Dad developed a sudden, different, and rather intense friendship with a younger church couple. I had never seen them involved with other couples like they were with Nancy and Larry. We had them over for dinner a lot and went to their house a lot. Very unusual. After they had a little baby, named Marianne, we gushed over her. But for some reason the friendship seemed "odd" to me. Then it ended as suddenly as it had started. No one explained why. In the back of my mind, some suspicious questions arose—had Dad had an affair with Nancy? Was Marianne his child? And then I felt guilty for even thinking such thoughts. Surely not. It was probably just my overactive imagination.

When I was in high school, Dad resigned from the Elder's Board at church. That really surprised me because he loved being highly involved and up in front of people. He didn't give us a reason, but again, my suspicions were aroused. He loved being the center of attention, so it puzzled me why he would suddenly step away from the spotlight.

Cheri dated Ed Heckman in high school. He was tall, distinguished and very likeable—a good guy. They were serious, but then Mom and Dad made her break up with him because they found out he was a very distant cousin. Had that happened today, they probably would have ignored that fact, since it was so distant that it wouldn't have mattered, but they weren't sure back then. I remember how Cheri cried herself to sleep. In later years, they wished they had let her marry Ed. Perhaps things would have worked out better. Cheri's best friend in high school was Becky Monroe, the minister's daughter. They were thick as thieves and it seemed to me they encouraged some "haughtiness" in each other. I witnessed the battles between Cheri and Diane Hegel. I suspect Diane wanted to be friends, but Cheri treated her badly, so they couldn't stand each other.

Cheri graduated from high school in 1965 and went to Manchester College for one year. She hated it there (her roommate was gay) so she transferred to Cincinnati Bible Seminary (CBS—our church-related seminary) for her sophomore year. She declared that Manchester was not the same school Grma Faye and Mom had attended—it had become quite liberal and had moved away from its Christian roots. Mom and Dad were resistant to that transfer because CBS was not an accredited school, and they feared her degree would be worth very little. That proved true—she got a teaching degree, but didn't student teach and was never able to teach due to lack of accreditation. Ralph, a guy we knew from church, also attended CBS, so he and Cheri traveled back and forth together. They began dating and soon became serious.

I can still "see" Cheri putting her nose up in the air and turning away slightly when she was irritated with something or was refusing to do what she was told. When she and Ralph were dating, Cheri shared with Mom that Ralph told her he saw Christ in her. She was thrilled, but I often wondered if that assessment came from seeing her in that pose—like she was turning away from what she perceived as evil? I thought she just looked snooty and stuck up.

Then something very interesting happened. Dad gathered us all together during my junior year to tell us some special news. Our family had been selected as the American Field Service family for our high school! We were going to host a foreign exchange student from Turkey for my senior year. But what surprised us was that we didn't even know Mom and Dad had applied for it. Normally, the AFS organization selected a family that has a senior student of the same gender to be the "sibling" of the foreign student, but since my brother, Brent, was a sophomore, they decided that was close enough.

Nuri came to us in July,1966, and stayed for a full year. Brent and I traded bedrooms, so Brent and Nuri could have twin beds and I took the double bed (Cheri was in college by then). Brent and Nuri rode Brent's motorcycle to school early every morning for football practice and they were on the wrestling team together.

There was one event I remember vividly from that year. It was in January, 1967, when we lost all power due to a major snowstorm. We huddled at our kitchen table playing games by candlelight, trying to stay warm while we listened to the battery powered radio. Nuri couldn't believe we would lose power in America! We were stunned when the news came on the radio about the space capsule catching fire on the launching pad. Astronaut Gus Grissom, from Indiana, and two others were killed. The Bunker Hill Air Force Base in Kokomo, Indiana, was renamed Grissom Air Force Base in his honor in 1968.

Nuri was a Muslim, so we were introduced to new things. He wasn't a strict Muslim, and didn't pray five times a day, but we did have to avoid pork all that year. I felt sorry for Mom having to cook with new restrictions. Nuri was very pleasant and got along with everyone, which made it easier for us as a family. But I noticed that for some reason, Mom wasn't quite as

Nuri, my Turkish brother

Nuri, Brent, and me (with a cat!) 1966

"taken" with Nuri as the rest of us were. She was nice, but more reserved about him. Nuri was easy-going and quite popular with everyone. But he certainly didn't understand assertive American girls! I grew concerned about what I was seeing at school. After I reported it to Mom and Dad, we sat Nuri down to explain to him what to do about the girls that were overtly flirting with him. We certainly didn't want him getting a girl pregnant while on our watch! We took Nuri to church with us a few times and he enjoyed it. He seemed open to a new view of a loving God.

When the school year ended, it was hard to say goodbye to Nuri. Even though we wrote to him for a few years, we got no responses. We assumed he had been killed while doing his required military duty after he got back to Turkey. Then, I suddenly heard from him 25 years later, in 1992! He was married with two teenage sons and wanted to come to our 25th high school reunion! So I hosted them (in Osceola) and we got reacquainted. I was not impressed with his wife or sons. They seemed distant, snooty and uninterested in Nuri's high school experience. Later, I heard he got divorced. He came to visit again a few years later (in Mishawaka) for another high school reunion with his new wife, Mine (Mee' Nay), whom we loved! Brent (and Nore) flew his plane up from Indianapolis to spend time with them, too, and took them for a ride in Brent's plane. In fact, Nuri and Mine came twice more for reunions. We laughed that he attended more high school reunions than most of the "in country" students! And when I took the girls around the world in 2000, we spent time with Nuri and Mine in Istanbul.

During our 35th class reunion in 2002, I was awarded the prize for "most interesting life"—what a kick in the pants! We had no medical doctors or lawyers in our class, which was very unusual. So I guess, my life seemed the closest thing to "interesting." Only two of us in the class of 1967 earned doctorates and Susan, the other gal with a doctorate, did nothing with it (that we knew of). I was a Dean at Bethel at the time, so that seemed to impress the committee (go figure!).

I did a lot of babysitting during my high school years (for 50 cents an hour!). I always hoped the parents would stay out past midnight so I could earn $1.00 an hour! I got my first "real" job the summer before my senior year in 1966. I worked at Heckman Book Bindery in North Manchester. I got the job because the girl before me mashed her fingers in the press. I stood on a hard cement floor eight hours a day pressing books in the book press. New covers had just been glued onto old books. I had to press the books and then inspect them to make sure no glue was oozing out. Then I had to sand down any rough places where the pages had been accidentally glued together in the overflow. I detested that job but worked there for five summers. It certainly made me appreciate my education when I left the bindery every August to go back to college. I so appreciated the fact that I wouldn't have to work there for the rest of my life, like those other poor factory workers. I was blessed to have other options.

I started out earning $1.30 an hour at the bindery. By the time I left, five years later, I was earning $1.50 an hour. They gave me a nickel raise every summer.

My worst memory of the bindery was the summer I was assigned to the hot press. As books came down the line, I had to calculate the appropriate temperature for the press—an extra layer of responsibility. One day, a doctoral dissertation come down the line. I calculated the appropriate time and temperature, and put the book in the press, but when I tried to open it for inspection, I found all the pages had melted into one solid lump. I panicked, and quickly looked to see if there were other copies of the same dissertation waiting to be pressed (usually, several copies of the same book came down the line together). There were no other copies! That was the one and only copy of this poor doctoral student's dissertation and I had just melted it! The bindery was very nice about it and said it wasn't my fault. The dissertation pages were all typed on onion skin paper, which was easier to erase, but they could not stand up to the heat of the book press. This, of course, was in the days before computers. He had typed his whole masterpiece on a typewriter! To this day, I have no idea what that poor doctoral student did for a dissertation. I'd hate to think he was denied his doctorate because of my actions. After all, he had no dissertation to verify his hard work. Fifty years later, I still have occasional nightmares about that incident! I made sure when I completed my own doctorate in 1991, that I sent several copies to the bindery, and they weren't on onion skin paper! Thankfully, I was able to make easy corrections on the computer so I could use regular paper.

I developed a valuable habit while in high school. I learned to delay gratification. It started out simply as a way of eating. I first ate the food on my plate that was my least favorite, so I could save my favorite till last and taste it longer. Then I began doing unpleasant tasks right away to get them over with. I began making my bed the minute I hopped out of it every day, so I didn't have to worry about doing it later. I did my homework in the library at school so I didn't have to do it at home. I also discovered what a nice feeling it was not to have those unpleasant tasks hanging over my head! Thus, I gradually learned to avoid procrastinating.

In my final (tenth) year in 4-H, I surprised myself by running for 4-H fair queen. Dad was so sure I would win that he didn't take any pictures during the various times I came out on stage. He planned to take photos when I was crowned the winner. I wasn't, so we have no photos! I really didn't care, but Mom was not happy with him! What a hoot.

I graduated from Northfield High School in June, 1967, ranking 24th out of 114 students, which put me in the top fourth of my class. That surprised me, since I viewed myself as just average.

One of the local businesses gave each graduating girl a small cedar box—like a mini "hope chest." I don't remember what they gave the boys, but hope chests were very common for girls in those days—usually larger chests to store linens and household items as a girl "hoped" for marriage. I don't know if they still emphasize hope chests today, but to me, it clearly pointed out the role girls were to aim for—marriage. A tiny shadow of resentment grew within me, even though I didn't recognize it at the time. I

Me on the right

Nuri, Cheri, me, Mom, Brent 1967

**Back: Joyce, Jenny, Sue, Linda
Front: Becky, Pam, me, Sally**

With Nuri

subconsciously wondered why being married was the only thing to aspire to. Couldn't a woman do anything else in life? The urge within me to be different than everyone else was growing.

My wonderful high school friends and I parted ways. Some of them went to Manchester College, and some to Goshen College, while I went my own way to Taylor University. Again, it seems I didn't want to be like everyone else, and didn't feel a need to go where my friends went, although I'm not sure that was a conscious decision. I just knew I wasn't afraid to venture out on my own, where I knew no one. I was ready for the next "room" in my life.

CHAPTER THREE
KITCHEN
TAYLOR UNIVERSITY
(Upland, Indiana)
1967-1972

Being in college was like being in the kitchen of my "house." I planned the menu for my life (my major), studied recipes for success (education classes), cooked up my philosophy of teaching, stirred the pot of what I believed, and my Christian beliefs became more baked in!

I moved into the dorm with just my clothes and my portable typewriter. No electronics or TV, no phone or radio, no records or stereo—quite different than college students today!

Taylor was not of the same denominational background I was used to, so much soul-searching was required of me. Cheri kept writing to me, urging me to transfer to CBS because I needed to be "set in the faith," but I preferred to stay at Taylor where I had to sort out for myself what I did and did not believe. Besides, I had visited her at CBS and wasn't impressed. It almost felt "in-bred" to me, and I felt stifled there. CBS wasn't accredited and I wanted my degree to be worth something. I remember one time I visited there, the main topic on campus was whether or not the administration would allow interracial dating. They finally decided to ban it. I was floored.

I had a wonderful experience at Taylor and made many new and lasting friendships. Taylor was conservative—no alcohol, smoking, drugs, or dancing—and that was fine with me. I was comfortable with those things anyway. Girls were only allowed to wear slacks on Sunday night. I still remember how cold my legs were walking across that windy, frozen campus in skirts and dresses. We attended chapel three times a week. I definitely deepened my faith at Taylor and learned ways to incorporate that faith into teaching. Yes, I wanted to be an elementary teacher. I loved kids and other than nursing, girls didn't have a lot of choices in the 1970's. I thought about being an architect, but my math skills weren't that good and females were not widely accepted in architectural programs. I wanted to be an artist, but again, I wasn't that good, and I knew making a living at that would be difficult. I eventually added art as a minor.

I was a self-starter. I didn't need outside motivation to get me moving. I had an inner sense of drive that satisfied and fulfilled me. I never skipped classes or chapel, was diligent in my studies and always did what was expected of me.

There was one recent "new" thing at Taylor. They had just acquired a computer that filled an entire room. We were introduced to it and briefly taught some basics about how to program it, but it was still so new, that what little I learned, didn't stick.

I stared out as an average B/C student at Taylor, but as time went on, I learned how to study better and graduated with honors (cum laude). I worked part- time at the switchboard in the basement of the library. In other words, I was the Taylor University operator and had to learn how to work an old PBX board. One day, I took a call from an operator in Hong Kong. I was so impressed to be speaking with someone on the other side of the world! Of course, I didn't know that years later, Hong Kong would become one of my favorite (and most visited) cities in the world. For several years after graduating, I still slipped and answered the phone "Taylor University."

I lived in the ancient MCW dorm (which has since been torn down). Kathi Oosting, my roommate, and I played hours of canasta during study breaks. When someone came to spend the night, we slid down the stairs on old mattresses (with cockroaches) collected from the attic. We became

In Kathi's wedding

I lived in the MCW Dorm for three years

Marching Band   **My Taylor job working a PBX board**   **Mrs. Owens, my switchboard boss**

lifelong friends. Kathi is a wonderful person and I was blessed to have her for a roommate. We still keep in touch today.

Other than marching band and chorus, I was not very involved in extra-curricular activities at Taylor. I worked almost 20 hours a week at the switchboard and studied a lot, so there wasn't much time to join clubs and other activities. Besides, Kathi and I had too much fun playing canasta during study breaks!

At the end of my sophomore year, I was approached by the Resident Assistant to be a dorm counselor for my third floor hallway. So during my junior year, I served as a dorm counselor. That was interesting! I was responsible for the girls in my hall, maintaining discipline and rules, running the weekly meetings, solving problems and being a mentor for the girls. It was not a paid position. It was my first position of authority and I learned a lot about working with difficult people and situations. Kathi and I roomed together for three years, till she had to find cheaper housing due to a family issue. So, I moved to an off-campus college apartment with three other friends for my fourth year. We had to cook our own meals, so I got to experiment with Mom's and Grma's recipes. I missed Kathi dreadfully and didn't bond as deeply with my new roommates. I didn't have a car, so I had to walk many blocks to and from campus. Brent enrolled at Taylor during my junior year and he did have a car. I could never understand Dad's reasoning that Brent needed a car because he was a guy, but I didn't. That seemed very unfair (and sexist) to me!

I was very proud of Brent when he joined Wandering Wheels and rode his bicycle across the United States with them in the summer of 1969. Quite a feat!

I dated a few times in college, but never felt very interested in anyone in particular. In my sophomore year, I noticed a guy named Dee, whom I was interested in. I invited him to the Sadie Hawkins party (by written note, as was protocol for that "girl invite boy" event). He wrote back and turned me down. I found out later he looked me up in the yearbook and found me listed with the senior class, so he thought I was older than he was. They had put my yearbook photo in the wrong class! He later married Ruby, the sister of my brother's future wife, Eleanore (both Taylor students)! We still joke about that misunderstanding!

While I liked boys, I wasn't interested in overt behaviors that some of my friends took. I got quite peeved at Jonni, when she would cross a street just to walk past a boy she liked. I thought that was ridiculous. If you were supposed to meet, God would arrange it without your help.

Back then, education students didn't set foot in a classroom for observation or field work until their junior year, so declaring a major in something you had never had a chance to experience was a bit risky, but I was fortunate and loved teaching. Years later, at Bethel, we made sure students were out in classrooms their freshmen year to help them decide if teaching was for them.

When Cheri started college, I remember Mom wrote her long letters every week, and even though I didn't know what they said, I suspected Mom was lecturing Cheri, trying to give her advice—a continuation of what she had been doing verbally while Cheri was still at home. When I moved to college, I assumed I would get the same kind of long, advice-laden letters. But I didn't. I just got warm, newsy, loving notes every week. It seems Mom didn't feel a need to lecture or advise me, like she had Cheri. By the way, Mom continued to write me weekly letters from 1967 through my days in Korea—until 1989, when I was back in the U.S., and we began weekly phone calls on Friday nights. That's 22 years of faithful letter-writing! What a treasure that was to me!

Cheri and Ralph's wedding 1969

Cheri and Ralph got married in June, 1969 (at the end of my sophomore year), and I sensed there was some family tension over it. Ralph came from a very dysfunctional family with some "odd" personality traits. He'd had a difficult childhood and had been mistreated. Years later, I found out that Mom and Dad (and even Grma Faye) tried to caution Cheri that she would be marrying into a "strange" family and could expect problems or even some inherited "odd" traits in her own children. Cheri refused to listen, and the seeds of resentment and bitterness were planted in her heart. We liked Ralph. He seemed nicer and more normal than his family, but Cheri accused our family of not liking or accepting him. We did like and accept Ralph, but the adults felt it their responsibility to caution her, as good parents should. She took it badly. She claimed she had always felt like the "outsider" of the family (because of her stubbornness and refusal to listen to Mom and Dad?). So this caution from her parents compounded her sense of not being accepted.

During my junior year at Taylor, I applied for and was accepted (along with Gayle, a gal I didn't know) for a new, summer, "teaching abroad" program in England. We flew to London in June, 1970. Mom drove me to the airport in Fort Wayne, and I know she thought she would never see me again. It was the first time I had ever been on an airplane, and I was so excited! A few times, Dad had flown to Cleveland on business, but otherwise, no one in my family knew anything about flying or traveling overseas. It was a new experience for all of us. To give you an idea how novel it was, during his entire lifetime, Grpa Ora only spent two nights not sleeping in own bed—one night in Indianapolis visiting Brent and one night at Cheri's in Ohio. And to cement how small his world was—while Brent drove him around in Indianapolis on all the elevated highways and winding overpasses, he asked in amazement, "What would anyone want to live down here for?" Traveling was a foreign concept to them. I was introducing new parameters to their way of thinking, and it scared them. My parents and grandparents had never uprooted their lives, moved to a new place, and started all over again—finding new doctors, learning new streets names, and making new friends. They had never had to adjust to a new life. They could not imagine why I wanted to do that.

In Farnborough, England, Gayle lived with the rector of the church and I lived with the Price family (the headmaster of St. Peter's Junior School, where we would be working). A junior school includes the equivalent of our first through fourth grades, so I got a nice variety of teaching experiences. I walked about half a mile to school every day and coined the phrase "guided chaos" to describe the British classroom. My new students were mesmerized by NASA's July, 1969, moon landing and constantly pumped me with questions about it. The teachers paused for a tea break every afternoon, so even though I had never been a tea drinker before, I learned to love hot tea (with milk!). Gayle and I accompanied various classes on field trips, so we learned some British history along with the students. I especially loved Stonehenge and the Tower of London. The church family made sure we were entertained on the weekends by inviting us to various homes and touristy sights.

The Price family was so kind to me, and I kept in touch with them for many years afterward. I visited them twice more—in 1975 (with two friends) and in 2000 (with my daughters).

I loved every minute of this new culture and I fell in love with all things British. Gayle and I also got to travel and sightsee not only all over London but the rest of England, too. My favorite trip was our excursion up to Scotland. The Isle of Skye was wild and barren, but absolutely gorgeous. Loch Ness amazed, scones delighted, and kilts intrigued. A special, unexpected treat happened as I stood in an aisle seat at church in Scotland. Queen Elizabeth passed within a few inches of me as she walked up the aisle! The entire trip was a blessing to me, and I came back to Taylor a more outgoing person and more confident in the classroom. That trip whetted my appetite for world travel.

I liked most of my Taylor professors. But one stood out as a negative—my math methods professor. One day in class, I answered his question incorrectly and he announced to the whole class that I should be "hung, drawn and quartered" for my answer. I vowed then and there that I would never be the kind of teacher who embarrassed her students. The sad thing was that he was British! I was quite disappointed in him and the terrible example he set. What was he doing training teachers?

One thing happened at Taylor that has had a life-long impact on me. One professor encouraged his students to make a "Life List" of things they wanted to attempt in life. This was long before people began calling it a "bucket list." To me, the name "Life List" sounds much more positive! And no, it's not the same as the life-list birders keep of all the birds they have seen in their lifetime.

That professor didn't explain just how a life list worked, so I made my own rules. I decided to break my life list into three parts—personal, professional and spiritual, and to include both large and small goals. Jeremiah 29:11 became my life verse. "For I know the plans I have for you," declares the Lord. "Plans to prosper you and not to harm you. Plans to give you hope and a future." If God had plans for my life, I figured He didn't want to keep those plans a secret from me, so I'd better find out what those plans were and act on them.

After much prayer, to make sure I was working within God's will for my life, I began my life list with some basics because I figured the list would evolve over time. I marked off each item as I accomplished it and immediately selected another item to work on. I was very pro-active. I didn't just "let" life happen but worked to "make" it happen according to my goals. In other words, I would constantly be working on one goal or another. I also decided that I wanted to avoid the pain and heartache I watched others go through when they made bad decisions. So I decided to do things right the first time around. I didn't want to pay "stupid tax" by making poor choices in life. I also decided several things on that list would be secret—just between God and me, but I will share some of the others here.

On my spiritual life list, I wanted to spend eternity in heaven with God—the first and most important item on any of my life lists! While I recognized that working on a life list would be a way of life, I knew Christ IS life. On my professional life list, I wanted to earn a teaching degree, and after teaching for a few years, get a master's degree. My personal life list included sky diving, giving blood, writing a book (although I had absolutely no idea what I would write a book about!), and traveling the

world! I'm retired now and have marked off most of the items on my life lists. I am still working to accomplish some of the others.

During my fifth (senior) year (1971), I student taught in first grade in Allisonville Elementary School in Indianapolis. We were not allowed to live anywhere near home or campus or even visit home during the semester. My

Taylor Sophomore   **Taylor Junior**   **Student Teacher**
1968-1969   **1970-1971**   **1971**

supervising teacher, Mrs. Greenlee, was kind to me, but was tough and had high expectations, so I worked very hard! She was a good mentor. I ran into her in a hallway at Ball State University many years later (1989) as I started my doctoral program. By then, she was an education professor at Ball State.

Since Allisonville School was using a new method of teaching children to read called ITA (Initial Teaching Alphabet), I had to memorize it overnight

Taylor Graduation 1972

and soon learned to love it. Unfortunately, that reading philosophy died out after a few years. My first graders were such a delight and I thrived in the classroom. I also started keeping track of funny things kids say. One day, the principal was hand-delivering paychecks to the teachers. When he handed Mrs. Greenlee her paycheck, one of my kidlets, Davy, asked what it was. Mrs. Greenlee told him it was her paycheck. He cheerfully asked, "Oh, do you work somewhere?" So adorable. And when I ran into one of my students in the grocery store one day, she was startled to think that her teacher bought groceries and had a life outside school. She thought I lived at school all the time.

Since I had to attend college one extra semester to earn my art minor along with my elementary education degree, I completed my degree in January, 1972, and missed graduating with my friends in the class of 1971. Mom and Dad couldn't afford to pay for that extra semester, so I had to take out a loan to pay for it on my own. It took me several years to pay back that $1000 loan! Yes, in 1972, college cost $2000 per year—an astounding amount! But that art minor served me in good stead for my entire teaching career.

I hated leaving Taylor, but since my friends had graduated before me, I was ready to move on to the next room in my life.

CHAPTER FOUR
BATHROOM
BENTONVILLE SCHOOL
(Connersville, Indiana)
1972

I relegate this short six months of my life to the bathroom. It was definitely not the most comfortable room of my "house" and it smelled a bit. I opted not to spend too much time there.

Since I finished my degree in January, finding a teaching job mid-year was difficult, but one day the Taylor placement office called to inform me of an opening in a southern Indiana town called Connersville. I drove down to interview and was offered the job. I taught fourth grade for one semester. I had a passion for first grade so there was a slight misfit to the position, but a job is a job! My very first teaching salary was $3,000 for that half year.

Bentonville Elementary was an old country school with one class of each grade. The former teacher had been moved to a new position and the students missed her. While they kindly gave me a chance (bless their hearts!) and I grew to love them and the grade level, I did not find any comradeship with the other teachers. When I first began there, they

**Bentonville Elementary School
Connersville, Indiana 1972**

My fourth grade class

invited me to one of their Friday night parties, where much to my dismay, one of the teachers forced lots of beer on her little 11-month-old son so they could laugh at his drunken antics. I was horrified and never socialized with them again.

I boarded with a rather strange family for a few weeks until I found an old upstairs apartment. I disliked my living situation, disliked the town, disliked the school, (but loved my students!), and disliked my teaching colleagues. The only positive thing from those six months was when Connersville High School won the Indiana state basketball championship in March!

At the end of the school year, even though the district offered me a first-grade position in a different school, I chose to leave Connersville completely. I couldn't wait to shake the dust of that place off my feet!

My sister, Cheri, who was living in Lancaster, Ohio, encouraged me to apply for a teaching position there. After interviewing there, I was offered a first-grade job in Lancaster and grabbed it. Teaching jobs were few and far between back then and most teachers had no choices. I knew how fortunate I was to have two choices! God is good. And so, I gladly moved on to the next room in my life.

CHAPTER FIVE
BEDROOM
NORTH SCHOOL
(Lancaster, Ohio)
1972-1981

I liken this period of my life to being in the bedroom of my "house." It was a safe refuge, a comfortable place to rest. Here, I reposed for a nine-year chunk of my life, made many lifelong friends, unpacked a lot of understanding about my adult self, repacked my world view through travel and a solid Christian environment, and learned to accept my single status through much time closeted in prayer with God. I emerged refreshed and ready to face the world—newly clothed in personal confidence and teaching skills.

During my first year in Lancaster, I shared a trailer with Cindi, the new kindergarten teacher at North School. We got along well. Then Cindi moved away, so for the next five years, I shared an apartment with Chris, another teacher at North School. We became lifelong friends. She remains a treasure to me. When she got married and moved out, I couldn't afford the apartment by myself, so I invited Caroline, a single gal from church (a

**The back wing of North School 1972
First floor on the right was my classroom.**

non-teacher), to move in. I didn't know her very well but did know she was still living with her parents and didn't even have a driver's license. I soon learned she had no idea how to "cut the cord!" and be out on her own. It did not work out and she moved out after a year. So, for my last couple of years in Lancaster, I lived alone and loved it.

I loved teaching first grade. What joy it brought me! I remember the very first day of school, I thought to myself, "Wow! These parents actually trust me with their children!" I don't know of any other grade that is as rewarding as teaching first grade. What a thrill to watch non-readers turn into fluent readers in just a few short months. To watch children with no inhibitions learn decorum, structure and self-discipline, and to watch children bloom into second graders brought me much joy!

As soon as I began teaching, I discovered two things:

1. I was a morning person. (That explained why I was never able to pull an "all-nighter" studying in college—I still go to bed early.) Mornings are the best time of the day—with the birds chirping so cheerfully and the peaceful, quiet atmosphere. Many years later I relished sitting on my deck in the quiet morning air, praying, talking to God, viewing my own personal Garden of Eden and watching the wild animals (many of whom I fed each day). What a peaceful way to start the day.

2. I couldn't arrive just 30 minutes before the students (school regulation) and be totally prepared. So, I developed the habit of arriving at six thirty or seven a.m., long before the other teachers came. I got twice as much done when I was fresh and energetic, and I didn't waste time standing around talking to the other teachers. They preferred to stay after school and work late, but by the end of the day I was too tired to be productive. That pattern stood me in good stead for my whole 45-year teaching career!

And so, I learned to always plan ahead (I was extremely proactive) and to be fully prepared. To this day, I don't feel on top of things unless I have everything well planned out and organized ahead of time, no matter what my project. And I hate procrastination. I am never late for anything. Procrastination drives me crazy. I agree with Mom—people who keep you waiting are rude and assume their time is more valuable than yours. I may have inherited Dad's "self-starter" genes, but I also know I got the "arrive early" philosophy from Mom.

FIRST GRADE TEACHER PHOTOS IN LANCASTER, OHIO AND A FEW OF MY CLASSES

1972   **1973**   **1974**

My first full year of teaching In Lancaster, Ohio 1972-1973

1975   **1976**   **1977**

NORTH   ELEMENTARY
1976-77
MISS WILSON,   GRADE 1
LANCASTER, OHIO

1976-1977 with student teacher

North School was an old building with two or three classes for each grade level. I moved into room 108—the room of a legend. Mrs. Friend had just retired and was quite well known and loved by all her students. I felt I

1978   **1979**   **1980**

My last year at North School in Ohio 1980-1981

had a lot to live up to inheriting that room. There were several other new teachers that year and we formed a nice cohort. Many of them were single gals, too, so we had a lot in common. We played volleyball every Friday after school (along with the principal, Mr. Packard, and other returning teachers) and then went out to dinner together. We also socialized in other ways, which was great. For several years, each spring, a group of my friends hosted a progressive dinner. We had appetizers at one house, main course at another, etc. It was classy and well done. What fun!

I loved working with teachers who shared my values. We formed a craft club and met once a month to stitch, sew, or work on our various crafts while we chatted away. We played euchre and went to movies together. I joined the church where my sister's husband, Ralph, was the youth minister and I sang in the choir there. I worked out at the Y with friends. So, my new life was full and comfortable.

My first teaching salary in Lancaster was $7,100 per year, so finances were tight. When Chris and I moved into our apartment, I bought a sofa, and she bought a table. I bought a used bed and a new mattress. Otherwise, I had nothing. For a long time, that's all we had in that empty apartment! I barely made enough to get by. It was difficult to set up a household without the benefit of bridal showers or wedding gifts like all my married friends had.

With a slight salary increase each year, I managed to get by, but I couldn't even afford the dollar-a-day lunches in the school cafeteria. Chris and I became known as the "casserole kids" because in our lunches, we always carried whatever casserole was left over from the night before. We each put $10 into the grocery kitty each week and that $20 bought what groceries we needed for the week. Sometimes I tutored students in the summers to supplement my income. By the time I left Lancaster nine years later, I was making $17,000. Things were still tight, but I always managed to find spare money to spend on my classroom. My students were so needy, and I loved providing for them.

Teaching in the 1970's was quite different than teaching today. I constantly had blue fingertips from the ditto fluid used to run off copies on the hand-cranked ditto machine. We produced our own materials as there were very few products available for purchase. I made most of the games and activities my students needed. Students were generally not mainstreamed, so there were not as many special needs to deal with. We had curriculum guides in our classrooms, but no one paid any attention to them. We were free to teach as we saw fit. We could teach units or not, test or not, and use the classroom hours as we wished. As long as our students were ready to move on at the end of the year, things were fine. I took advantage of that freedom and experimented with some wonderful approaches and ideas.

I drove a cheap used car for many years. But after I taught for a few years, I bought a "new" car. It cost $4000. I was stunned how expensive cars were. That was nearly a third of my salary at the time! It took me several years to pay that off.

The principal, Mr. Packard, came many times to observe, of course, and my yearly evaluations were always good. He seemed very pleased with how I was doing. Sometimes, when he had to be away, he had me serve as the acting principal for the day. I didn't know it at the time, but he twice nominated me for Outstanding Teacher of the Year (for Lancaster City Schools). I didn't know that until he told me after the second time that I had come in second. I remember wondering "Who, me?" Another year, he selected Chris and I to be honored participants in the Jennings Scholar program. We went to several stimulating conferences about education and heard many great speakers.

After I taught for five years (the minimum at which colleges considered you "qualified" to supervise), Ohio University asked me to supervise student teachers in my classroom. I hosted three student teachers at various times. One gal was so overtly religious it caused problems—you know, the kind of Christian that gives Christians a bad name? For example, she was to begin teaching her unit on oceans on Monday, so the week before, I reminded her to have her unit bulletin board up by Monday morning. When I came in on Monday, there was no bulletin board. When I asked her why not, she said she was a Christian and she didn't need to do that bulletin board. God would do that bulletin board for her. I was dumbfounded. I told her it doesn't work that way. I'd been a Christian for a long time and God had never yet done a bulletin board for me! It was like talking to a blank wall. Or sometimes her lessons weren't prepared for the day because she had spent the night "praying someone through." I gave her a D in student teaching but the university raised it to a C so she could pass. I heard later that she did get a teaching job after graduation, but the parents got her fired during her first semester. Seems she didn't do any work. Hmm . . . I could have told them that would happen!

My other two student teachers were just average. I didn't see a lot of promise in either of them, so even though they improved, they still only managed to do O.K. I worked hard to improve their knowledge and skills, but they didn't seem to "get it." They lacked "with-it-ness." But even then, they came a long way from where they started, while working in my classroom. I couldn't tell if their lackluster performances were indicative of their personalities or of Ohio University's teacher preparation program. Either way, I wasn't terribly impressed. Were my standards too high? It had never dawned on me before that my teaching might be more than just average. Sure, I always got great reviews, but since I didn't know what reviews the other teachers were earning, I had nothing to compare myself to. Over the years, I had spotted a couple of teachers in our building who seemed like poor teachers, but that was only my guess. But after working with the Ohio University student teaching supervisor, I began to think about how much fun it would be to do her job—to supervise student teachers in the field. A seed was planted.

I was tickled when, year after year, parents requested me as their child's first grade teacher. There were three first grade teachers, so I felt honored to be singled out by parents. One year, a parent offered me an old four-legged bathtub for my classroom. Since I had a student teacher at the time, I gladly accepted and spent considerable time sanding it down, painting it bright yellow, and designing two Peanuts cartoon scenes for the sides. In one of them, Lucy is yelling, "READ!" I then hand painted the adorable scenes, and lined the tub with carpets and pillows for students to read in. They loved it and a reporter came to school to take a picture of it for the paper.

Another year, our librarian invited the staff to paint a large mural on the library wall. It consisted of eight-foot-tall African animals all reading books. We spent many fun hours painting that wall and got our picture in the newspaper, too! I remember that was the time when fashion dictated short "mini-skirts" for girls. I didn't wear mine as short as some, but Dad had a fit about my skirts if they were much above my knees. The newspaper photo I sent Mom and Dad showed me with a skirt shorter than he was comfortable with. I frequently heard lectures from him about my morals and how a short skirt would send guys

The "Reading Tub" I painted

the wrong message. He also disapproved of us piercing our ears. His view was that only loose, immoral girls pierced their ears. Even Mom wanted to pierce hers. He lost that battle.

During my time in Ohio, my Grpa Ford, passed away. It was my first loss of a family member. Having family five hours away was hard, but when Mom and Dad came to visit, Dad always fixed whatever needed fixing. I drove home to Wabash for holidays and summer visits.

During one Easter visit home to Wabash during the 1970's, I had a heart-to-heart conversation with Mom. I asked her point blank if Dad had had an affair with Nancy back in the 60's. She finally opened up and admitted he had—more than one affair, but she would only confirm that one name. I was heartbroken for her. She wouldn't tell me much, but I know she had suffered terribly over the years. For some reason, she thought she should keep it quiet, so she bore the burden alone. I still loved my Dad, but at the same time, I was quite frustrated with him. But I, too, decided not to mention it to anyone else, mostly to protect Mom. If it got out, I was afraid Dad would take it out on Mom. One thing that frustrated me, however, was having listened to Dad preaching about sexual purity all those years we were growing up—about not having sex outside of marriage. That was one of the pillars of my morals. If I could live by it, why couldn't Dad live by what he preached?

As adults, my siblings were quite different from each other. Cheri remained "difficult," but Brent was a wonderful guy, whom I liked a great deal. He was easy going and pleasant. I appreciated having one sibling I could relate to.

King Arthur's Round Table (Winchester Cathedral) • Tower Bridge (London)

England

Stonehenge (England) my favorite

Tower of Pisa (Italy)

Venice, Italy

Colosseum (Rome)

Italy

Notre Dame's Rose Window(Paris,France)

Little Mermaid (Denmark)

Holland

Scandinavia

My first summer in Ohio (1973), Chris, Sandy (another teacher) and I went to Europe, visiting a dozen countries. We rode trains (with Eurail passes) all over Europe, having a wonderful time and learning a lot. We purposely did not want to be seen as "hippies," like many of our generation, so we never wore jeans or carried backpacks. We dressed in slacks and kept ourselves neat and tidy. We were not traveling to relax and be pampered. We wanted to learn history and see the sights. That kind of traveling is hard work! I was thrilled to experience other cultures, visit places I had heard about, and see how others lived. So, I added a new item to my life list—someday I wanted to live and teach overseas.

My sister, Cheri and her husband, Ralph, lived in Lancaster the first couple of years I was there. Their son, Peter, my first nephew, was born shortly after I arrived in Lancaster. What joy it brought me to be an aunt! I sewed a few maternity tops for Cheri. Her sewing skills weren't the best (but her cooking skills were wonderful—I learned a lot from her!). I helped them out quite a bit. But she took advantage of me being there in the same town. I loved my nephew, but I was asked to babysit for free on a regular basis and was expected to drop other plans to meet her babysitting needs. It seemed she thought her needs were more important and greater than mine. After all, I was single and had nothing else to do, right? She was married, so that trumped my singleness. In her view, I was not worth as much as she was. Her activities were more important than mine. The tension between us began to increase.

Sometimes, I attended Ralph's youth group, at Cheri's request, so I could see him at work. I remember he would call out, "Attitude check?" and the kids would shout, "Praise the Lord!" He was encouraging them to praise God in all circumstances. Cheri was a tremendous help to him in his job since she was musical. She played the piano, created and directed

**Pete (age 2) riding
on my shoulders**

Mom's visit to Lancaster

the Maranatha Singers, and did all sorts of jobs for him. After they had been there about four years, Ralph was fired from his job. I was told the church board wanted to start with a clean slate after the senior minister (married) had an affair with the church secretary. I wasn't surprised since the minister had made passes at me and even come to my classroom to "chat." I let him know I wasn't interested and that his visits to my school were inappropriate. What fascinated me is that Cheri was so verbally critical of the minister, but not of the church secretary, who was a good friend of hers. I didn't get that since it takes two to tango. So Cheri and Ralph moved to a different youth ministry position back in Indiana. Peter was only two when they left, and I missed him terribly! But I was also a bit relieved they had moved on.

After they moved, I changed churches, where I was happier, and made many new friends. I taught VBS, worked at church camp, sang in the choir, played in the hand bell choir, spoke at a Women's Retreat about being a single Christian woman, and volunteered for several other church activities. One thing did irritate me, however. Since I was an elementary teacher, church people just assumed I would love to teach little kids in Sunday School, too. The problem, as I saw it, was that I needed some adult interaction one day a week!

The first time I drove five hours back to Indiana to visit Cheri and Ralph in their new home in Converse, Cheri ran to me and hugged me tightly. That is the only time I can remember her doing that. Thereafter, she resumed her normal attitude of being cool till I moved to hug her. I loved playing with Peter, having him ride on my shoulders, while he hung onto my braids. I loved being an aunt!

I distinctly remember the time I found a lump in my breast. I was scheduled to have surgery to see if I had cancer or not. Cheri was conducting a major choir production at her new church in Indiana. I was expected to attend, and I offered her much praise, but she never once mentioned my upcoming surgery. She was so consumed with her choir production and happy that she was pregnant again, that those two things took all her attention. The fact that I might be struggling with a potential cancer diagnosis never seemed to have occurred to her. (Luckily, the tumor was benign.)

Brent and Nore's wedding Feb. 1974

My brother, Brent, married his college sweetheart, Eleanore, in Feb., 1974. Cheri and I sang at their wedding, although I don't think we did a very good job (and I always suspected that having us sing was Nore's way of appeasing Cheri).

I loved Nore. She was so sweet and a "small spit-fire," only 4' 11" tall, but with lots of personality and charm. I noticed that Cheri was never very nice to Nore. I didn't know why, since Nore was such a treasure. Nore sensed it, too, and did everything she could to be kind to Cheri, but it did no good. Brent and Nore have lived in the Indianapolis area ever since.

Since none of us lived close to Cheri and Ralph, we maintained civility from a distance, but continued to invite them to family gatherings. Cheri was not interested in anything about Brent and Nore's life (or mine), so she never knew any of the amazing things Nore was able to accomplish in life. Her life and family were more important than ours. In fact, several times over the years, she told me that her children/family were better than either Brent's or mine. I just had to shake my head and sigh over her attitude. It was like she wore blinders and refused to see that we were all doing well in life. Proving herself better than the rest of us seemed to be her mission in life. I could only guess that her attitude sprang from her bitterness at the family.

One summer, Grma Faye and Grpa Ora presented each of us three grandchildren with $1000. I was dumbfounded and very touched. How

in the world had they saved up enough to do that? They lived frugally and never had any extra for extravagances. I put mine directly into savings to earn interest. Cheri spent hers on a china cabinet. I got the feeling Grma wasn't very happy that Cheri spent hers.

One year for Christmas, I assembled two books for Dad, and had them bound at the bindery where I used to work. One was

Why you shouldn't wait until retirement to travel!

titled "Anecdotes from the Life and Times of DeVon Wilson." I put in stories of his childhood, pictures and special memories. The other (as a joke) was titled, "All I Know About Wine, Women and Song," by DeVon Wilson. The pages were completely blank (as a joke)! We all had a blast reading the first book. Little did I know how prophetic the second book was.

In 1975, Chris, Barb (another teacher) and I went back to Europe and Scandinavia. I began seeing a method to my madness. In fact, my friends teased me about being a miser because I saved every penny I could for a year or two, and then took a big trip. I opted to do without during the year, so I could afford another overseas cultural adventure. People asked why I was traveling so much. They said I should wait till I retired to travel. But I didn't want to do that. I wanted to see the world while I was young and able-bodied.

In 1977, I went on a Caribbean cruise with my parents. It was their first time out of the country and they seemed relieved I was with them since I was fairly experienced in international travel by then. In 1978, I went to

**Elephant footprint
outside our tent**

Masai tribe

the Philippines with my brother, his Filipino wife, Nore, and my parents, to visit Nore's culture. Cheri and Ralph declined the offer to go with us. Mom, Dad and I also traveled up to Hong Kong (it was to become my favorite

city in the world!) so Brent and Nore could have some time alone with her family. One memory stands out for me. I bought an oil painting from a street painter of two Chinese "junk" boats floating peacefully into the sunset. I still have that painting hanging in my living room! It always gives me a sense of peace and contentment when I look at it and it reminds me of my favorite city in the world.

While we were in the Philippines, when we had about a week left in our trip, Dad suddenly decided he needed to get back to his carpet store and insisted he be driven to the airport. We were nowhere near the airport, so it was a major inconvenience for Nore's family to meet his demand. In my heart, I suspected he just wanted to get back to Mae, his store assistant. Mom said nothing, but I knew

On the equator

she was quite embarrassed by his decision to leave a week early. I felt so sorry for her.

In 1979, I experienced one of the most memorable and impressive trips of my life. I joined an NEA (National Education Association) tour group going on a photographic safari in Kenya. What a fantastic experience that was, even though I knew no one in the group beforehand. I remember waking up in a tent, hearing lions and hyenas on the other side of that thin canvas wall, knowing they were not in cages! One morning, we found a huge elephant footprint right outside our tent. He had visited during the night, and we never heard a thing.

Another morning we woke to find a herd of zebras right outside our door. I learned the difference between reticulated giraffe and masai giraffe, as well as many animals I was not familiar with before. I did not have a zoom lens on my camera, but took some amazingly close photos of lions, zebras and elephants. What a thrill that trip proved to be! Two of my photos won blue ribbons at the fair the following year.

I conducted one experiment while we were staying in a hotel in Kenya situated right on the equator. The hallway sat right on the equator. My room on the north side of the hallway, was just north of the equator and when I held a bottle upside down, the water in the bottle swirled out clockwise into the sink. When I did the same thing a few feet away, across the hall, just south of the equator, it swirled counterclockwise. The pull from the north and south poles affected the direction the water swirled!

Two of my African photos won a blue ribbon

Just those few feet made a big difference! I loved learning things like that to take back to my first graders. They thought that was pretty cool!

Another vivid memory was staying in Tree Tops Hotel—a hotel built in the tops of the trees! We had to climb stairs to get up into the hotel and they pulled the stairs up after us so wild animals couldn't get up (except the monkeys on the roof, of course, who loved to steal whatever we had in our hands or pockets). We spent several nights watching the well-lit watering hole down below as all the wild animals came to drink. Tree Tops Hotel is famous because in 1952, Princess Elizabeth spent the night there. Her father, the King, passed away while she was there, so she went up into Tree Tops a Princess and came down a Queen!

I had many great experiences teaching at North School. I loved my kidlets and their many hugs. First graders are so wonderful and I loved the funny things they said and did. My most vivid memories are of specific students. Little Mary Ruth was such a dear. One day, she accidently shook her thermos as she opened so the liquid splashed all over several of us. I unthinkingly exclaimed, "Oh, Mary Ruth!" She was crushed and burst into tears. I quickly told her it wasn't her fault and apologized for my unkind response.

Little Russell lived in poverty. He wore the same smelly clothes every day. They reeked of urine because he wet his pants every day, and since he was wearing no underwear or socks, it ran down his legs and into his shoes, mixing with his foot odor. I always sent him to the nurse who put him into a set of clean clothes. But the next day, he always came back to school in the old smelly outfit and never returned the borrowed clothes. We learned that his father was frequently arrested for "streaking" down Main Street—a popular nude activity in the 70's! Poor kid. He didn't have a chance at any kind of better life.

The principal was laying out a map of where each of our students lived, so he had the students come to his office one at a time to ask them specific questions. One of my boys told him he lived right next to that "Walk, Don't Walk" sign!

Another student, David, made me chuckle one day. We were learning new vocabulary words in reading group. I tried to introduce the word "herd" by asking what we would call a group of cows. David piped up with "a cow crowd!"

Little Tammy (a midget) literally ate her pencils. At first, I thought she was just chewing them, but they disappeared at an alarming rate. We finally figured out she had Pica, a vitamin K deficiency, and got her help for it.

Mark was so curious to know if the frost on the playground equipment tasted like ice cream that he stuck his tongue out to lick it. Of course, his tongue stuck to the frozen pole. I had a terrible time getting it loose without him sacrificing too many taste buds!

Little Becky was partially deaf, so I wore a microphone around my neck that transmitted to her hearing aids. However, I frequently forgot to turn it off while at lunch. When people called me "Becky," she assumed it was for her and quickly looked around to see who was talking to her.

Little Oleta was a delight (and I got to be friends with her aunt), and we reconnected many years later after she became a well-known singer.

One year, I stayed with Molly for a few weeks, while her parents traveled. That was a treat to be in a big luxurious home.

Some of my students were from nice homes, but several were from poor ones. One of my goals was to make them more aware of the world around them since most of them didn't know what city or state they lived in. As I traveled during the summers, I learned to count to ten in various languages and then came back and added that to the ones I taught my kidlets. We identified each country on the world map, sampled food from each culture, and on recitation day, they could count to ten to earn a certificate. They were so proud of themselves! I hope it broadened their horizons a bit. By the end of the year, they had mastered counting in about ten languages (it varied from year to year). I was so proud of them!

Over the years, Cheri had frequently criticized me and given me unsolicited advice—telling me what college I should attend, that I was too old to wear my hair long (after 30) , that I should be less picky, that I needed to get married, who I should marry, that I made too much noise (when I accidentally dropped the toilet lid), that I should stop "wasting" money on expensive trips, etc. And one day, after they brought newborn Peter home from the hospital and I was over there cooking dinner for them, I called up the stairs to ask Cheri something. Ralph scolded me thoroughly for being so loud—I might wake the baby. Since I hadn't called out very loudly, I was quite taken aback by the reprimand. I mentally thought to myself that Peter would learn to sleep through whatever they taught him to sleep through.

I tried to accept Cheri's criticisms as constructive and examined myself to see if her concerns were valid. I always considered her advice and then made my own decisions. Since she felt free to "counsel" me, I assumed she wanted the kind of relationship where we were honest with each other. Some of her actions, behaviors and attitudes concerned me, so I made a very stupid mistake. I wrote her a heartfelt letter after they moved to Indiana, expressing my concerns. For example, when they left their rental house in Lancaster, they took the coffee table, which belonged to the landlord, because she felt he had mistreated them and therefore they "deserved" to take it. I viewed that as stealing, no matter how badly he treated them (and I doubted he had). She did not receive my letter well. In fact, she was livid and responded with a very nasty letter. I decided to just drop the matter instead of responding to her and making our relationship even more strained. So our relationship remained quite lop-sided. She could and did criticize me freely and tell me what I should and shouldn't do, but I wasn't allowed to criticize/advise her on anything. I deeply regret that I did not save copies of those letters for future reference.

Several times (after they moved to Indiana), Cheri mentioned that they wanted to get rid of an old stereo cabinet and wanted me to "have" it (implying "free"). Finally, I loaded it into my car and took it back to Lancaster. A few weeks later, she wrote and told me they wanted $50 for it. I didn't have $50 and would never have taken it had a price tag been mentioned up front. But to avoid further hard feelings, I scratched up the money and sent it to her.

I began jogging while in Lancaster. I was never a long-distance runner but did manage to run in a couple of 5K races. I also learned to play racquetball and loved it! It became my favorite activity.

I dated while in Lancaster. During my first year, someone set me up on a blind date. The guy seemed nice enough, and in my attempt to get to know him, I asked him what his goals in life were. He said he didn't have any. I never went out with him again! I wasn't interested in that kind of approach to life. He was just going to let life happen at random? No thanks. Not my kind of guy.

What amazed me is that during those years in Lancaster, there were six guys who wanted to marry me—and I had never even dated some of them! One Sunday afternoon, Dave, a guy from church, stopped by my apartment to propose to me. It took me completely by surprise because

I only knew him vaguely and we had barely spoken before. Another guy, Bill, a divorcee in his late 30's, wanted to date me and let me know up front he intended to marry me. We went out once, but I didn't care for him. Steve, a guy about my age, kept hanging around (we never dated) even though I gave him absolutely no encouragement. He finally got the hint and gave up. Then there was the strangest one of all—Art, a guy I met accidently when I was babysitting my nephew. He called to talk to my brother-in-law, Ralph, and we ended up chatting for quite a while. He sounded nice on the phone, but I later found out he had been arrested a few times for beating up his mother. It took me a long time to get rid of him and only after he harassed me for over a year, giving me flat tires (at the very least, I learned how to change a tire!), and making repeated threatening phone calls.

My sister, Cheri (in Converse, Indiana) set me up on a blind date with a veterinarian (Terry) where she lived. We dated when I was there visiting (I even met his parents) and he came to visit me twice in Ohio. He was nice enough, but I wasn't thrilled with him—he was rather "blah." His parents were disappointed that he wasn't able to marry me like he wanted. And Cheri wasn't happy with me, either. She gave me her "snooty" look.

One time, while I was in Converse visiting, Mom called to report that Grma Faye had been swindled. While she was home alone one day, a guy dressed in some company uniform knocked on her door, saying he needed to make a repair. He went out to the side of the house and did something, then, he asked her to get her checkbook to pay him directly. She made out the check to him but left the amount blank, per his instructions. He did tell her to go ahead and sign the check and then to go upstairs and pull her records. While she was upstairs, he left with the check, went directly to Roann, filled in the amount, and cashed the check for $5000. When the bank cashier questioned him about it, he said he was building a pole barn for Ora. He wiped out their life savings. As soon as she realized he had tricked her she tried to call the police, but he had cut the phone lines. Grma was devastated. Those kinds of things didn't happen in those days, and she was so embarrassed she didn't want anyone to know except Mom. I don't think she ever lived down her shame.

Then, after a few years, Ralph was fired from his youth ministry job in Converse, too (for reasons they said were a repeat of Lancaster, but who knows?) so they moved to Wabash and lived on and farmed the estate farm his parents had lived on. His Mom and Dad arranged for Ralph to take over the estate farm. After managing the estate farm for a few years, they moved out of the estate farmhouse, and into a house Ralph's mother owned near N. Manchester. They farmed her place and took over farming Grma Faye's acreage. Charlotte lived in Florida. I have no idea if they paid her rent. So that was twice Ralph's mother (his father had died by then) had helped them with housing. I thought it was very kind of her, but they bad-mouthed her at every turn. And Ralph had absolutely no relationship with his brother or sisters. He had completely disowned his family.

While they lived on the estate farm, they ran up a huge vet bill with one of their dogs. Cheri voiced concern that they couldn't afford to pay the bill and didn't know what they were going to do. I stopped at the vet's office on my way back to Lancaster one time to pay off their bill for them, but it was closed. So I sent some money to a friend in another state (someone Cheri didn't know or I had never spoken of to her) and had her send them a cashier's check from a local bank. I knew they would have no idea where the money came from and therefore my contribution would remain a secret. She never mentioned that someone had sent them money. I never told her it was me.

By then, Cheri and Ralph had two boys—Peter and Jason. One summer I went up for an overnight at the lake cottage where they were staying for a week's vacation. There were only two bedrooms, so Cheri moved Jason to the couch and had me sleep in Jason's bed, which was fine, except Jason was a bed wetter. His sheets were dry but reeked of urine and Cheri made no effort to change them for me. I said nothing because I knew it would hurt Jason's feelings. But I was stunned that Cheri would put me in that position.

I remember when Cheri bought a microwave oven. I had never heard of such a thing before. She was the first person I knew to own one. I frequently heard Ralph say, "Buy the biggest and the best," and they always did. When Cheri wanted a new sewing machine, she bought a huge one, even though she didn't sew that well. She used that $1000 from Grma and Grpa to buy the biggest china cabinet she could find. She always decorated her home nicely. She always decorated her kitchen bulletin board for the seasons, but one time, she decorated it with items describing a person with "class." I took that to mean she felt she was an example of someone with class. Unfortunately, I never witnessed her doing any of the things on that list! She definitely thought highly of herself, or at least gave that impression. I remember once Mom wisely commented that Cheri must be deeply unhappy but tried to cover it up with her haughty attitude.

Mom and Dad put in an above-ground swimming pool in their back yard, thinking it would bring their grown kids back home more often. Cheri took her boys over to swim in it. One time, Jason accidentally fell in. Dad saved Jason's life by diving in fully clothed to fish him out. I don't remember if Cheri ever fully understood what Dad had done for Jason. She certainly didn't comment on it.

Mom and Dad commented to me once that Cheri only stopped to see them if she wanted or needed something. Otherwise, she ignored them. And the conversations were always about her family. She rarely asked about or showed interest in how they were doing or in the rest of the family. I remember there was some kerfuffle when Ralph asked Dad to loan him money so he could buy a car. Dad did, but Ralph never paid him back.

By now, I was tired of defending myself to everyone who constantly asked why I wasn't married. The implication was that I would never be "accepted" unless I was married. Mom and Dad even asked when I was going to get married and "settle down." I tried to patiently explain that I was settled down. I was the only one of their three children using the college degree they paid for. While my two siblings moved around and changed jobs frequently, I had held one job successfully and lived in one location for nine years. I think they finally accepted my singleness and stopped pestering me about it. But the pressure to be married was exhausting. People actually told me I should lower my standards and "settle" for a less than perfect guy. I wasn't looking for a perfect guy! But if I had my act together, what was wrong with trying to find a guy who had his act together too? Besides, I'm not sure God wants his children to "settle" for second best in their partners.

Then a new problem began creeping up when folks asked me, "Why aren't you married yet?" they hinted there must be something wrong with me. People assumed (and said) that if I was single by chance or choice, I must be gay. During the 1970's, the topic of homosexuality (formerly a taboo subject) was becoming more openly discussed. Since I didn't know how to "fight" that stigma, I just ignored it. I knew I wasn't gay, so why bother with what other people might think?

Being single in a "married" world was difficult. I struggled with that for several years as my siblings and friends got married and had children. I grew to resent Mother's Day because it reminded me that I wasn't even close to being a mother and that depressed me. My self-concept suffered as a result of not fitting in to social expectations like everyone else. In past generations, a woman had to be married to be "accepted" and financially secure. It was rare for a woman to work outside the home. Grma Faye never did. Mom was the first "working" woman in our family and then just for 18 years, till her children were through college.

Many women feel they have no value or are incomplete unless they are married. Since I valued who I was, that wasn't part of my thinking. And I had proven to myself that I could support myself and make my own way in life. I finally realized that I didn't have to be married to be happy. In fact, it dawned on me that I'd rather be single and happy than married to the wrong guy! What an eye-opening realization that was for me! I figured there were probably many unhappily married women out there who wished they were still single!

Grma Faye had made lots of beautiful quilts during her life but saved six of them—two for each of us. Years before, we had each picked out the two we wanted. She gave Cheri and Brent theirs when they got married, but she held on to mine "until you get married." Finally, I asked her if I could just have mine now, since I didn't know if I would ever get married. She finally relented and gave them to me.

After realizing I could be single and happy, my life list soon included a new entry—if I wasn't married by the time I was 30, I wanted to adopt children. I saw no reason why being single should keep me from being a mother, but with my Christian values, I chose not to have pre-marital sex, which might produce a child by birth. I wasn't interested in messing up my life (or my child's life) that way. That left me with the adoption option.

I met Rob Libbee at church and dated him for four years. He was a sixth-grade teacher at a different school. We were good friends, did a lot of things together, and did a lot for each other. I typed his master's thesis and made shirts for him, since his arms were long, and he couldn't find "off the rack" shirts that fit him well. We worked a week at church camp as cabin counselors during the same week. We worked together to paint few houses for extra income in the summers. Rob and I went out every

Saturday night. But I felt no romantic interest in him, even though he planned on us getting married.

Rob and I were great friends with John and Carol, a couple we met at church. We played lots of euchre with them, went to movies and generally enjoyed double dating. Then one year, their son, Shawn, was in first grade at my school, but in my colleague Cheryl's classroom next door. Cheryl and her husband, Terry were good friends of mine, too. I grew puzzled when I saw John coming in frequently for parent conferences without his wife, Carol. Their son, Shawn, was a great kid, so I couldn't imagine he was having problems in school. I noticed they always closed the classroom door. Then suddenly, John and Carol stopped doing things with Rob and me. No explanation was given and when we confronted them asking what was wrong, they denied any problem. So, it remained a mystery to us until suddenly it became obvious that John and Carol were having marital problems and John and Cheryl (my colleague) were seeing each other. Eventually both couples divorced and John and Cheryl got married. Rob and I were devastated that people we thought we knew, with the same morals we had, could destroy two marriages and cause such a rift in their children's lives. We were heartbroken.

While in Lancaster, I continued working on my life list—adding items such as being a blood donor, learning to needlepoint, and learning to drive a stick shift. I began donating blood regularly and completed five gallons (40 donations—the allowed five times a year) by the time I left Lancaster. Dad and I began having a contest to see who could give the most blood. Dad had been giving for years, so I knew I'd never catch up to him, but I tried. As for driving a stick shift, Rob tried to teach me, but the lesson never "took." He wasn't very patient with me or a very good teacher! I think I could have learned it with a different teacher. I finally gave up that idea! So, no, I haven't been successful at everything on my life list! I think it's attempting things that makes life interesting and builds character.

I also began collecting sayings or quotes that appealed to me and that went along with my life verse (Jeremiah 29:11).

"If you don't know where you are going, any road will get you there." (attributed to Lewis Carroll, Theodore Roosevelt and Henry Kissinger, et al.)

"Attitude is more important than circumstances." (Charles Swindoll) (Phil. 4:12-13)

"Life is 10% what happens to you and 90% how you react to what happens to you." (Charles Swindoll)

"Destiny is not a matter of chance, it's a matter of choice. It's not a thing to be waited for, it's a thing to be achieved," (and that implies action on your part!) (William Jennings Bryan)

"The measure of a person is the size of the thing that gets her down." (variation of several quotes)

Along with collecting sayings that fit my philosophy, I also found that first and last stanzas of the poem "The Road Not Taken" by Robert Frost exactly summed up my desire to do things differently than everyone else:

Two roads diverged in a yellow wood,
And sorry I could not travel both
And be one traveler, long I stood
And looked down as far as I could
To where it bent in the undergrowth;

I shall be telling this with a sigh
Somewhere ages and ages hence:
Two roads diverged in a wood, and I—
I took the one less traveled by,
And that has made all the difference.[1]

In the summer and fall of 1980, I began to experience a restlessness that was new to me. I took me a while to figure out that God was urging me to pursue another item on my life list—teaching overseas—but I had no idea how to go about doing that. Then one day, I saw a tiny ad in the paper about a Cleveland job fair for overseas teaching positions. I contacted them (the placement bureau), drove up to Cleveland over Christmas break, interviewed with Don, and was accepted as their client. Don was very

---

[1] Robert Frost, "A Group of Poems", The Atlantic Monthly (August 1915). Accessed 2021-03-18

confident about my chances of finding an overseas teaching position. He explained that superintendents and headmasters from various countries came to the U.S. every spring to interview prospective teachers. After returning to their countries, they called their most promising candidates to offer jobs. I signed up for the February interviews in Cleveland.

During the 1980 Christmas dinner at Mom's and Dad's house, I announced that I probably wouldn't be there for the next few Christmases because I would be interviewing in February, and would likely be moving overseas to teach. The whole family was stunned. What was I thinking? It really hit them hard—especially Grma Faye and Grpa Ora.

Grpa Ora passed away suddenly a month later, in January (1981), only aware that he had three great-grandsons, without knowing there would be three great-granddaughters added to his family in the future and before knowing where I would be moving. I wondered what he would have thought, had he known where I would be living. I'm sure that with his restricted worldview, he would not have been able to relate to the changes soon to take place in my life.

At least I got to be there for Grpa's funeral. Cheri got upset when Grma Faye held her head up and got through the funeral without breaking down. She was appalled that Grma didn't show some emotion, which would have been Cheri's reaction. But I knew inside Grma was grieving privately. They had been married for 61 years.

I broke up with Rob in January, 1981, because I knew our relationship was going nowhere and I would soon be interviewing to teach overseas. I tried to break up with him several weeks before interviewing so the people at church would not associate our break-up with me moving overseas. It didn't work. Rob didn't tell anyone we had broken up. So the news about me moving overseas and our break-up hit at the same time. It was awkward!

Those interviews in February, 1981, made for an exhausting, whirlwind weekend! On Friday, I selected 11 countries, interviewed with them all on Friday and Saturday, and received eight job offers on the spot! I was shocked, since Don had indicated that would not be the protocol! It did a lot for my ego but left me overwhelmed. Besides the hour-long interviews, I also had to attend an hour-long orientation for each of those schools/countries. It was an overwhelming and exhausting experience. By Saturday night, I knew I'd better accept one of those job offers or the headmasters would move on to other interview sites and hire someone else. I prayed hard about it. I yearned to accept one of the two job offers in Africa, but I felt quite strongly that for some reason, God wanted me in Korea. I had no idea why.

I called the headmaster from Korea (Mr. Underwood) and at 11:00 Saturday night, I signed a two-year contract (for $15,000—a $2,000 pay cut from my current salary) to teach first grade in Seoul, Korea! I was stunned! Had I really done that? All the way back to Lancaster, I prayed I wouldn't be sorry about my hasty decision when I got back to my "real" world. I never was.

The joke going around my school was that I didn't know a soul in Seoul, but everyone was so excited for me. I wasn't completely sure where Korea was. I knew it was in Asia, but I had to look it up on a map to find out exactly where I would be moving!

Teaching was very hard those last few months as I packed up my classroom and prepared to leave the life I knew and loved. Some of the teachers joked that the school should retire my classroom number like they do with the jersey numbers of famous sports figures. What a hoot.

Before moving to Korea 1981

But even though it was tough leaving what I knew and loved, I never once doubted that I should do this. There is security being smack dab in the middle of God's will for your life.

In March, I got a call from my sister, Cheri. She was in tears. As she and her husband, Ralph, (who had taken over farming Grpa Ora's fields) had been burning out fences (to make more room for his large equipment in the fields), a spark flew up and set Grpa's barn on fire. No one was hurt, but the barn and all Grpa's farm implements were destroyed. Grpa had retired, but his implements remained, as well as all the items Dad had stored in the barn when their old church was torn down. Luckily, there were no longer any animals in the barn. I tried to calm Cheri by reinforcing that no one was injured, and "things" could be replaced. I learned later that Ralph had not asked permission to remove any fences (from Dad, the new owner) and was foolish to be burning on such a windy day.

When the newspaper reporter came to take pictures and interview the owner, Dad, about how the fire started, Dad just kindly said "we" were burning out fences—leaving the impression he had been involved in the work. The reporter questioned Dad about the wisdom of burning fences on such a windy day. Ralph was standing right next to Dad but said nothing—in other words, he let Dad take full responsibility for starting the fire.

We later learned Ralph figured Dad wouldn't lose anything, since insurance would pay for everything. However, Ralph didn't know that Grpa had canceled all his insurance when he retired, so Dad lost a great deal, financially, in that fire, as well as losing face in the community for starting the fire. Ralph never apologized for starting the fire and it caused hard feelings in the family for many years, although it wasn't discussed openly. We all still remained civil and kind to Cheri and Ralph, but that incident increased their already growing bitterness and anger with the rest of the family.

The fire affected Grma Faye terribly. Every day she had to look out and see the missing barn while still grieving the loss of her husband and learning to live alone. Then she fell and broke both of her wrists. I wished so badly that I could be closer home to help her during that terrible time. But I can still remember one thing she said about all the trials she was going through. She said, "Please God, don't let me waste this experience." In other words, she knew she could learn something even amidst her sorrow and grief. What a testimony that was to me!

In May, I packed and mailed a couple of big boxes of school things to Korea, not knowing what teaching supplies would be available there. I wanted my classroom to have all the games, puzzles, and activities I had made for my students.

I applied for a two-year leave of absence from my teaching position in Lancaster, since I didn't know if I would be returning there after my two-year contract expired. But they would only grant me a one-year leave, per their standard practice. I found a young couple to sublet my apartment for two years, to keep that door open, as well, and stored most of my belongings in the basement of the apartment while I was away. I sold my car to a nice couple who kindly let me use it until I left. My friends and church gave me a big send-off. It was with a heavy heart that I said goodbye to North School, my church, my friends, and Lancaster. I left North School with 180 unused sick days! I almost never missed school. I had developed wonderful memories and friends living in Lancaster.

In August, my parents drove over from Indiana and they, along with four of my friends, drove me to the Columbus airport to see me off. I reunited with Donita there, whom I had met at the Cleveland job fair. She was hired as the new music teacher at Seoul Foreign School, and we had communicated for a few months and asked SFS to arrange our flights together. However, the Air Traffic Controller's Union had gone on strike a week before we were scheduled to fly, so all our flights were canceled. We were put on a small eight-seat commuter plane going to Detroit and weren't sure we'd even have a flight after that. We were only allowed one suitcase on the small plane. I grabbed one, not knowing if it held summer or winter clothes. As it turned out, I had to wear the same clothes for the first four days I was in Korea till the rest of my luggage arrived. I had opted

Setting off for Korea!   **Friends to see me off!**

to carry my things with me, rather than send a shipment, so I had pared my belongings down to bare bones—just two suitcases, one trunk, and my trusty sewing machine.

Leaving Lancaster and all my friends was very hard, but I was thrilled to move on to the next exciting room of my life.

CHAPTER SIX
DINING ROOM
SEOUL FOREIGN SCHOOL
(Seoul, Korea)
1981-1989

Korea was like the dining room of my "house." What started out as a two-year meal (contract) morphed into an eight-year smorgasbord. During those eight years, I was well fed (physically, mentally, emotionally and spiritually), gathered wonderful new friends around my table, shared challenging new cultural "dishes" with people who relished those new experiences as much as I did, and feasted on the most thrilling and life-changing period of my life. I compare those dramatic changes in my life to eating nothing but plain bread before and now gorging on succulent meats, creamy sauces, delectable vegetables, and rich desserts! Because it was such a rich experience for me, I kept extending my contract, so I could delay leaving the table.

Since my eight years in Korea are related in great detail in my two books, *Seoul Searching* (2019) and *Re-Searching Seoul* (2020), through my monthly newsletters to folks back home, I won't go into as much depth here. Those books contain a lot of information and detail that will help the reader better understand this period of my life. I highly recommend readers also read those books.

Just as I had with England, I fell in love with Korea. It was the most unique culture I had ever experienced. It's hard to explain why the challenge of figuring out a new culture appealed to me. It was exhausting and exhilarating all at the same time. It was incredibly hard, but so rewarding. Nothing around me was familiar—street signs, language, alphabet, approaches to problem solving, clothing, food or customs. I didn't speak the language, couldn't rely on my surroundings or signs in my environment to get around, didn't understand the culture, had no car, and was overwhelmed and exhausted by culture shock. It was a very steep learning curve, but I persisted, and it impacted my life in huge ways. Korea had a profound effect on my life.

I know I offended a few times without understanding what I was doing. For example, when I first arrived, I graded my student's papers with red ink and usually wrote their name on the top of papers, such as, "Good Job, Hu Won!" I was soon advised that is offensive to Koreans. Writing a name in red or black ink signifies blood or death (in the Shamanistic religion). And when I laughed out loud with my mouth open, I was being rude by Korean standards. Koreans giggle behind their hands.

The Korean gate at SFS

I taught first grade for five years (again in room 108—what a coincidence!), then moved to second grade for three years. Seoul Foreign School, (with over 700 students, pre-kindergarten through high school), had students from over 30 countries, with an interesting mix of backgrounds. There were children of businessmen, missionaries, embassy workers, and a few military-related personnel (most military dependents attended the DoD—Department of Defense—schools in the area), but none of our SFS students could hold Korean passports (hence, "foreign" school). Some of my students spoke no English and had come from backgrounds that astounded and impressed me. I was used to working with lower and middle-class families and suddenly I was working with the upper echelons of society—kids who had drivers and wore Gucci accessories! What a difference! I was also used to teaching in the public school system and now discovered the delights of working in a private school, with much more freedom to experiment and great support from parents, who demanded more from their children and their teachers!

I was delighted to teach children from so many different cultures and countries. It was very challenging. While there were many names I struggled to pronounce, some of the more challenging over the years were Resvaninijad, Athanissiadou, Quaeyhaegens, and Charutrakulchai. It was quite normal to have children from 15 or 20 different countries in my class.

My kidlets, for the most part, were bright, alert, eager and delightful. Their world views were quite different from my students in Ohio. They had been everywhere and experienced a great variety of life, thus their "schemata" (or schema—background knowledge) made learning easier and more fun. I thrived teaching them! In contrast to my kidlets in Ohio, these children were able to master counting to ten in 15 languages by the end of each year. I worked hard to keep ahead of them! Their hunger to learn was inspiring. There were two first grade classes, and I loved Mary Pat, the other first grade teacher. We became lifelong friends. By my second year there, parents were again requesting me as their child's teacher. I felt honored.

I taught in the "old" building for the first couple of years, then they tore that down (during the school year!) and built a new elementary school. That transition was difficult and inconvenient for everyone, but we managed. I also lived in five different apartments while in Korea, so it seemed I was in a constant state of transition, moving and settling in, during my eight years there.

KOREAN CULTURE

Carrying a baby o-ba-ba

Buddhist bell

Kimchi, national dish of Korea

Sec dong fabric

Kimchi pots

Shoes off at the door

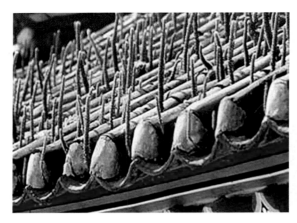

Weeds growing out of a tile roof

Bride and Groom in a traditional Korean wedding

**Temple with the Buddhist
symbol (NOT a Nazi swastika!)**

**The elderly are
greatly respected**

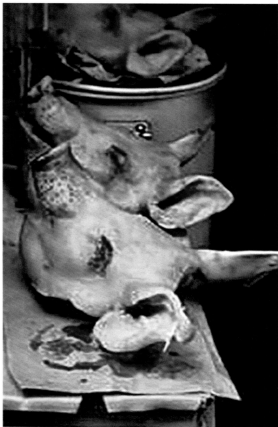

**Offerings
to
Buddha**

Planting rice is never fun.
Bent from dawn till the set of sun.
Cannot stand and cannot sit.
Cannot rest for a little bit.

Drying garlic   **Dried fish**

**My
chicken
lady**

**Carrying heavy loads
on their backs**

Running to catch a bus

On a city bus

Seoul traffic jam

Both old and new in Seoul

Farmer's Dance

Korean drums

Farmer's Dance

At the 1988 Olympics

My favorite Olympic poster

Harubang (stone grandfathers), Chejudo

Beautiful Korea

Typical Korean road sign

Buddha's birthday lanterns

My absolute favorite picture of Korea!

Koreans are not as informal as Westerners are. They rarely address others, even friends, by first names. It is always "Miss Kim" or "Mr. Oh." And in many situations, Koreans seem to do the exact opposite of what we do. For example, we motion "come here" wagging one finger with our palm up. That is extremely offensive in Korea. Instead, you wag all four fingers with your palm down (like we "shoo" someone away). One Korean woman was shot and killed by soldiers at a checkpoint, after they motioned for her to leave (shooing her away) but she thought they were motioning for her to come nearer.

Putting your feet up and showing the soles of your feet is considered very rude. It is offensive if you hand someone a gift or item with only one hand (this is a hold-over from the old days when the other hand could be holding a weapon). Either offer the item with both hands or hold the item with one hand while touching your wrist with the other hand. It is offensive to touch a Korean child on the head.

In years past, it wasn't unusual for a Korean businessman to board a city bus after work, find a seat, and begin to disrobe. In a city where crowding is such a problem, you can attain privacy by undressing! You become "invisible" when you disrobe (no one will look at you). Therefore, the businessman could have a few minutes privacy and peace before arriving home. While that is rare today, it is still quite common for shoppers to disrobe in the aisle of a crowded store to try on a new outfit. When undressed, you become "invisible" to other shoppers.

Korean toilets are quite different than Western ones. Instead of a seat on a raised platform, it is an oblong hole in the floor. You need to squat to do your business. Hence, "squat pots!" Many Koreans, when traveling to other countries, still put their feet up on a toilet seat and squat there. Toilet paper is never put in the toilet, but in a wastebasket nearby. Thus, Korean toilets smell! And many Korean toilets are unisex. Women are expected to walk past men at the urinals and proceed to a squat pot with a door.

We take our hats off in a home, but Koreans take their shoes off at the door. We clean our plate to show we are done eating (and how much we liked the food). Koreans leave a bit on the plate to indicate they are done. If they eat it all, it is assumed they want more. Westerners pronounce their family names last in sequence (Min Ah Kim), but Koreans give their family names first in the sequence (Kim, Min Ah). In Western society, youth is highly valued. In Korea, the elderly are highly respected. Westerners say, "excuse me," when trying to get around someone. Koreans think it is much more polite not to intrude on your private thoughts by speaking to you, so they push you out of their way instead. I was pushed into busy city streets many times and I thought Koreans were the rudest people I had ever met, until someone explained to me the reasoning behind it. That made it much easier for me to handle.

We carry loads in our arms, but Koreans carry loads on their backs—which is much better for your back! We shake hands while Koreans bow. When two people are talking and a third person needs to pass through, Westerners will move together so the third person can pass behind. Koreans move back so the third person can pass between. Western parents discipline their children from an early age and prefer that schools do not punish their children. Korean parents do not discipline their children at all and expect teachers to do that after age six. Therefore, small Korean children are sometimes quite "bratty." Westerners blame teachers for everything. Koreans hold teachers in high regard (even though they pay them poorly!)

One cultural habit I struggled with was that Korean children will not look you in the eye when you are scolding them. Our tendency is to put a finger under their chin and say, "You look at me when I'm talking to you!" But by not making eye contact, they are showing you more respect. And they giggle when you are scolding them! They aren't being rude and making light of what you are saying to them. They are embarrassed and cover that by giggling. Those in positions of authority are addressed by their position rather than their name, so my students rarely called me, "Miss Wilson," but "teacher," to show me respect.

I took Korean lessons for two years, and while I never became proficient, I managed to get by. They say Korean is the second hardest language to learn after Finnish, (but I don't know if that's true.) My language skills were compartmentalized—talking to shop keepers, ordering groceries over the phone (I had to learn the Korean words for foods, weights, amounts, brands, etc.), discussing baby and household topics with my adjumonie (nanny, housekeeper, maid), finding the restroom, and basic conversation with strangers. Early on, I memorized a very basic sentence syllable by syllable, to help me out of difficult situations—"I'm so sorry, I only speak a little. Korean is very difficult and confusing!" ("Me an ham ni da. Cho cum ha sayo. Han gook mal ajoo pok chop hayo.") Koreans always reacted with laughter and kindness at my stupidity. They were amazingly forgiving and just tickled that I made an attempt to learn their language.

Learning Korean is different than learning French or Spanish, because there you can rely on the same alphabet while learning new vocabulary. But Korean requires a three-fold thought process—learning to read a new alphabet, learning new vocabulary (and grammar), and knowing which level of language to use, depending on whom you are speaking to!

The Korean alphabet (Hangul) was invented in 1446 by King Sejong and is the only alphabet in the world that has a special holiday to celebrate it! Korean is phonetic and is much easier to learn than Chinese, where the characters stand for an idea. I memorized the Korean alphabet in a day. In Hangul, there are 14 consonants and ten vowels. The vowels make a different sound than in the English alphabet. For example, a short "a" in English says "a" as in "apple." But the Korean "a" says "ah." The "i' makes a long "ee" sound, as is true in several other languages. In Korean, each letter makes only one sound, which makes them more stable than English letters. Letters are grouped into syllables with a space between syllables. There are no capital or lower-case letters.

Korean can be written left to right or top to bottom. Sometimes words are transliterated rather than translated. For example, I spent most bus

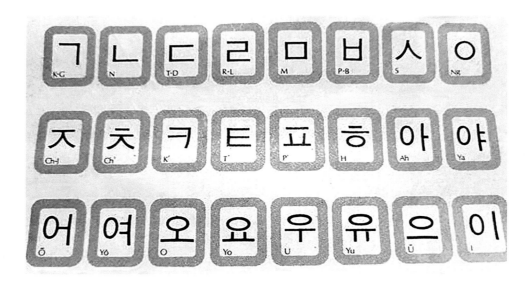

and taxi rides practicing my skills at decoding road signs. One day, I translated a word on a shop as "tah ee ah." I couldn't figure it out until I realized the word had been transliterated (written in Korean but using an English word)—"tire." It was a tire shop! Koreans tend to make more syllables out of words than we do in English. Hence, "tire" (two syllables in English) became three syllables in Korean! We pronounce "Seoul" as one syllable, but Koreans make two syllables out of it—"Sa' well."

Since there are seven levels in the Korean language, you not only have to learn vocabulary, but also need to figure out the correct level to use, depending on the age/position of the person you are speaking to. You can say the same thing at seven different levels. Thus, Koreans need to know how old you are (and usually how much money you make!) so they know which level to use in speaking to you. Westerners consider it rude to ask those personal questions, but Koreans ask it for a reason! I frequently embarrassed myself by using the wrong level when talking to children, adults my age, or someone older than me.

Much of a Korean sentence is understood. So if I want to say, "he will go tomorrow" all I need to say is "tomorrow go." There are no pronouns in Korean, so when trying to learn English, Koreans have a terrible time understanding and using pronouns. I frequently had parent conferences where the parents of a daughter kept referring to their daughter as "he" or "him." And the order of words in a Korean sentence are different than in

English. We place words in subject, verb, object order, but Koreans put the verb last. I always came away from my Korean lessons with a headache!

Koreans also use two different counting systems. For simple counting, amounts of money, minutes in an hour, bus numbers, apartment numbers, telephone numbers and addresses, "Chinese" numbers (not really Chinese, but adapted from Chinese to Korean) are used. But for hours of the day, and counting objects or people, Korean numbers are used. My head hurt from trying to sort all that out, too.

For all Koreans, your age changes at the New Year. A child is one year old when born and becomes two the next January. Thus, a baby born in Dec. becomes two years old the following month. So when I ask a child how old he is, he/she usually asks, "My Korean age or my American age?" It gets quite confusing.

Koreans are a proud and stubborn people. They think very highly of themselves. That is evident in the words they use. The Korean word for the Korean people is, "Hahn gook" (number one people); the national costume, "hahn bok" (han boke) (number one outfit); the Korean language, "Hahn gook mal" (number one language); and the Korean alphabet "Hahn gul" (number one alphabet). But my favorite is their word for God—"Hahn na neem" (number one honorific "being").

Koreans use different logic than Westerners do. For example, one of our teachers found a small hole in her apartment wall where water was trickling in. She called maintenance to come, assuming they would simply plug up the hole. Instead, they drilled another hole right below it so the water could run back out again! It worked!

Koreans eat some form of kimchi (the national dish) at every meal. There are over 50 types of kimchi. The most prevalent is cabbage kimchi. In the days before refrigeration, when they had no form of vegetables during the winter months, they made kimchi. It is cabbage, radish, cucumber or other forms of vegetables, marinated in garlic and red pepper and allowed to ferment. It is very spicy! It is stored in stone jars (kimchi pots) and buried in the ground up to the brim. Koreans eat so much kimchi that it is no longer just a matter of bad breath—they sweat the garlic smell out of their pores! Your only defense to avoid smelling it is to eat it, too, and then you don't notice how they smell! Getting on a city bus without having some kimchi in your system is a most unpleasant experience!

You should never eat kimchi by itself. A bite of rice first, then kimchi. Drinking water to cool your mouth is not as effective as eating more rice.

We ex-pats adopted a saying that someone who was in big trouble was in "deep kimchi!" It seemed most fitting.

I watched Korean children playing a game called "kiyee, biyee, bo" which later became quite popular in the U.S. but there was known as "rock, paper, scissors."

My friend, Becky Anderson, and I usually went to the business office together to pick up our pay (in cash) and pay our utilities. Becky was a towheaded blond and I had brown hair, but poor Mrs. Kim could never tell us apart. She remarked, "Oh, all you foreigners look alike!" I had to laugh because I thought all Koreans looked alike when I first moved there! We at least had different hair color! They all had black hair.

One day, out on my balcony, I found colored propaganda leaflets from North Korea which had probably been dropped from spy planes. They were fascinating and of much better quality than the ones I had found previously. South Koreans will not pick them up or touch them in any way because showing any interest in North Korea is very frowned on in South Korea.

KEN JENNINGS

My first year at SFS (1981), there was an "unusual" (OK, nerdy!) second grader named Ken Jennings. Since I was teaching first grade, I missed having him as a student, but did have his sister, Gwen, and his brother, Nathan, in first grade in subsequent years. I got to be good friends with their mother, Cathy, and later helped them adopt a Korean child, whom they named Miranda (can you tell dad was a lawyer?). Many years later, Ken Jennings became famous for his incredible winning streak on the TV show, "Jeopardy." Then he won the GOAT (Greatest of All Time) tournament and hosted the show after Alex Trebek passed away. What a hoot to have known him and his family many years earlier!

My favorite story about Ken was when my friends, Jay and Dusty, went to Kenny's parents' house for dinner one night and saw Kenny going up and down the outside stairs. When they got inside, they asked Cathy what Kenny was doing. She laughed and explained that Kenny had trouble going up and down stairs like other people—he stepped down with one foot and then the other foot onto the same step, instead of one foot on

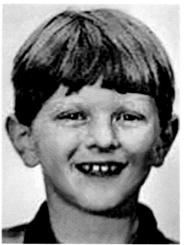

Grade 2   **Grade 3**   **Grade 4**

one step and the other foot to the next step. He knew that wasn't how everyone else did it, so he was making himself practice to get it right. Oh, the problems of being super brilliant!

It's rare you get to see the school pictures of someone famous! So, just for a hoot, I've included elementary and middle school photos of Ken Jennings.

TEACHING AT SEOUL FOREIGN SCHOOL

I made a point of visiting Korean schools while I was there, because I wanted to experience the difference in educational philosophies. Korean schools have 80-90 children in one room, but there are NO discipline problems. While Korean parents do not discipline their children at all, they tell children that when they get to school, they will mind the teacher. So, these children sit perfectly still in a cold room with colorless walls and recite everything the teacher says. Learning is rote. Their philosophy is that if the teacher says it and you repeat it, then you have learned it. There is no provision for special needs or to cement understanding. Children with special needs are sent to special schools and kept out of sight of regular society. Teachers are held in high esteem, but paid poorly. The higher the grade you teach, the more respect you earn.

One year, my friend Evy moved from teaching fifth grade to high school English and all the school adjumonies were tsking and shaking their heads over it. When I asked why, I was told that Evy got a promotion, but

Grade 5

Grade 6

Grade 7

2022 SFS Alumnus of the Year

Grade 8

her poor husband didn't—he was still teaching sixth grade. They felt so sorry for him! Koreans assume you get promotions to teach the higher grades. They didn't understand our system. So they must have thought I was a really lousy teacher to still be teaching first grade!

One of our teachers related how frustrated her husband got with the way Koreans said his name, which was Jerry Wilms. But since Koreans frequently interchange the "r" sound and the "l" sound, his name was usually pronounced "Jelly Worms." And you'll just have to understand and take this next one in the right context. To buy a subway ticket to the City Hall stop, don't try to enunciate it slowly in the hopes of getting your point across. It won't work. Instead, you have to say "Shitty Whore," and they understand perfectly. And then there were the Lionel Richie tapes prominently displayed with his name clearly printed as, "Rionel Lichie."

1982

1983

1985

Top: First Graders 1982-1983 • Bottom: First Graders 1983-1984

Second Graders 1986-1987

Hu Won Wang and friend (I love his musical sounding name!)

With Dean, the principal

Faculty dressed up in hanboks for Korea Week

After my first year in Korea, I wrote to Lancaster requesting an extension of my one-year leave of absence. They refused—they were laying off teachers and had no jobs to "save" for me, so I resigned from Lancaster permanently. During my second summer home to Ohio, I moved all my belongings to storage and gave up my old apartment.

Seoul Foreign School is the oldest foreign school in Korea and I was blessed to be there for their 75th anniversary. It was quite an impressive celebration, complete with a time capsule. However, we all arrived coughing, sneezing and crying from tear gas since we drove through a demonstration on the way there.

I was quite disheartened to run across some "dishonest" missionaries. One such couple was in the U.S. during the summer, and I heard they were presenting at a church in Ohio, so I decided to go, just to see them. It was a long drive and I got there late, so I slipped into the back pew. During their presentation they showed slides of their church (not accurate) and their home, showing a poor, run-down place. I immediately realized that was false, too, because I had been to their home. After the presentation, I slipped out without talking to them, so they wouldn't know I had been there. I was stunned they would present their situation inaccurately. I suppose it was an effort to drum up more support.

Another missionary taught Bible classes at SFS. One day over lunch she mentioned they wanted more money to live on, so she said she was going to tell her church board their electric bill had gone up, so they would send them more. I was stunned.

One missionary friend, Pat, had eight children and they had recently built a huge new home. The Korean neighbors jokingly called it the "mansion on the hill." I briefly worked with her while trying to adopt, until I learned some of her methods were suspect.

Evy's (teacher friend) mother came to Korea to visit and was able to meet some missionaries she had sacrificed to support for years. When she found out how well they were living, she felt completely betrayed. But she said she would continue supporting them; it was her job to be faithful. It was up to God to deal with them. I thought that was a very mature attitude.

Bachelor Creek Church, where I grew up, supported the Burney family in Japan for years. I vividly remember Grma sacrificing to support them financially. But they seemed to win few souls to Christ in Japan. Although I know Japan is a difficult place to win souls, I remember wondering if they were just "living" in Japan and not really doing any work. While at SFS, I met the Burney's son, Joe, who was married to the daughter of the SFS headmaster. He was a very strange guy, disliked by many and strangely lacking in social graces. Very interesting.

On the other hand, I met many wonderful and dedicated missionaries. I learned missionaries are just like the rest of the population—some good and some bad!

I collected some hilarious things my kidlets said and did. Those are all related in my first two books, but I'll include a few here.

Little Ernest, whose black Korean hair typically stood straight up, came to school one day with bad red marks around his neck. Seems he was playing with a rope. . . he could have strangled himself. Ernest was always in trouble (not malicious, just a typical "boy" but also clueless!) and had been paddled the year before in kindergarten. One day, the principal announced over the intercom system (first graders usually think that is the voice of God!) that someone had been writing on the bathroom walls and if anyone was caught doing so again, the "severest punishment would be meted out." Knowing that my kidlets would have no idea what that meant, I followed up with a discussion.

After explaining what "meted out" meant, I asked, "What is the worst thing the principal can do to you if you write on the bathroom walls?" My kidlets thought and thought but didn't know. I figured Ernest should know since he'd been paddled the year before.

Finally, Ernest gasped and shouted out, "He'll break all our pencils!" I made sure to let the principal know that he had wasted his time paddling Ernest; he should have just broken all his pencils.

Since I had a directive from the principal to send Ernest to him for any misdeeds (he remembered Ernest from Kindergarten and wanted to step on problems before they developed too far), the next time I sent Ernest to the office, the principal (with a straight face) told Ernest that if he didn't straighten up, he would come to the room and break all his pencils. Ernest was shocked! When he came back to the room and the kids asked him what had happened, he replied, "The principal solved all my problems!"

When the principal did my annual evaluation, he made a point of asking two or three of my students what kind of a teacher I was. Naturally, he picked Ernest, who told the principal I was very strict and tough. Then he smiled and said, "But it's only 'cause she loves me!" Whew!

Little Becca, a Korean girl adopted by Lutheran missionaries, was extremely shy and never spoke up in class. One day, we were writing two-line poems about a picture of a turtle who had crawled out of his shell and was shivering. When I asked who wanted to read their poem, Becca's hand went up. I figured I'd better take advantage of that since she never volunteered for anything! She proudly read her poem, "What the hell, I lost my shell." I almost choked, but had to maintain my composure so as not to embarrass her and make her "lose face." The daughter of a missionary? In a Christian school? Where in the world had she even heard such language?

At recess, I went down to the office and showed her poem to the principal, who knew her parents from church. He roared with laughter. However, that action backfired on me. Unbeknownst to me, the principal shared that poem with the pastor, who, the next Sunday in church, read Becca's poem from the pulpit to the total surprise of her parents, who knew nothing about it. I felt awful. I should have kept my mouth shut. That poem spread through the foreign community like wildfire.

A few months later, the same family adopted another Korean girl (three years old) and named her Michelle. One day, Michelle wanted to walk to school with Mom to pick up her brother and sister after school, but Mom told her to just wait at the compound gate instead. When Becca and Mark got home, they asked where Michelle was—she was not waiting for them at the gate. The whole compound turned out to look for Michelle. Then Mom got a call from SFS saying there was a little girl at the school—was it their daughter? Little Michelle had walked down the mountain they

Nathan Jennings (Ken Jennings brother)

Becca Susan (turtle poem)

Ali Khanbashi

lived on, through Yonhi Dong, crossed eight major lanes of traffic and then up the SFS mountain to the school—a trip she had only made a few times before with Mom. Everyone was quite surprised she managed to find her way.

So then the joke going around the foreign community was, "What the hell, where's Michelle?" That poor family endured a lot of ribbing. And it was all my fault for not keeping my mouth shut.

The parents of little Ali Khanbashi (from Iran) told me they were raising him to be the foreign minister of Iran. The family moved to Bahrain a couple of years later, where my friend Donita was teaching. She related that she had his sister, Lilly, in school. Then the family moved back to Seoul. Our teachers reported that Lilly was mesmerized by Christianity and that her family called her, "Little Mary," because she constantly talked about it. I asked if that bothered her family. They said, "No," because she is just a girl and her opinion does not matter. I hoped and prayed she would be able to make some inroads into her family's beliefs and win them to Christ in future years.

Little Alice (from Australia) was very adventurous. She made a habit of getting off the school bus I put her on at the end of each day, then getting on a different bus and getting off somewhere in the city (of ten million people) wherever she felt like. The first time resulted in a serious talk and a warning, but after the police found her the second time, the principal

 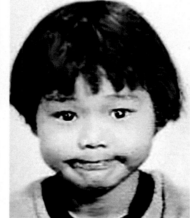 

Gwen Jennings
(Ken Jennings sister)   **Woi Chien Lim**   **Bonani Basu**

decided to give her one extra swat on her bottom every time she repeated her trick. He got up to eight swats before she finally stopped doing it. And this from a six-year-old! I couldn't always be there to make sure she stayed on the bus I put her on and the school bus drivers were of absolutely no help in the matter, since Koreans do not discipline children at all. That is the teacher's job. The drivers refused to keep her from getting on their buses or stop her from getting off somewhere in the middle of Seoul.

Little Woi Chien ("way-chin") was certainly a delightful handful. He was from Singapore and was one of the most cheerful children I had ever met. So cheerful, in fact, that it made me want to pull my hair out. For everything I told him to do, his answer was always, "OK!" while smiling with big eyes and nodding his head agreeably and then going on his merry way, totally ignoring what I told him to do. I realize you aren't getting the full effect when you can't see him in action. He had an extremely short attention span and couldn't concentrate on anything. But I did love that kid—he was such a hoot!

I gave Woi Chien more than adequate time to settle into first grade and learn good work habits, using several different methods to encourage him to get his work done, but nothing worked. I finally had a conference with his mother and she suggested that I should give him a time limit every day and if he didn't meet it, she wanted me to send him to see the principal. I didn't make a habit of sending children to the principal, opting instead to solve issues myself (so as to maintain the authority in my own classroom), but Woi Chien simply wasn't "getting it." The first two times Mr. K., the principal, merely talked to him, but I knew that wouldn't last long. The third time I sent him to Mr. K, I think Woi Chien realized it, too.

I said, "Woi Chien, I sure do hate to send you to the principal."

"Wow, I sure do hate to go, too!" he chirped cheerfully, with a broad smile on his face. But Mr. K. wasn't in at the time, so I had to send him back down after lunch, by which time Woi Chien had become pretty shaken. Having that hang over his head had only served to increase his anxiety. The rest of the class was in music and I was out in the hall hanging up student papers when Woi Chien returned. He sauntered down the hall with his hands in his pockets, and I could tell by his actions that not much had happened.

"What happened, Woi Chien?" I asked.

"Oh, boy, I sure do hate to tell you!" he sang cheerfully.

"I know you do, but don't you think I should know?" I urged.

"Yeah, but I sure do hate to tell you!" he repeated, shaking his head. By this time, I was having great difficulty keeping a straight face.

"I really do think you'd better tell me, Woi Chien," I coaxed.

"Well, Mr. K. said he was going to paddle me the next time!" he sang smilingly. "Boy, I sure was worried!" To drive home just how worried he had been, he turned, walked into the classroom and threw up on my desk. I'd like to think it wasn't a malicious act, but simply a matter of timing. Anyway, he perfected his aim nicely, I thought. That seemed to be the turning point in his awareness of his lackadaisical behavior and he became a bit more studious and reliable after that. I feared he would never set the world on fire with ambition, but at least he tried harder.

When he was in second grade, Woi Chien often stood with me while I was on recess duty. We discussed such heavy topics as the political situation in Singapore or did I know that street in Singapore where they sell batiks from Indonesia? He was thrilled when I could respond with, "Arab Street?" and then we'd carry on conversations about the different things to see and do there, like the Jurong Bird Park or the Telok Ayre Market. I was pleased I could remember those things so I didn't disappoint him. I think I learned more about Singapore from him than he did from me in all of first grade! What a sweet kid, but he certainly didn't relate to his peers.

Little Bonani (from India) couldn't jump rope when the school year started. All year, at recess, I watched her make slow progress until she was finally able to get all the way through the jump rope rhyme and then begin counting. I was so proud of her one day when she got all the way up to 18, but then her underpants fell down around her ankles. She calmly pulled them back up and walked to the back of the line for another turn. I was dying laughing inside, but the students didn't even seem to think anything of it.

One day, shy little Jean (a Korean), a new student, stood behind me while I was in reading group, to complain that she didn't feel well. Before I knew it, she threw up on my back. She felt so badly about it. Luckily, I could slip home to change quickly.

One of my saddest memories is of Ronald (an American). He was a depressing little boy and showed alarming signs of being suicidal. I was able to talk to his parents and they got him some help. I still wonder what happened to him.

Brent, me, Cheri 1982   **Cheri, Me, Brent 1983**

With my two precious grandmothers 1984

During my second summer home in Indiana, I also spent time in Ohio with my friends. Rob, my old boyfriend, wanted us to get together for dinner, so I went. He showed me the house he had just purchased and said I could fix it up any way I wanted. What????? Somehow, he had convinced himself that I was coming back to Lancaster and would marry him now. I gently, but firmly let him know that was not going to happen.

That fall, as I began my third year in Korea (1983), KAL flight 007 passenger plane was shot down by the Russians just before our school year started. SFS lost students and one of them was little Noelle (and her whole family), who was slated to be in my first grade class that year. We were as shocked as the rest of the world. We held a memorial service at SFS and my first graders sang Noelle's favorite verse of "Away in a Manger"— "Be Near Me, Lord Jesus." We also placed a plaque in her honor near the elementary school playground. It was a tragic start to our year. The international uproar over that incident was scary. Many thought Korea or the U.S. should attack Russia. It was an extremely tense time in Korea.

Then I got a phone call from Rob (back in Ohio). That was very unusual since no one could afford international calls. Rob adamantly demanded I resign my job and come home to Lancaster—Seoul was not safe. I turned him down again. I can only assume he thought being assertive and putting his foot down over the issue would win me over. Not happening.

Mom wrote to me every week, like she had while I was in college and in Ohio. She typed her letters on an old typewriter where she had to pound each key hard to make it go down. We couldn't afford long-distance phone calls and there were no computers then, so no e-mail. I looked forward to the daily mail with a passion. Those letters (which took about ten days to arrive) from my friends and family were a lifeline for me. One year, on Grma Faye's birthday, I splurged and called her ($100 for a ten-minute call). She couldn't believe she was talking to someone on the other side of the world! It thrilled her to death.

Korea was a shopper's paradise—eel skin, celadon pottery, brass, clothes, tennis shoes, jogging suits, jewelry, lacquerware, mother-of-pearl inlaid pieces, antique chests, etc. (I later heard that Korea sold all its antique chests to foreigners and there were no more left in-country—how sad.) And prices were very reasonable. It was very easy to fill up your apartment and I definitely took advantage of the situation. And Hong Kong was only a four-hour flight away. I made it to Hong Kong at least a dozen times during my eight years in Korea. What joy to shop there as well! I especially loved the Jade Market. I soon established my own personal jeweler in both Seoul (Turtle Hong—a wonderful Christian man) and Hong Kong and began stockpiling "real" jewelry that I never would have been able to afford in the States. I even designed some of it and had it made just for me.

I dated a couple of soldiers while in Korea. I beat one of them at racquetball, which did wonders for my ego! Me? A physically poor specimen beating a physically fit soldier? What a hoot. I'm not sure what it did to his ego!

After the grandkids began arriving, Mom's name, Marcella, got shortened to Grma Marcy. I was never sure she liked that, but she let the grandkids call her whatever they wanted! Dad retired from General Tire in 1984. I couldn't be there for his big retirement party, but they sent me a cassette tape of all of his roasts. Mom actually pulled off quite a surprise, which was hard to do with Dad. She held it a month early and he had no idea. Shortly after retiring, he bought and managed a carpet store (Wabash Interiors) shortly after retiring and went to work there every day. He had an attractive younger gal, Mae, working for him and I began to suspect trouble. Mom didn't say so directly, but I could read between the lines, to know that she was jealous of Mae and the attention Dad gave her. My antennae were already up, so it didn't take much for me to figure out why.

If you read my two books (*Seoul Searching* and *Re-Searching Seoul*), you'll learn that God gave me a new restlessness soon after I arrived in Korea. I recognized that feeling from when He urged me to teach overseas. This time, I felt like He was telling me it was time to work on another life list item—adopting! That was not why I had moved to Korea, so it surprised me, but I was 31 when I moved there, and the timing seemed right, according to my life list desires. However, I soon learned that by Korean law, it was illegal for single parents to adopt Korean children, so while I was busy teaching, and earning my master's degree, I spent four long, frustrating years fighting a legal battle to adopt a daughter. One of the issues that came up was that the adoption agencies hinted that I should bribe them under the table. Since that went against my values, I chose not to do that, even though it might have moved things along more quickly. George (friend) suggested I provide the man at the adoption agency with a bottle of bourbon, but that wasn't my style.

As a cheaper way to get home to the U.S. for the summer (it still wasn't free!), I applied for two orphan flights (through Holt Adoption Agency) in 1982 and 1983. Both times, I escorted six babies to Detroit (with another worker). It was exhausting work, with no time to eat or sleep for over 30 hours, but it was so rewarding to hand those precious babies over to their excited new parents! However, it made my desire to adopt more pronounced.

Another teacher, Flo, had a very traumatic orphan flight. Besides her six babies, there was another Korean man who had six babies. He left them sleeping and one of them suffocated in the pillows. She was a twin. Her poor parents in New York were expecting to receive two new children, but only got one. So heart-breaking. Since it happened in international airspace, no one was allowed to disembark till the authorities had investigated the accident.

I was blessed to sing in two very special cantatas with South Post Chapel (on the army base). They were both professionally staged, included actors and costumes, and were sung from memory. The Easter Cantata and then the Christmas Cantata were incredibly moving, and singing those songs about baby Jesus was so precious to me. I got to be good friends with some of those folks and they followed my adoption process with interest. They wanted to know how my "four-year pregnancy" was going.

WORLD TRAVELS

Before I became a mother, I took full advantage of traveling in Korea and to more foreign countries. Over weekends, fall breaks, Christmas, Easter, and summer breaks, I traveled a lot. I took a graduate class in Hawaii one summer, stepped across the line into North Korea a few times (very sobering), and went to Hong Kong (dozens of times—it became my favorite city in the world!). I visited Taiwan (incredible museums!), Malaysia, Indonesia (love those batiks), Bali (where we slept in a straw hut with no electricity or running water and lost all track of time), Thailand (wore a python around my neck in Bangkok on Christmas Day and rode an elephant through the jungle in Chaing Mai). In China, I climbed the Great Wall and marveled at the newly discovered life-sized terra cotta statues in Xian—we were one of the first tour groups into China after it opened to foreigners in 1982. They did not know how to deal with tourists! In Nepal, I went trekking in the Himalayas and rode an elephant through the jungle. Singapore was the cleanest city I've ever seen. Japan was gorgeous covered by cherry blossoms in the spring, while the Hiroshima Museum was very sobering. On my way around the world twice, I visited India (the Taj Mahal!),

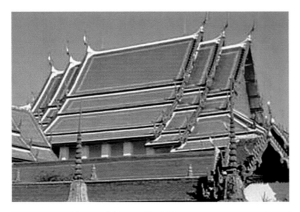

Bahrain (sand everywhere but lots of gold jewelry), Italy (the artwork is phenomenal), Egypt (rode a camel around the pyramids), and Greece (loved the Parthenon). What wonderful things I saw. I have treasured memories of those trips and of my fellow friends and travelers. And every time I flew to Hong Kong, I came back carrying another Chinese hat for my "hat wall." Travel broadens your horizons—what an education!

Wearing a python in Bangkok!

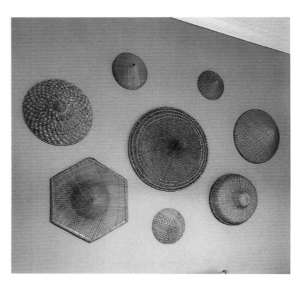

Chinese hats

Temples and cherry blossoms in Japan

**Himeji
Castle,
Japan**

**Life-size
terra
cotta
figures
in Xian,
China
1982**

Temple of Heaven, Beijing

Pokhara, Nepal

Katmandu, Nepal

Goats on the main street, Katmandu, Nepal

Great Wall of China 1982

Greece

TRAVEL BUDDIES
Me with Donita and Becky

Himalayas, Nepal

Nepal

Singapore

Egypt:
Riding a camel around the
Pyramids

India

At the 38th parallel (DMZ) in Korea

Riding an elephant in Thailand

I had to laugh at my friend, Dusty. The first time I visited the Great Wall, I collected a few souvenir pieces of the wall, where it was crumbling. She jokingly reprimanded me be saying, "Becky, if every visitor took a few pieces of the Great Wall, it would be gone in five million years!"

I did manage to get home every summer while I lived in Korea. I remembered when Cheri and Ralph used to go home to visit family in Wabash (when they lived in Ohio), Cheri got upset if people didn't come to visit them where they were staying. She didn't want to have to go to other people to see them—people could come to her. So when I was home, according to her logic, I just assumed they would come to see me, but no. Cheri was quite offended if I didn't go to see them. She was just too busy to stop what she was doing to come see me. And she didn't really want to hear anything about my life in Korea. She always changed the subject to what she and her family were doing. If we only talked about her family, we got along fine. I soon learned not to talk about Korea at all. And I could tell by her conversation that she had never bothered to read my monthly newsletters. They just didn't interest her.

While I was overseas, Cheri and Ralph bought a house in Roann, when Ralph left farming and bought an insurance company. They attended a Brethren Church in Roann, which really surprised me since they were so dead set on the Church of Christ doctrine. Did this mean they weren't "set in the faith?"☺ It didn't last long, however, and they went back to Bachelor Creek Church where Mom and Dad worshipped. But Cheri and Ralph hardly spoke to Mom and Dad at church, and I got reports that they walked around church with chips on their shoulders. Their bitterness seemed to be growing worse. I also got a report many years later that the folks at the Roann church found Cheri rather "bossy" and weren't too sad to see them leave that church.

Living in Roann, it was not a long-distance call for Cheri to telephone Grma Faye to check on her. She rarely did, though, which frustrated Mom, who couldn't afford to call Grma Faye long distance each day. In fact, Ralph and their boys took advantage of Grma by using Grma's old hen house to house some pigs, and then not cleaning it out when they removed the hogs. That added to Grma's stress. Peter, Cheri's oldest, did mow Grma's yard, but expected to be paid well for it and Grma couldn't afford that.

Cheri and Ralph began distancing themselves more and more from Mom and Dad and treated them poorly. I heard things like, "There is no excuse for the way we were treated," and, "We've had to put up with Dad's reputation for years." But she would never explain what she meant by that. I wondered if she knew about Dad's affair with Nancy but couldn't be sure. Since Cheri and Ralph were in the same church and in the insurance business, they may have heard rumors about Dad's infidelities from board members or others who knew Dad in the community.

One time, Mom went over to Cheri's house when she hoped Ralph would not be there. She wanted to ask Cheri directly what the problem was, why Cheri was so angry with the family and what could be done to improve things. But Ralph came in, then, and just stood there (like he was protecting Cheri?) so Mom never got an answer. Cheri refused to discuss it.

Another time, over a period of several weeks, Mom wrote Cheri anonymous letters of encouragement and support. She was trying (I think) to help Cheri be more positive and kind to others. Cheri liked them, thinking she had an admirer, till she found out Mom had sent them—then she was just irritated.

Cheri had worked several temporary jobs over the years—as an AAA clerk, as a pre-school aide (I was alarmed by the things she said about those youngsters and how she handled some situations), and at a bank. When a secretarial job opened up at Bachelor Creek Church, she applied, but was not hired. I suspect they had witnessed her attitude at church and had learned how difficult she could be. Cheri fumed about not getting that job. "I can't even get a job as a church secretary with a degree from a Bible college?" I suspect that was the final straw. They left Bachelor Creek Church and drove all the way down to Converse to worship. The family gap widened. Cheri finally began working at Ralph's insurance agency.

Cheri was an excellent cook and I had gotten several recipes from her over the years, but her sewing skills were just so-so. Trying to show her I was interested in her other artistic ventures, (she was quite talented at weaving baskets), I paid her to make me a large basket and several small baskets to hold my marble eggs. They were beautiful. It must have taken her hours. I appreciated them so much, and still have them. In later years, Cheri left basket-weaving behind and began making silk flower arrangements. I wasn't wild about them, but sweet Nore (in a bid to appease Cheri?) ordered and paid for several bouquets to give to her nurses.

One day, I got a letter from Cheri informing me that I was no longer to call my nephew, "Peter." He now wanted to be called "Pete." It seems some kids in his school were making fun of his name. He caved under the bullying. I was concerned that perhaps she had taught him to be as emotionally hyper-sensitive as she was. Many years later, Pete married Laurie. In my opinion, she was a very selfish, controlling, spoiled young lady. After they were married, she wouldn't let Pete have a key to her house (she owned it before they were married). He had to wait outside until she got home. Later, she divorced him and he became one of the "walking wounded."

By the late 1980's, Grma Faye had moved to Peabody Retirement Community in North Manchester. Cheri rarely visited her there, either, which really hurt Mom. And Grma didn't understand why Cheri was ignoring her.

Brent and Nore had two children—Chad was a year and a half when I left for Korea, but Kara (the family's first granddaughter!) was born while

I was overseas. I couldn't wait to meet and hold her and showed her photo to everyone.

My friends and I had a marvelous time together. We played euchre, ate out, explored Korea and generally enjoyed one another. One time, we were laughing so hard that Dusty wet her pants, which of course set us off even more! What a treasure my new friends were!

George and Lois Blanks (teachers) were great fun. George used to run a zoo and regaled us with funny zoo stories. They also liked to collect unusual objects from their travels around Korea. As a group of us gathered at their home one evening for games, I saw two large green glass balls used as ocean buoys, so I excitedly asked, "Oh, George, where did you get your balls?" I was quite embarrassed when the room exploded with laughter.

My principal, Dean Kauffman, gave me excellent reviews each year and in one of them, he commented that I should be teaching teachers. His comment made me remember that thought I'd had back in Ohio that supervising student teachers would be fun. I had never thought about teaching future teachers, but began mulling that over and praying about it, and soon I added three more items to my life list—getting a doctorate, teaching at the college level, and supervising student teachers. But having just finished my master's degree while teaching full-time, I was ready for a break from going to school, so I moved those new life list items to the back burner for the time being.

MASTERS DEGREE

I earned my master's degree through the University of Southern California (USC) at an extension on the army base in Yongsan. It was very hard getting to and from classes (two buses each way) and I wasn't always able to get through the gate onto the base, so I sometimes missed classes. And attending night classes while teaching full-time during the day was exhausting. I took several weekend classes as well. We met for eight hours on Saturday and eight hours on Sunday. I was usually brain dead by Sunday night!

For my master's thesis, I chose to study self-concepts in children and used my first-grade students as my subjects. I compared children's drawings of a person (which I scored to determine their intellectual maturity), and their views of themselves. I used a self-report survey, to see if there was a correlation with their academic achievement; it was interesting stuff! The worst part was not being able to find any research materials in Korea. Of course, this was in the days before computers, and army base libraries didn't have what I needed. Korean libraries, which were not heated in the winter, didn't have many resources in English. I was quite the spectacle in Korean libraries where foreigners seldom ventured. I finally got a friend in the U.S. to mail me one book I needed.

During the summer of 1984, I took a graduate class in Hawaii. The Moana Loa volcano was erupting then, and our class took a trip out to the area. We were able to stand in the middle of a highway that was blocked by the lava flow, and we watched the hot molten lava sluggishly inch its way across the road just a few inches from us. Quite an experience!

For graduation, in May, 1985, I was asked to give the student speech since I had the highest GPA in the group (4.0). I suppose I was the "valedictorian," but I don't think they use those terms for graduate school. What fascinated me about the group I graduated with was that none of them had undergraduate degrees in education and had never been teachers. They had absolutely no idea what teaching was like. Our classroom discussions were contentious, frustrating and fascinating, as I tried to get them to understand teaching. Why those folks wanted a master's degree in education was beyond me.

Master's degree, Seoul, Korea 1985

1985 turned out to be a particularly spectacular year. I traveled around the world, graduated with my master's degree and became a mother!

AMANDA

After four long frustrating years fighting the Korean government, God provided a miracle. I adopted my first daughter, Amanda, in November 1985. (See *Seoul Searching* for all the details.)

I want to make a special commendation here for my friends John and Gwen Johnson. On both of my adoption days, they went with me to pick up my new daughters. John is an excellent photographer and to this day, the pictures he took on those special occasions are precious to me. I would never have been able to remember all those special moments had he not captured them for me. Thank you, John!

That precious little ten-month-old girl changed my life drastically and I fell in love. Overnight, I went from being a carefree single woman with plenty of free time, to being a mother. I had never had to think of anyone else's needs or cook for anyone else, or restrict my activities, or lose any sleep. Suddenly, I was consumed with changing diapers, making baby food (which wasn't available in Korea), fixing bottles, going to doctor's appointments with no car, lugging my baby up and down that mountain, teaching full-time, getting no sleep, never having a moment to myself— and I had never been so happy in my life. Once I became a mother, I took skydiving off my life list. I figured my daughter had lost one family; she shouldn't have to risk losing another.

I had no "baby" equipment when I adopted—no playpen, no highchair, no stroller, no baby monitor, no toys, nothing. I bought a crib, and my friends threw a lovely shower for me, where I got lots of clothes, diapers, and toys, but I just did without the larger paraphernalia most new mothers have. I figured she'd grow up so fast we could do without those things for a few months. I borrowed a highchair and a friend loaned me a stroller one time to get down the hill to the doctor—who scolded me soundly for using a stroller—claiming the baby would get less pollution if I carried her on my back! I never did figure out how that could be, but I never used a stroller again—it was too much work over all the uneven sidewalks anyway. I just carried her "o-ba-ba" on my back.

One nice thing about living on a communal campus was that all the other teachers became aunts and uncles to the kids on campus. What a nice support system!

I got quite a reaction from Koreans after I adopted. Koreans do not adopt for any reason. That's why there are so many Korean children available to foreigners. Bloodlines are too important to them. So, for the life of them, they could not figure out why I would adopt, especially without a husband! I was quite the novelty to them. To their way of thinking, that would effectively ban me from ever getting married. While on city buses, Koreans would sometimes take Amanda out of my "o-ba-ba" back sling, pull down her pants, and check to see if she was a boy or a girl. A Caucasian woman with a Korean child was strange enough, but why in the world would I want a girl? Boys are much more valuable. And I'm sure they were horrified that I didn't wrap her in several layers of blankets. Koreans overwrap babies to the extent that the child literally sweats.

I got feedback from the parents in my classroom. They asked if there was a new student named Amanda in the class. Seems their child talked about Amanda constantly! What a hoot.

I also got feedback from the foreign community about their children's reactions to me "having" a child. The elementary school principal was tickled when his middle school son said, "But I thought you had to be married first!" He said it restored his faith in his son's innocence.

Koreans love babies and doted on Amanda. The assistants (girls) that roamed the grocery store aisles at Saruhga always took her away from me when I went in. They loved holding her while I shopped. One time, Hannam grocery store kindly gave me a real treat—a ride back up that steep mountain side (I found out later that they took sympathy on me because they thought my Korean husband must have died). Carrying bags of groceries up that mountain while carrying Amanda on my back was a real chore. So I soon learned to order groceries over the phone and have them delivered.

**Day I met Amanda
(8 months old)
October, 1985**

Adoption Day, November, 1985

Pure joy!

With Mrs. Nah

I got a call from Don, my agent in the Cleveland Teacher's Placement Office. He had heard I adopted and wanted to highlight my story in his magazine. So I wrote it up and sent him the article and a picture. What a hoot!

Carrying Amanda o-ba-ba   **One year old**

The "baby brigade" on campus

Carrying her babies o-ba-ba

First birthday!

Our beloved Mrs. Nah—beautiful inside and out!

She was so tickled with the silk blouse I brought her from Hong Kong.

My new adjumonie, Mrs. Nah, was an absolute treasure! What a sweet, kind woman. She fell in love with Amanda and proudly showed her off to all the other adjumonies on campus. Amanda loved her, too. First, she called her "Nah Nah" but that changed to "Missa Nah" as Amanda grew older. I didn't have Mrs. Nah cook for me very often, because she fixed too much. But I loved that she did my laundry and took care of Amanda while I taught. She even ironed my underwear! What a treat!

When Amanda began talking, Mrs. Nah held her as I'd leave for school every morning, and I told Amanda, "I love you!" For weeks she replied back, "I ... you!" The fact that she left out the middle word was quite consistent with the way children learn. They initially hear the first part of a new word or sentence and then they hear the last part. The middle part is the last part they attend to. So Amanda was doing just that by leaving out the middle word. She eventually included the middle word.

While in Korea, I didn't own a car and was supplied with a rent-free apartment, so for the first time in my life, I was able to save money! I did have to pay for utilities, (which were expensive), and constantly had to pay for taxis and bus tokens. That all added up quickly, but in general, my expenses were much lower. We were paid half in dollars into a bank account in the U.S. and half in Korean Won, in cash. I lived fairly easily on the Korean Won part of my salary. While the salary wasn't excessively large, it was adequate. But my financial picture changed drastically when I adopted my girls (1985 and 1988). Suddenly I was the only person on campus paying a full-time adjumonie from a single salary. Teaching couples who hired a full-time adjumonie for their children had two salaries to use! Things were more than just "tight" after I adopted. I earned extra income by administering GMAT, GRE and TOEFL tests on Saturdays to Korean adults, by private tutoring in English, doing Voice of America audio taping jobs, and then writing English textbooks for Korean middle schools. I also co-starred in the video cassettes that accompanied our textbooks. While I hated being away from the girls, the extra money helped us survive.

I had previously applied for the "First Teacher in Space" program with NASA. On January 28, 1986, the day I held an open house to celebrate Amanda's first birthday, the space shuttle Challenger exploded shortly after take-off. I was devastated. My students didn't understand why I was so upset all that day. It became quite clear to me that it was a "God thing," I was a new mother instead of on that space shuttle.

My family had no idea I had been trying to adopt but were thrilled for me (I sent telegrams). I took Amanda to the U.S. in June, 1986, to meet her new relatives. First, we flew to Hawaii to meet Amanda's new grandparents, who had flown there from Indiana to meet us. I had been working to set up her U.S. naturalization ceremony in Hawaii, but the adoption paperwork was delayed, so things did not work out. Then we stopped to visit my dear friends, Dean and Gaila Kauffman, in California. What joy they give me! I managed to secure another date for her to become an American citizen—on July 4th, in Indianapolis! The whole family turned out and we had a joyous day. Since that was the 200th anniversary of the Statue of Liberty, the crowd was too large for a normal courtroom, so the whole ceremony was held in Union Station in Indianapolis. Then, I worked furiously to secure a new U.S. passport for her, as well as a visa back to Korea for mid-August. One funny thing—Amanda didn't warm up to Grpa DeVon very

Four Generations:
Left: With Dad and Grma Charlotte
Right: With Mom and Grma Faye

**Amanda's winning
baby picture 1986**

**Quite the model!
2 years old**

well in Hawaii, that summer. But when we landed in Indianapolis, she immediately went right to Uncle Brent—a total stranger. I suspect it was because he looked like Uncle John at SFS. Grpa was quite hurt by that.

That summer, while in Indiana, I had Amanda's photo taken at K-Mart, where they were having a state-wide baby photo contest. I got word later that Amanda's photo won for the state of Indiana!! I put that $150 prize money into her college fund.

That fall (1986), I decided I needed a change after 14 years in first grade, so I "graduated" to teaching second grade. I was amazed at the difference! These kids knew how to stand in line, could tie their own shoes and never wet their pants! How refreshing! And I got to teach cursive writing! I was so excited to teach cursive and my kidlets were thrilled to learn how to write like adults. A few decades later, I was quite frustrated when schools had the option to stop teaching cursive. What a disservice schools are doing to children. Cursive requires a higher level of thinking than printing and our kidlets need to know how to read it.

One of my current second graders, Samir (from Pakistan), was talking to me at recess one day and said his family was moving to the U.S. in the summer, to live with cousins. When I asked where they would live, he told me, "Right beside the alley."

"What city, honey?" I patiently queried.

"I forget, but you know that alley?" I would have expected this from my former first graders, but Samir was almost a third grader! Sigh.

I included many of the sweet, precious and funny incidences with Amanda in my first book, *Seoul Searching*, so I won't mention them all again here, but will include a few.

Amanda was quite precocious. Friends took us out to eat when she was 13 months old. They were stunned that she was trying to hold her knife and fork correctly when cutting her food (even though the utensils were in the wrong hands)!

When she was about two, someone gave Amanda a new toy that had a set of plastic shapes, each a different color. The child was to put the shape through the matching hole. But Amanda did it differently. She said, "Red square," or "purple triangle," or "green oval" or "yellow rectangle" as she put each shape in the correct place. I was amazed she knew both shapes and colors.

Another time, when Amanda was two years old, I came home from school and she was reading out loud! I was stunned, because I had not taught her to read. I suspected she was extremely bright but did not expect this! And I knew Mrs. Nah, the adjumonie, didn't speak enough English to teach her how to read in English! I wondered if she had memorized the page from hearing me read it aloud so often, so just to make sure, I pointed to a few words at random and she knew what they were. I even wrote some of the words on another paper, thinking she might have memorized the words by their position on the page. She knew them all! She had taught herself how to read. I was stunned! I don't think she even knew all the letters of the alphabet by name. Very interesting. But then, I could read Korean and I certainly didn't know the names of the Korean letters!

After I got Amanda, a friend sponsored me to attend a "Tres Dias" (Spanish for "three days") weekend at the Army Retreat Center. Friends kept Amanda so I could focus on my own spiritual growth. It was an awesome spiritual experience and one I have treasured ever since.

I could tell Amanda was very bright. She mastered one-to-one correspondence more quickly than average. She also asked some very intelligent questions. One time, she asked why sometimes, it was "one, two, three," but other times it was "first, second, third." So I explained about ordinal and cardinal numbers. She caught on right away. But other times it took her a bit longer to catch things. One night we were playing on the floor, and I asked her to rub my back. When she refused, I added, "Pretty please, with sugar on it!" Later in the evening when she wanted me to do something, she said, "Pretty please, with peas on it!" She figured it was supposed to have food on it, I guess!

Parents all seem to develop funny names for their kidlets and Amanda became a "stinker binker." One day she said, "Mama, I'm a stinker binker, and Cami is a twerp and Jonnie is a buggie boo. What is Christi?" She simply would not let it rest till I sheephishly called Mary Pat and asked. Turns out Christi is a squirt pies and Jamie is a turkey buzzard. It satisfied Amanda to know.

One funny memory I have of traveling with married friends and fellow teachers, is when Barry, Evy and I decided to take our two kidlets (ages two and three) on a Christmas trip to Kuala Lumpur. When we arrived at the K.L. airport, Cammy and Amanda, our two daughters, encountered men in turbans and robes for the first time. They got so excited and exclaimed,

"Look, Mommy! It's Joseph and the wisemen!" We had to hold them back from running up and hugging them. Can you tell we had been reading them lots of Christmas Bible stories?

But my funniest memory happened one night as Amanda (about two) sat on my lap, leaning back against me as we had our "bebotions." After I read the children's devotional, I asked her to pray first. She wrung her hands together, squeezed her eyes shut, screwed up her face, and with exaggerated expression said, "Oh, dear Jesus! Thank you my momma has big boobs!" She had been leaning against me and it must have been quite comfortable, but really? Where had she ever heard the word 'boobs?' I almost choked with laughter and barely got through my prayer.

For Amanda's second birthday, I let her invite four of her little friends and we held the entire party in the bathtub! That contained the mess quite well and I wasn't running around by myself trying to corral little kidlets all evening! I took a photo of them lined up at the edge of the tub. After I got the picture developed, I did a mean thing. I asked my principal (in a secretive manner) if he wanted to see a picture of five naked females in a bathtub. His eyes lit up as he nodded eagerly. When I showed him the photo, he was so disappointed!

Five naked females in a bathtub!

We were able to move into the newest apartment building on the SFS campus in 1986, a year after I adopted Amanda. There, we lived in a spacious fourth floor walk-up for a year. But then we had to move to a smaller third-floor apartment for our last two years, because the headmaster insisted we weren't a family because I didn't have a husband. Sigh. We lived there when I adopted Abbi. It was her first home with us and the first time she had ever lived in a real building.

My apartment building 1982-1986

Our apartments in Korea from 1986-1989

I was so blessed that my parents came to Korea twice to visit me. The first time was in 1984, before I adopted Amanda. Dad was invited to come work in Korea as a rubber consultant after he retired. We figured it was a "God thing" that he was invited to work in the country where his daughter

Mom and Dad in Seoul, 1984

just happened to be living. He worked in Pusan and came home to visit Mom and me on the weekends. I had a delightful time showing them my orld and I think it helped allay their fears about where I was living. The second time they came was after I had adopted Amanda. Dad was working again but we managed to find lots of time together and Amanda loved having Mamaw and Papaw there. Otherwise, I was unable to convince any other family members to come see me. But what a special treat it was for me to share Korea with Mom and Dad. Amanda talked constantly about, "Papaw DeBon," after they left. She hadn't been too taken with him the summer before, when we went to the U.S., but now she adored him.

ABBI

In the summer of 1986, I told Eastern Adoption Agency I wanted another child. They were quite upset with me anyway because they had lost face after I won my first adoption struggle, despite their refusals to help me. So this time, they completely restricted where I could look—no orphanages, foster homes, or children with living parents. In other words, I had to find a child living on the streets and apply for the exception to the policy by myself. After having dealt with me for four years, you'd think they would have learned I was persistent! I had learned the

**The day we adopted Abbi
Our first family photo
March 24, 1988**

**Eun Hwa was living in a cardboard/plywood
shack on the streets of Won Dong with her
teenage brother and sister**

**The day I first met
Eun Hwa
March 9, 1988**

Leaving her old home to begin a new life!

New sisters!

A healthier Abbi, a few weeks later, April, 1988

**Meeting her great grandmas
July, 1988**

hard way that persistence carries more weight than intelligence! So I began my second legal battle. This time, it took me 2½ years to find and adopt Abbi. But God provided another miracle. Detailed information about that struggle is presented in my book, *Re-Searching Seoul*. The little girl we found living on the streets of Won Dong was named Kim, Eun Hwa. But we had called her Abbi in our prayers, so I knew we'd be changing her name. We brought her home in 1988.

To gradually change Eun Hwa's name to Abbi, we called her Eun Hwa Abbi for a few weeks. Then we switched it to Abbi Eun Hwa. Finally, we dropped the Eun Hwa part and just called her Abbi. She didn't even notice the change and we avoided the pain of taking away her Korean name.

Amanda was three when I adopted Abbi (who was seven weeks shy of turning five). At first, Amanda was tickled to have a new sister, but that wore off quickly after she realized Abbi wasn't leaving! Her jealousy set in with a vengeance. There was one incident where Amanda bit Abbi (no damage), but otherwise, nothing too major. I understood that poor Amanda suddenly had to share her mom, her bedroom, her dresser, her toys and her clothes. We had a few difficult times, but managed to weather them.

Both of my daughters were miracles. I love this poem by Fleur Conkling Heyliger that explains adoption:

Not flesh of my flesh
Nor bone of my bone
Yet still miraculously my own.
Never forget for a single minute
You didn't grow under my heart
But in it.

The year before, when Amanda had turned two, she began what I recognized as the "terrible two's." She flew into rages over nothing and was inconsistent in what she wanted. For example, one day, she flew into a rage if I helped her brush her teeth, but the next day she raged if I didn't. I tried to be patient with her adjustment to being two and then later adjusting to having a new sister. This new situation wasn't just hard on Abbi, but on Amanda, too!

In my books (*Seoul Searching* and *Re-Searching Seoul*), I wrote about the many struggles with Abbi's adjustment to our family and to entering the English-speaking world. Adopting a five-year-old was quite different than adopting a baby. Abbi was going through more than just a regular adoption adjustment—she was experiencing culture shock, too, since she had to listen to English all day at school and all evening at home, and she was homesick for her brother and sister. Sleeping in a bed up off the floor scared her. Her new situation was overwhelming for her. I was frequently startled awake in the middle of the night when I felt her standing by my bed staring at me. She woke up and couldn't remember where she was, poor baby. She suffered from malnutrition and we found out a few days after I adopted her that she had tuberculosis. We were quarantined for a month while she got enough meds in her not to be contagious. Unfortunately, we had exposed everyone on campus in the meantime. I was so relieved a few weeks later when everyone tested negative for TB.

While we were quarantined, we played games, read books, and did everything we could to help Abbi accumulate English (Amanda taught Abbi her ABC's on the computer), but the going was slow. Abbi had been culturally deprived in her first culture and was now being thrown into a totally new one—she was in such culture shock she couldn't attend to learning a new language. She had never been in a car, never eaten in a restaurant, didn't know how to hold scissors, and I had to show her how to run!

Abbi had been told (by her brother and sister?) that since she was being adopted by an American, she would be rich now and could have anything she wanted. That meant every time we were in a store, she begged to have everything she saw. And that, of course, made Amanda take up the crusade, too. I was bombarded with begging children. I finally had to have a Korean friend sit Abbi down to explain that teachers don't make a lot of money. I could afford to buy what she needed, but not everything she wanted. She improved after that.

By far, the most moving incident with Abbi came as a result of a gift her brother and sister had given her when I went to get her. They couldn't afford much so they gave her a small pencil/crayon box with a plastic cover. Abbi carried that box everywhere. I knew she had an emotional attachment to it since it came from her brother and sister, but I sensed I was missing something. One day, I noticed a small slit in the plastic and tried to tape it for her, but she became hysterical over that, so I left it alone, still not understanding what was going on. Then one day, as I walked into the girl's bedroom, I saw Abbi put her finger in the slit and pull out two tiny pictures of her brother and sister. Finally, I "got" it. She looked up right then and saw that I had seen her pictures and panicked. I stood there thinking to myself, "What I do now is very important." I went to my room and found a small brass picture frame that would hold two photos and I helped Abbi put those pictures in the frame. She was so relieved that I didn't care if she had pictures of her brother and sister—who had probably told her to hide them from her new mommy since they figured I wouldn't want her to have them. She quickly discarded the pencil box and carried that picture frame around with her all the time. As she adjusted to being with us, she sometimes left that frame in one room while playing in another, but frequently ran back to check on it. Gradually she checked on it less and less often. Eventually she no longer felt the need to check at all. She still has that little frame, as a reminder of her former life.

After my month of maternity leave (and our quarantine was over), I went back to teaching (in April) and Abbi entered Junior Kindergarten (preschool) at SFS. She came up to my second-grade classroom every day so I could give her the nasty TB medicine. It was messy since I had to mix the powder with honey to make it palatable, and I didn't want her teachers to have to mess with it. She loved having me in the same building. She only had two months in Junior Kindergarten before the school year ended and her teachers (friends of mine) wanted to retain her. She had learned very little English and was very immature. Not knowing if the problem was a lack of intelligence or a lack of English, I opted to give her the benefit of

The girls loved Mamaw and Papaw!

Abbi meeting Aunt Cheri and falling in love with cats

Abbi (5), me, Amanda (3) in 1988

In our hanboks

Grma Marcy and Grpa DeVon with their six grandchildren 1988

the doubt and move her on to Senior (regular) Kindergarten, hoping she would accumulate some English over the summer. I was able to get her a Korean passport and we traveled to the U.S. that summer (1988) to meet her new relatives.

Abbi had a bad burn scar on her right wrist from when someone spilled hot soup on her as a baby. I took her to Severance Hospital for plastic surgery, but it was unsuccessful and they had to go back and operate again. Her skin "rotted" instead of healing. It was a very trying time for both Abbi and Amanda, who was at home with babysitters. I had to stay in the hospital with Abbi, per Korean custom, where it is the family that feeds and takes care of the patient, not nurses.

In the fall of 1988, Abbi (five) started Senior Kindergarten at SFS and Amanda (three) started preschool at Seoul British School. Abbi continued to have a blast socially, but made little academic progress.

Amanda excelled, but she started a pattern that would follow her in school for many years—she refused to talk to her teacher(s) until about March. I don't know if it was shyness, stubbornness or insecurity, but there you are. I learned she was an observer—standing back and watching before getting involved.

I enrolled Amanda in pre-school because she needed to work on her social skills. Mrs. Nah, our adjumonie, walked her over to school every afternoon, since SBS was close by and shared the SFS campus. One day, Mrs. Nah brought Amanda to my second-grade classroom in the middle of the day, because Amanda insisted she was going to wear her slip on the outside of her British school uniform (we had to learn how to tie the tie on her uniform!). I spent quite a while trying to convince her to change it. She was stubborn. Koreans are a very stubborn people and Amanda got a double dose of it!

Amanda's teacher, Miss Southerst, raved about her abilities, which didn't surprise me. Both her advanced vocabulary and logic amazed me, so I knew she was extremely bright. For example, once (at age two) when we were walking on uneven sidewalk, she said, "We must walk carefully so we don't trip!" and "If I go too fast, I could easily fall down!" (Seriously, adverbs?) Or the time she told me I was being "unrealistic." What? Did she even know what that meant? She loved big words and often used them. When she was in second grade, she told Abbi not to believe what I was saying because I was just being facetious (not normal second grade vocabulary)!

My brother, Brent, and his wife, Nore, had two children (Chad and Kara) who were half Filipino and now I had two Korean daughters. My sister, Cheri, had two Caucasian boys (Peter and Jason). So I teased my parents and asked them, "In your wildest dreams, did you ever think that four of your six grandchildren would be Asians!" That wasn't something that usually happened in Wabash, Indiana! What a hoot!

When I taught first grade, one mother approached me at a social gathering to tell me they were considering moving back to the U.S. But she said if I could promise her that I would remain at SFS for another two years, they would stay in Seoul so I could teach her daughter, who was in Junior Kindergarten at the time. I was flabbergasted and humbled.

By now, I was teaching my second-grade class with some important people watching me. Four sets of SFS parents requested me as their child's teacher—the school board president (daughter), a school board member (daughter), the high school principal (son), and a high school teacher (daughter). I felt very honored that they had all requested me out of the three second grade teachers.

WRITING KOREAN TEXTBOOKS

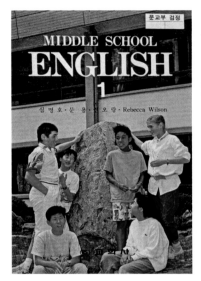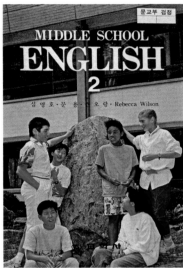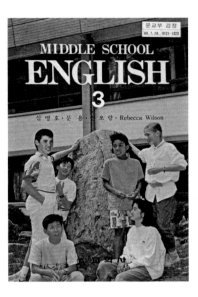

The top-selling English textbooks (for Korean Middle Schools) in Korea! 1988. Our textbooks were used for six years.

What a hoot! ↗

Taping our textbooks

In the meantime, I had spent the summer before (and part of the school year) co-authoring a set of three English textbooks for Korean middle schools (working on a team with three Korean men who had doctorates in English). Our many months of hard work proved both culturally frustrating and enlightening for me. By far, the most frustrating part for me was the way my co-authors treated me. In their view, I only had a lowly master's degree and was merely a woman, so therefore I "knew nothing."

Besides writing parts of the three books, I was to proofread their writings. One day, as I was proofreading, I found these two sentences:

This is my son who is a doctor.
This is my son, who is a doctor.

When I asked what they were trying to teach with these two examples, they said the first sentence (without the comma) meant that I have one son and he is a doctor. The second sentence, with the comma, meant that I have more than one son and this particular son is a doctor. I jokingly asked, "So, the comma gives you more children?" They said it did! When I pointed out that was nonsense (in a more tactful way, of course), they argued that they had doctorates in English and they knew what they were talking about. I said I didn't have a degree in English, but that as a native speaker, I had never heard of this rule before and was pretty sure it wasn't correct. Inwardly, I was thinking that even if such a rule exists, first, second, and third-year English students don't need to know it! Two decades later, I learned there is such a rule, but it is very obscure and certainly wasn't for beginning English speakers.

We argued about those two sentences every day for three solid weeks! I dreaded going to the office because I knew we would argue about them all over again. I finally realized it was a cultural problem that I needed to solve culturally. They were having trouble being corrected by a woman and the fact that I only had a master's degree made it doubly insulting to them. So the next time I went to the office, I said, "Let's not argue any more. Let me call my friend, who is an English teacher (not providing a name or gender). They thought that was a good idea (assuming my friend was a male—the norm for English teachers). Talking on the phone (with Evelyn, whom I had forewarned), I read the two sentences and their explanation and asked if that was right. Over the phone, Evy said, "No." So I turned to my co-authors and said, "My friend, who is an English teacher, says that's not right." Without hesitation, they replied, "Oh, OK!" Because they thought it came from a man, it was easier for them to accept. I seethed inside. Three weeks of arguments simply because I was a woman and "knew nothing."

The Korean government then locked the textbook judges in a hotel room for a month, while they selected the top five textbook sets from the 64 sets submitted. Every middle school in Korea would have to choose one of those five sets. In other words, the other 59 teams of writers had wasted their time and energy. We were delighted when ours was one of the five sets chosen! However, ours also ended up being the best-selling textbook in the country, capturing 40% of the market, while the other four teams had to share the remaining 60% of the sales. The other textbook authors were not very happy with us because they lost profit.

Unfortunately, at the last minute, the government decided to publish the books without my name on the cover. So I had to fight my third legal battle with the Korean government (and won) to keep my name on those books. I also taped all the videos that went with the books. It was a "real kick in the pants," (as my friend Lois would say), when Korean middle school students recognized me on sidewalks and asked for my autograph! Or when our Korean aides at school brought their child's textbook for me to autograph. It was my 15 minutes of fame, I suppose!

The three of us frequently lay on the couch together reading books or snuggling. One night, before we started reading, the girls "fixed" my hair with several of their colorful barrettes so my hair stuck out all over. Later, when the doorbell rang, I forgot my hair was a mess and answered the door. The dry cleaner man, who came to collect our clothes each week, looked at me very strangely! First, I had been single, then suddenly had a baby and then had two Korean children and now looked like this? He did not understand. "Way gooks" (foreigners) were very strange!

One time, Amanda and her little friends were discussing their Grmas and Grpas. They agreed that their Grmas and Grpas lived in "an airplane in the sky," which is logical for three-year-olds! After all, they had seen their grandparents come to visit by getting off an airplane!

While working in the kitchen, I loved eavesdropping on the girl's conversations (after Abbi's English improved).

Abbi: I don't wanna go to college! I want to stay with Mommy.
Amanda: Yeah, but we have to mind our Mommy.
Abbi: Yeah.
Amanda: And besides, I have to get my master's degree.
—

Abbi: God is right here in this room.
Amanda: Yeah, but we can't see Him.
Abbi: Yeah. And heaven is a lovely place. And we'll get new bodies.
Amanda: And we won't have to go to bed! And we can ask Grandpa Ford to sing us silly songs like he did for Mommy when she was a little girl.
Abbi: Yeah. And we can meet Grandpa Orny (Ora), too. She was Grandma Marcy's daddy. (Abbi still hadn't sorted out pronouns!)
Amanda: Yeah. I wonder if God minds his Mommy.
—

Amanda: Some people have daddies.
Abbi: Yeah. And some people don't have mommies.
Amanda: We'll get married someday.
Abbi: Yeah, but first we have to meet the right person.
Amanda: Yeah. Some people get married for the wrong reason.
Abbi: Yeah, you have to love somebody.

In front of my girls, people frequently told me how beautiful my girls were. I usually responded with a thank you, but that I was more interested in their inner beauty—the quality of their character. I wanted them to hear me say that to reinforce that outer beauty only counts for so much.

MY GIRLS THROUGH THE YEARS

1988 SEOUL OLYMPICS

The 1988 Seoul Olympics were a once-in-a-lifetime event. How many people get to attend the Olympics? Brent's kids were too young, but I wrote to Cheri and asked her to let her two sons come. Peter was 16 and Jason was 12. All she had to do was put them on a plane in Chicago and I'd meet the plane in Seoul. They were old enough to fly by themselves and I wanted to stretch their horizons a bit. I offered to pay for their flights, housing, meals and tickets to events. She refused. It broke my heart to have those boys miss such a huge opportunity. She had criticized me before for "wasting money" traveling the world, so I suppose she thought that experience would be a waste of time for her boys.

I attended several Olympic events (mostly gymnastics). The tickets were not expensive! I took Mrs. Nah to one of the tumbling events. She was thrilled. Barry, Evy, Pam and I got to attend the Closing Ceremonies. What a treat! I didn't bother taking my girls—they were too young. But they loved Hodori (the Olympic mascot) and got to watch the Olympic flame as it passed us on the streets of Yonhi Dong.

The Olympic torch passing through Yonhi Dong

KOREAN CLOSURE

**Me, Barry, Evy, and Pam
at the Olympics**

In 1989, after eight years of teaching in a foreign country, three successful legal battles against a foreign government (without an attorney), adopting my two precious girls, getting a master's degree in one year, going through two unsuccessful surgeries on Abbi's arm, writing three textbooks, recording lots of audio and video tapes, and proctoring GRE, GMAT and TOEFL tests on Saturdays, I was exhausted. I began weighing my options. I could continue teaching at SFS, apply for the new assistant principal position, apply for a sabbatical, or leave Korea permanently (to move to another country, teach in an elementary school in the U.S., or earn my doctorate). I prayed long and hard about those options asking God to lead me to the one He wanted for me. He led me to start my doctorate. So, with the headmaster's understanding and permission, I broke my contract (something I would normally NEVER do) and we were set to move back to the U.S. in June. Abbi was six and Amanda was four.

The spring of 1989 was a terrible, emotional time for me. No one told me, but I accidentally found out Abbi's adoption had been "stopped" and no one could/would tell me why. First, I spent hours on the phone, just trying to find out what the problem was. Then I spent weeks trying to figure out how to fight it. After I'd had Abbi for a year, the Korean government decided they were going to take her away from me and let her grow up in an orphanage. Their reasoning was that I hadn't really gotten permission to adopt her in the first place--that Eastern and I hadn't interpreted their letter correctly. They lost face due to an error on their part and were now trying to correct it. So, I began my fourth legal battle with the Korean government, this time to keep her. I petitioned the Blue House (like our White House), spoke with numerous lawyers (who could not help me), and the U.S. Embassy (who could not touch it because it was a Korean matter, not an American one). I hit deadends everywhere.

But God specializes in miracles. He provided a U.S. embassy worker (who called me in his "off" hours) who volunteered to assist me. He refused to tell me his name because he was not allowed to help me "officially" and didn't want this kindness to come back and bite him. We conferred numerous times on the phone. His investigation found that my adoption paperwork was lying on the desk of Dr. Kim, the top adoption official in Korea, just waiting to be approved or rejected. So, he devised a very strange plan— one that would never have occurred to me. He sent an American friend to meet with Dr. Kim. This friend told Dr. Kim he was a Western journalist working on an article about this Rebecca Wilson over at Way Goo Geen Hakio in Yonhi Dong, who, a year ago, out of the kindness of her heart, had adopted a Korean child living on the streets. He had heard the Korean government was going to take the child away from her now and let her grow up in an orphanage. He wanted to present both sides of the story, so he was there to learn the Korean government's position, "to make sure he reported it correctly in his article."

Korea was so afraid of the Western press at the time, that they capitulated and I got my exception the next day! I was allowed to keep Abbi! See *Re-Searching Seoul* for more unbelievable details. It was a God thing—He provided another miracle. I had fought for 2½ years to get her and another year and a half to keep her, so her's was a four-year battle, too. That legal battle took us right up to the time we were leaving Korea, so it was a close-run thing.

In the meantime, Abbi's arm surgeries to treat her burn scars were not successful and the skin on her arm was literally rotting. I was studying to take my GRE, and applying to grad school back in the U.S. to start my doctorate. I was finishing the taping jobs for our textbooks, and I was trying to enjoy my last semester teaching elementary school. We were saying good-bye to our many beloved friends, I was trying to find a mover to "pack us out" in June, Abbi's teachers again wanted to retain her in kindergarten, and I was working under the constant threat of losing Abbi. The stress from these many challenges was overwhelming. I cried in private (while my students were out at recess and when the girls were asleep). I was highly stressed, but knew I had to keep it from the girls to maintain their stable home-life.

Abbi's teachers didn't think she was mature enough to proceed to first grade. She had learned some English, but still hadn't learned much academically. Since we were moving to the U.S. that summer, I decided to give her the benefit of the doubt one more time and enroll her in first grade in Indiana. If she did poorly in first grade, I would retain her then. Besides, knowing how intelligent Amanda was, I figured at some point the schools would want to advance her a grade. If I held Abbi back, they would be in the same grade, which was NOT a good idea.

A couple of days before we left country, we went back out to visit Abbi's older brother and sister. We purposely didn't tell them we were coming, so they wouldn't have time to plan something if they wanted her back. Even though the adoption was final, they could still get her back if they wanted to. (The final break would be when she became a citizen of another country.) Sister wasn't home, but brother called her to come home quickly, and he went out and bought Abbi an ID bracelet. They hardly recognized Abbi. She was so shy and hesitant around them both, not remembering them very well. It had been over a year since she'd seen them. I suspect in

**We loved the Harubang (stone grandfathers) on Chejudo.
I started a collection!**

her heart she was afraid she'd have to return to them. It was a hard visit, but I'm glad we made the effort; I know they appreciated it.

I tried to prepare the girls for our move to the U.S. I knew it would be more complicated than just moving to another house! We also talked about how we would get homesick for Korea. Abbi remarked, "Yeah and we'll have to eat with plastic silverware." I puzzled over that for a week. Why would she link being homesick to eating with plastic silverware? Finally, I realized that when she first came to us she was dreadfully homesick. That was also the week we discovered she had TB so she immediately had to use disposable eating utensils to avoid infecting us. So, bless her heart, she thought I made her use plastic silverware because she was homesick. She didn't speak any English so I couldn't communicate with her very well. She must have thought her new mommy did some strange things!

The moving company, that I had selected with great care after hearing some of the horror stories of others leaving country (ships sinking, severe damage to belongings, etc.), came to "pack us out" in one day. It was an unbelievable experience watching them build a box around each Korean chest, carry it down three flights of stairs on one guy's back and fill our shipping container. Our apartment was soon empty, so we took Mrs. Nah to Chejudo (an island off the southern tip of Korea). She had never been on an airplane or to Chejudo (Koreans can't travel freely), and she was thrilled. The girls fell in love with the local "harubang" (stone grandfathers)

The day we were to fly to the U.S., an unforeseen major legal problem arose that almost kept us from leaving Korea (see *Re-Searching Seoul*). I had been worried we might have problems due to issues with Abbi's paperwork, but it ended up being a surprise legal problem with me! We literally prayed our way through customs. It was definitely a "God thing" that we were able to leave Korea. I was an emotional wreck on the plane. What a terrible way to leave my beloved Korea.

A week later, after we had moved in with Grma and Grpa in Wabash, Indiana, I was taking classes at Ball State University, beginning work on my doctorate. I was dizzy from the rapid transition to the next room in my life.

CHAPTER SEVEN
GARAGE
BALL STATE UNIVERSITY
(Muncie, Indiana)
1989-1991

Being back in graduate school after teaching for 17½ years, was similar to sitting in my garage waiting for someone to come fix my car. Regular life seemed to come to a halt while waiting for improvements in my vehicle (my educational knowledge). Not only did I have to adjust to being in the garage—a strange environment (a complete change of culture), but the switch from teaching to studying was like changing from being the mechanic to being the car. The hood of my car (my brain) was wrenched opened to replace broken parts and fix oil leaks in my understating and expertise. I had been out of the country for eight years, so trying to grasp the meaning of new education philosophies and practices (like prime time, ISTEP, LEA, or whole language), was like trying to learn car mechanics.

Every day of those two years I woke up asking myself, "Why am I doing this?!?!?" I felt like I was banging my head against a brick wall. And then I reminded myself, "Oh yeah, I'm doing this so my girls can go to college." As a single mom and teacher, I knew I would never be able to afford college for them. But I also knew they could get free tuition at a college where I was a professor. So I was spending my savings on my education instead of theirs. There was a method to my madness! But that did not make the undertaking easy!

I had no idea what they were talking about in half my classes (especially statistics and administration), we had no income, my girls were still young enough to need a lot of my attention and I was suffering from re-entry shock in a huge way. Just going to the grocery store was overwhelming.

Unlearning some of the cultural habits I had assimilated while living in Korea was difficult and took concentration. For example, I had learned to bow my head instead of shaking hands. To this day, I still find myself bowing slightly when meeting new people. But my most embarrassing faux pas was pushing students out of my way as I walked down the sidewalks at Ball State. I had to quickly unlearn that habit!

I had been warned that re-entry shock (going back home to my original country) would be worse than the original culture shock I experienced when moving overseas in the first place. I didn't believe it, but it turned out to be quite true! It took me much longer to adjust to being back in the U.S. than it had for me to adjust to living in Korea. The girls adjusted better and faster than I did because theirs was regular culture shock, while mine was re-entry shock.

We lived with my parents in Wabash for a month while I commuted an hour and a half each way to classes. To secure a parking space, I left at 5:30 every morning, went to classes, and came home in the evening, exhausted—just in time to read to the girls and tuck them into bed. I could see that the situation was very hard on Mom, so I began looking for a rental house in Muncie. During that first month with Mom and Dad, Grma Charlotte (99) passed away. Again, I was glad I could be there for her funeral and to be with family. I was fortunate there had been no family funerals while I was overseas.

It was so wonderful to be with family for holidays again! But I quickly learned that Cheri did not want to hear anything about my doctoral studies, just like she hadn't wanted to hear anything about Korea. We always talked about her family to keep the peace. I also noticed that Eleanore, who was very talented, never talked about her family or job when around Cheri, because Cheri acted completely disinterested in Nore's life. While Brent worked as a CPA, Nore (who later earned her master's degree) became the head nurse of a large hospital in Indianapolis, and was in charge of more than 400 nurses. She helped design and orchestrate a new hospital, and was acclaimed for her administrative skills. Her nurses loved her. She had an interesting life and was an accomplished woman. It was always fascinating to talk to her. One time, she was in a bank when a robbery occurred—and we all wanted to hear about it. But she didn't bother to mention it around Cheri.

Not many people could have successfully moved to a foreign country as a teenager, learned a new language thoroughly (till she dreamed in English), adjusted to a new culture, learned how to cook, gotten two degrees in a foreign language, and been a success in their profession.

Nore was remarkable and I respected her completely. But Cheri showed no respect or interest in her. It was Cheri's loss.

After I found a small rental house for us, we moved to Muncie. I planned to share the house and the rent with another doctoral student named Ann, but two days before she moved in, she was dismissed from the doctoral program, so I had to bite the bullet and pay the rent by myself. I had no childcare, so I found after-school care for them and hired babysitters when I had night classes.

This rental house in Muncie became my first home purchase, 1989

Our new neighbors were an elderly couple named Bill and Carol. They fell in love with my girls and the feeling was mutual. They quickly became "Grpa Bill" and "Grma Carol." We made many good memories with them. Their granddaughter, Megan, sometimes came over to our house to make cookies with us. We kept in touch with Bill and Carol for years after we left Muncie and they came up to Osceola to visit us a few years later.

I learned that nationwide, the success rate for doctoral students actually completing a Ph.D. is only 40%. The other 60% either drop out, are washed out of their programs or end up ABD (all but dissertation). In a master's program, if you do all the work, you get the degree, but in a doctoral program, you may do all the work but still not be allowed to get the degree. Standards are high and the pressure is intense. In our "doc room" at Ball State (education division), there were exactly ten of us doctoral students. Only four of us ended up with a degree. The statistics held true in our situation. Ann, my intended roommate, was one of those who didn't make it.

I formed my doctoral committee early and carefully. Dr. Sue Drake was a Christian, so I chose her to become my committee chair. She then helped me form my committee. Besides her husband, Dr. Ted Drake, we found another Christian to include—Dr. Jay Thompson. So of the five members of my committee, three were Christians. What a blessing that was to me!

I began writing my dissertation almost from the beginning of my doctoral program, since I wanted to finish as quickly as possible and I knew it would take me two years to write it. I did not want to be one of those students who completed all their coursework but ended up ABD and never finished—many gave up without finishing the dissertation. So I chose to work on both dissertation and classes at the same time. I "double dipped"—making all my research papers for other classes apply to my dissertation research. I had written my master's thesis about self-concept in children, and I decided I wanted to pursue the same subject matter in greater depth. I chose a published instrument that measures children's self-concepts, designed my research tool, and found a treatment program to assist children in improving their self-concepts. Once again, through my research, I was reminded just how important a child's early years are in developing a healthy self-concept.

I was awarded a doctoral fellowship, which included teaching in the Ball State Living Learning Lab pre-school, working in the ERC (Educational Resources Center), assisting professors in their classes, grading all the professor's papers, and supervising students in their field work. For that I was awarded a measly $400 a month. I did not consider it a salary. It kept a little food on the table, but did not pay the car bills, rent or utilities, so we ate through my savings quickly. I also substitute taught in the local schools during those two years (elementary through high school).

When we first moved back to the U.S., I noticed a tremendous difference in the political situation. The two political parties were attacking each other instead of working together. I didn't remember that happening as much before I moved overseas, but things had changed in those eight years. Most of the criticisms seemed to come from Democrats. It was unsettling and as I now know, has only gotten worse over the decades. It seems that being the party in power is more important than working to solve the country's problems. How sad.

That fall (1989), when Amanda was four and a half, she started school at the Ball State Living Learning Lab (preschool) where I taught part time as part of my fellowship. Amanda excelled in all things academic, but spent a lot of her play time alone, reading. Her intelligence became more evident.

Abbi, who started first grade in Muncie, was acquiring English well. In fact, I figured she had "arrived" when she began making the same grammatical errors other six-year-olds were making—"I cutted my finger." But I also knew that because she was six years behind in English acquisition, she was in the "buzzards" reading group. That was my facetious name for the lowest reading group—the bone-pickers of society, the kids who would never go to college. So I used her as a guinea pig in one of my graduate school projects—LEA (Language Experience Approach). Our six-week project literally turned her reading around. Before we began, she knew zero words by sight. When we finished, six weeks later, she knew 106 sight words! I was delighted when her teacher called me shortly after that to say she didn't know what had happened, but she was moving Abbi up to the "Bluebirds" reading group (my facetious name for the top reading group—those ready to take off and fly!). From that point on, Abbi was a great student, and graduated from college with honors. That little project was enough to give her the leg up she needed to succeed in reading (and thus in life!). I wrote an article about our project and published it. (Wilson, R. Spring, (1993). *Using LEA with my ESL daughter: A case study.* Indiana Reading Quarterly.)

Those two times in Seoul, in pre-K and Kindergarten, when Abbi's teachers wanted to retain her and I wondered if it was due to lack of English or lack of intelligence, I always chose to give her the benefit of the doubt and moved her on to the next grade. Now I was glad I had done that. She wasn't dumb but just needed time to adjust to her new world and learn English!

On a side note, I also tutored a little girl from Kuwait. Her parents had been vacationing in Europe when Iraq invaded Kuwait in 1990. They knew they didn't dare go back home, so they moved to the U.S. I used LEA with that girl, too, and had the same amazing results. Her reading skills improved greatly! LEA was designed to assist native English speakers, but my projects proved it also worked wonders with ESL (English as a Second Language) students!

Amanda's intelligence continued to impress me. I remember one time we were in some office filling out paperwork for something, and I needed her social security number. I didn't have it with me, so I turned to her (a four-year-old) and just asked her what her SSN was. The lady behind the counter dropped her mouth open at that, but recovered quickly when Amanda rattled it off to me. I had only told Amanda her number one time, but I knew she would remember it! The girls had both learned how to spell their names, recite their address and their phone number (a safety issue) because I set them to music, which made it so easy for them to memorize.

On another day, Amanda came to me and said, "Mommy, did you know that the California condor only lays one egg every two years?"

"No, I didn't know that," I cautiously replied. "How did you know that?" She showed me where she had read it in the encyclopedia. I knew she was reading well above her age level but had no idea she was reading encyclopedias for fun. How strange for a four-year-old who wasn't even in kindergarten yet!

At the time, I was studying the six levels of thinking in my grad classes (knowledge, comprehension, application, analysis, synthesis and evaluation) and I recognized her thinking level immediately. While it was remarkable that she could read an encyclopedia, she was only thinking at the basic knowledge level. Then her next question floored me. She added, "Do you suppose that's one of the reasons they're becoming extinct?" I quickly looked to see if there was anything in that article about extinction, but there wasn't. It was an old encyclopedia. I immediately recognized that she had jumped from the basic knowledge level (the lowest level of thinking) straight to synthesis and evaluation (the highest levels). She had combined the fact that one egg every two years might not be enough to keep the species going, with what she had seen on TV about animals becoming extinct. She was combining information from more than one source—that's synthesis. And to recognize that as a potential problem was evaluation! I was dumbfounded. Normal four-year-old's don't think at higher levels!

I quickly signed her up for an I.Q. test through the Ball State Psychology Department. I watched the whole test administration through a one-way mirror. The person administering the test was a graduate student, but obviously she knew nothing about a four-year-old's attention span. She gave Amanda no breaks and even though Amanda was so tired, put her head down on the table and cried at one point, the gal just plowed on. I wanted to bang on the window and scream at the gal, but I didn't dare. Based on that inappropriate test administration, I was afraid the results would be invalid. However, Amanda scored just over 150—well into the genius range. It made me wonder how much higher her score might have been if age-appropriate guidelines had been applied.

The following year, Abbi was in second grade and doing well, while Amanda started kindergarten, already reading at the second-grade level. For the third year in a row, she was "introduced" to the alphabet, which must have been incredibly boring for her.

I used two schools in the Wabash school district to administer the self- concept tests (both pre and post) and the treatments, so Mom could watch the girls while I worked in those schools. It worked out fairly well, even though it was an hour and a half drive from Muncie on a fairly frequent basis. Since there were a lot of tests to score, I held grading parties with Mom and my friends helping me to speed up the tedious grading process. It was exhausting work, but revealed some interesting data. I included my girls in the research data and found that Abbi's self-concept was off the charts! She thought very highly of herself! I also discovered that even though the test was advertised as "culture free," it really wasn't. The way my own two girls scored their self-concept about their eyes told me they had experienced some prejudice because their eyes were "slanted." That is cultural bias.

We settled into a nice church and made new friends in Muncie. The girls were devastated, however, when we did not win the mother/daughter look-alike contest at the Mother's Day banquet. They were convinced we looked just alike!

Ray, the husband in one of the families we grew to love at our church, was a private pilot assigned to fly the Ball State president whenever and wherever he needed to go, so he was gone a lot. But his wife, Toni, and her mother, Grma Frances, became very special to us.

Abbi started piano lessons while we were in Muncie. Amanda was just a bit too young yet.

Amanda continued to show some strange behaviors. She didn't seem to have grown out of her "terrible twos." I was getting concerned about her. Her unpredictable temper tantrums and rages seemed abnormal to me. It simply was not possible to reason with her. I am not a yeller and screamer, and always dealt with her calmly and rationally, but it did no good. Abbi and I began to feel like we were "walking on eggshells" around her, not knowing what might set her off. It was usually little things. If I moved her notebook to wipe the counter, she flew into a rage. But she could also be the sweetest thing on earth. Such a contradiction. We never knew which side of Amanda we would be dealing with.

I found it quite interesting that her meltdowns always occurred at home, never in public. Did that mean she could control her behavior somewhat or just that she felt safe to unload on us at home?

Now I reasoned that her high intelligence, combined with her lack of patience contributed to her rages. Learning came too easily for her. She usually caught things the first time and had no patience for trying again if she failed (which was rare).

As a teacher, I had several discipline techniques/behavior modification tools in my arsenal. I tried them all and none of them worked with her. In all my 20 years of teaching, I had never encountered a child who didn't respond to at least one approach. I was stymied.

In the middle of my doctoral program, I bought our rental house from our landlord—he was selling it and I couldn't stand the thought of moving in the middle of my doctoral program. I was 40 years old, and it was the first house I had ever owned. Fortunately, I was able to assume his mortgage, so that helped me a great deal. I would never have qualified for a mortgage with no income. I took May term off from classes and spent the month remodeling the house—doing physical work instead of mental. What a welcome change!

One day, I had been working in an empty, stripped-down bedroom with no clock. Then I got a call from the school that I had forgotten to pick Abbi up after school (Amanda was at the sitter's). Abbi sobbed and sobbed, and I felt horrible for abandoning her. Poor baby. I was afraid she'd be scarred for life, but with her usual cheerful personality, she bounced back fairly quickly.

God is so good. During my doctoral program and financial struggles, I got my first royalty check from the Korean textbooks I co-authored back in Korea! It wasn't huge, but I breathed a brief sigh of relief.

One semester, we hosted an exchange teacher from England. Nikki Turner (later Baslington) was delightful, and the girls loved her. She quickly learned the bus routes so I didn't have to drive her to and from school and she had several friends in the program with her, so her social life was full. The income from hosting her helped me out a bit.

In July, 1990, Abbi proudly became an American citizen in Indianapolis. That's when her name officially became Abbi Kim Wilson, and it broke her final legal tie to Korea. Her brother and sister could never get her back now. I was so relieved. I had to laugh because during her naturalization interview, the lady asked Abbi (six years old) if she was a member of the communist party! Abbi didn't even know what that meant.

We had been toying with what her middle name should be. One day, she asked if her middle name could be Rapunzel. Can you tell what we had been reading? I almost choked (to keep from laughing) as I explained that she might like that now, but she wouldn't like it when she grew up! We finally decided to keep her Korean family name, Kim, as her middle name.

I did well in my classes, but it was not easy being a single parent and earning a doctorate. Sometimes, I had to take Amanda to classes with me while Abbi was in school. On more than one occasion I asked the girls what kind of cereal they wanted for supper because I simply couldn't find the time or energy to cook. Since I knew I needed to get back out into the working world as soon as possible, my aim was to finish my doctorate in two years. I went to bed at 9:00 p.m. when the girls did, slept for four hours, then got up at 1:00 a.m. and studied the rest of the night. It was a hectic and overwhelming time for me and only getting four hours of sleep a night for two years destroyed my sleep habits. Years later, I am still dealing with the aftermath of that!

There was one gal in another doctoral program at Ball State who had a set of twins and a set of triplets all under three years old. Then her husband left her. We all decided he should be hung, drawn and quartered! And there was another gal in her 80's earning her doctorate! I was so proud of her for doing that!

I took my written preliminary exams in January, 1991. I spent several weeks studying to get ready for them, not knowing exactly what my committee would ask—it could be anything in the field of education, a very broad subject. I was locked in a room for five days and wrote (on the computer) for eight hours each day to answer the various questions my committee posed. It was very stressful, but I passed those successfully. My committee chair, Dr. Drake, let me know that she was praying for me every day during my pre-lims. It was rare to find a Christian in the secular halls at Ball State, so having her on my side was a real blessing!

One interesting and funny side note—while I was researching in the Ball State Library, only one computer was earmarked specifically for educational research—the ERIC Computer, and you had to reserve a time to use it. I spent so much time with ERIC that the girls thought it was someone I was dating! What a hoot! But it was worth the time. My dissertation bibliography was ten pages long and my dissertation was 108 pages. I was proud of myself! However, after spending so much time on it, I have absolutely no desire to ever read it again! Ha.

My dissertation, titled, *The Effects of a Self-Concept Treatment on Global and Specific Areas of Self-Concepts of First and Third Graders,* was dedicated to my girls:

> This dissertation is lovingly dedicated to my two precious daughters, Abbi and Amanda, who willingly uprooted their lives, cheerfully moved halfway around the world so I could go to school, patiently endured the times I couldn't play with them, and faithfully cheered me on through each milestone of the doctoral program. I hope that my attempts to study the self-concepts of children hasn't somehow, through neglect, damaged theirs. Of all the people my studies inconvenienced, they understood the least, but loved the most. I promise to do my best to make it all up to you, girls. Thanks (kam sa ham ne da). Dr. Mom adores you (sa rang ham ne da). (Wilson, R., June, 1991, *The Effects of a Self-Concept Treatment on Global and Specific Areas of Self-Concepts of First and Third Graders,* Ball State University, Muncie, In.)

I will never forget my oral dissertation defense in June. After presenting my research and findings, answering the questions and concerns posed by my committee (defending my research), I was sent out of the room so they could discuss my presentation, and decide my fate. Then I was called back into the room and Dr. Drake, my chairperson, introduced me to the committee as Dr. Rebecca Wilson! Such a huge relief! I had made it!

I was told I set a new record at Ball State by earning a doctorate in just two years. Most students spend seven to ten years earning their doctorates, but I was driven by the need to return to the work force and earn a salary so I could support my family. By God's grace, I was able to finish on time and graduated in July, 1991 with a 3.86 GPA. Mom, Nore, and Cheri brought food to my house for a reception after the graduation, but I could tell Cheri wasn't thrilled about being there. She didn't have her boys come at all. That shocked me. How many times in life do you get to watch someone be awarded a doctorate? Mom told me later that watching me be awarded my doctorate was the proudest moment of her life. I was so touched by that.

**Newly minted Dr. Wilson
July, 1991**

I wanted to get my girls settled somewhere so we wouldn't be moving any more during their school years. I had moved them around enough. Knowing that I wanted to stay within an hour of my parents after graduation (so the girls would have grandparents and family nearby), I applied for an elementary principal position there in Muncie (mostly because it paid well). But knowing that I also wanted to be able to share my faith with my students, I also applied to Christian colleges within an hour of my parents and was offered a position at Bethel College (now Bethel University) in Mishawaka, Indiana. My starting salary would be $25,000 –a $3,000 pay cut from Korea two years earlier! And that was moving from a master's degree to a doctorate! I knew Bethel was a small private, Christian college (600 students) and couldn't pay what state schools were paying, but even then, I was shocked at the low salary.

The story is told of a group having dinner together. One gentleman was expounding on the fact that teachers must not be worth much since they make so little money. He turned to the one teacher in the group and asked, "Seriously, Donna, what do you make?" After a thoughtful period, she responded, "I make a difference. What do you make?"

I had not gone into teaching for the money; teachers don't teach for the income, but for the outcome. Some things are more important than money. Educating children and future teachers are two of them. My mission in life did not involve becoming rich. My mission was to serve God, educate children and train future teachers.

Several years later, Shannon, one of my advisees at Bethel, who excelled at golf, was invited to play golf professionally, but she turned it down. She decided she'd rather teach. I was so proud of her for putting children ahead of making money.

One week after graduating from Ball State, we moved to the next room in my life. I was quite happy to leave my "Ball State" room. I began work as the Director of Student Teaching and Associate Professor of Elementary Education at Bethel College in August, 1991.

CHAPTER EIGHT
LIVING ROOM
BETHEL COLLEGE
(Mishawaka, Indiana)
1991-2015

I equate my Bethel years to the living room of my "house." For the next 25 years, I sat in various chairs in my living room—professor, director of student teaching, associate dean, dean, and then back to professor. The most comfortable chair was my "professor" recliner, while the most uncomfortable was the prickly, straight-backed wooden "dean" chair. In my "living room," I watched an age progression as I witnessed my college students changing from green freshmen into quality teachers. I entertained a lot of people in my living room—students, faculty candidates, administrators, and friends. I had a wealth of experiences at Bethel and lived a whole, rewarding life in that "room."

Our house in Osceola 1991-2001

The girls and I settled into a house in Osceola, so they could attend schools in the Penn-Harris-Madison School District. Cheri very graciously came up for three days to help me paint and wallpaper my new house. Amanda started first grade and Abbi third grade at Bittersweet Elementary School, while I began learning how to be a professor. I had one month to create syllabi for courses I had never taught before, but I learned quickly and fell in love with Bethel.

Being at a Christian college was so refreshing after being uncomfortable in the worldly atmosphere at Ball State. Bethel is conservative—no alcohol, smoking, drugs or dancing, and chapel three times a week. Bethel, a Missionary Church school, was founded in 1947 to train Missionary church pastors. Even though they did not emphasize baptism or weekly communion, I felt quite comfortable with their evangelistic stance.

TEACHING COLLEGE

During the fall of my first year at Bethel, I got a call from Ball State, asking if one of their student teachers in the South Bend schools could sit in on my student teaching seminar each week. I was also to supervise her student teaching. I agreed, but she only lasted one week in seminar. She complained to Ball State that she had to listen to devotions and prayer at the beginning of class and that violated her rights. Ball State immediately withdrew her from seminar, which I considered silly. They could have easily fixed the problem by just having her arrive five minutes after class began. It also frustrated me that while earning my doctorate, I sat in classes at Ball State and listen to professors and students take the Lord's name in vain and denigrate Christianity, but she couldn't listen to a five-minute devotional. I did continue to supervise her student teaching, but her quality was definitely not the same as my Bethel students who were committed to their students and the profession. It wasn't just a job. Such a difference.

Over the next 25 years I taught a variety of courses—Children's Literature (my personal favorite), Art for Teachers (my second favorite), Reading and Language Arts Methods I and II, Student Teaching Seminar, Sophomore Practicum (Multicultural Education and Exceptional Child), Emergent Literacy, and Elementary Curriculum. From 1991-96, I was the Director of Student Teaching and supervised student teachers in the field. For nine years, I also taught four graduate courses as an adjunct professor for Indiana Wesleyan University on Saturdays. Then, after Bethel started a master's program, I taught graduate courses for Bethel in Curriculum Development and School Improvement, as well as Folklore and Children's Literature. I loved my language arts courses.

One of my favorite memories of observing my student teachers in their classrooms was when I visited a middle school social studies student teacher. He had them listen to current events on the TV news each morning before beginning their lesson. The day I was there, the news was about a serial killer. After he turned off the TV, there was no follow-up discussion and he simply told students to get out their books. One girl, in the back of the room, tentatively raised her hand and asked what a serial killer was. My student teacher simply said it was someone who killed over and over and then he went on with the lesson. In the meantime, I was mentally squirming in the back of the room because of the "teachable moment" he had missed. During our follow-up conference afterward, I asked him what the student really wanted to know when she asked that question. He didn't know. It was a perfect opportunity for me to reinforce that as teachers you have to be able to "crawl inside a student's head" and figure out what it is they don't understand. When I told him the girl was thinking "cereal" instead of "serial" and wondered why anyone would want to kill Cheerios, he was dumbfounded! And if she was brave enough to ask the question, you can be sure there were others in the class who were wondering the same thing. He could have discussed the difference between the two homophones "serial" and "cereal", connected "serial" to the word "series," and praised her for being bold enough to ask for clarification. He asked me how I knew that was what she was thinking. I told him to check with the girl to make sure that was really her question. He came to student teaching seminar the next week to report that's exactly what she thought. Years later, he told me that lesson stuck with him and he has made good use of "teachable moments" ever since, as well as learning how to understand what students don't "get."

The subject of single parent families came up often in my classes—usually with a negative connotation. Children in single parent homes tend to have more emotional and behavioral problems than children from two parent homes because they have suffered through a tragic death or a painful divorce. However, I was a single parent, but my children hadn't suffered through either of those traumas. I made sure to encourage my college students not to leap to generic conclusions about children's home lives. Not all single parent homes are dysfunctional or produce children with "issues." Many of the girl's teachers commented that they didn't even know my girls lived in a single parent home! I took that as a compliment that my girls functioned normally and did not seem damaged by not having a father.

Over the years, most of my elementary education students reported that their favorite course was Children's Literature. What fun we had delving into the various genre's, values and uses of that delightful literature in a classroom. When the Harry Potter books first came out, I avoided them due to what Christians were saying about witchcraft in the books. But by the time the third book came out, I knew I had to read them to be able to discuss the pros and cons in class. I fell in love with them and clearly saw the struggle of good vs. evil. As I researched more deeply, I discovered the wisdom of John Granger, now the world's most well-known authority on the Harry Potter books. (Granger, J. (2006). Looking for God in Harry Potter (2nd Ed). USA: Tyndale House). He is a Christian who saw the same thing in those books I did—the story of Christ! See Appendix D for greater detail.

I have since done my best to let students (and the general Christian public) know it's o.k. to read the Harry Potter books. If we can accept witchcraft in The Lion, The Witch, and The Wardrobe, why can't we read about witches in the Harry Potter books? In my experience, Christians sometimes object to things before they have checked them out. J. K. Rowling intentionally did an amazing job presenting the story of Christ in an imaginative new way so we can look at "the greatest story ever told" with fresh eyes. And she kept her mouth shut about the Christian theme in them until after the last book was published, because she knew non-Christians would stop reading them. I was and am impressed!

I tried so hard to save some money to replenish my savings we had used up while I was earning my doctorate. I had the bank take $25 out of each paycheck and put it into a savings account. It wasn't much, but it was all I could spare. However, I was never able to leave that money in savings. Some need always came up with the girls and I ended up taking it back out again. We were living on the edge financially, even though I scrimped every way I knew how. We managed to survive on my low salary. But we could rarely eat out. I cooked homemade meals and we always ate family dinner together. If we did eat out, it was usually on Sundays after church and was a real treat.

One of my favorite memories of when the girls were little was when I poked my head in their rooms at night to check on them. I loved seeing them cuddled up with one or more of our cats. Doogie was always curled around the girl's heads or snuggly buried at their feet under the covers. Such contentment!

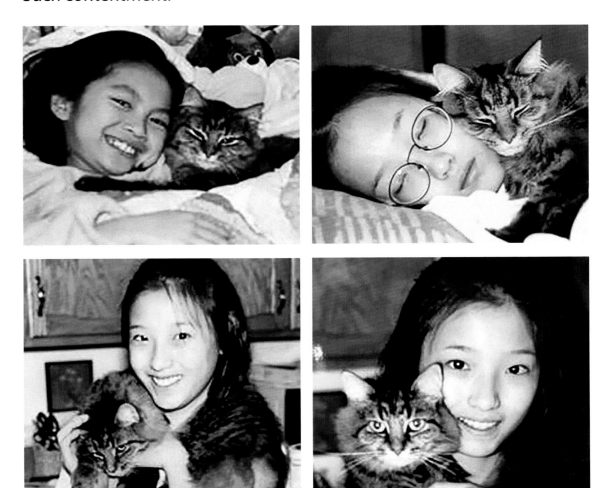

Abbi and Amanda with their beloved Doogie

My faculty evaluations and course evaluations were always great, and my advisees loved me, so I felt I was making a difference for these future teachers. What joy it gave me to share my faith in the classroom! I seemed to "fit" at the college level, for which I was both pleased and relieved. Several people asked me if it was difficult to move from teaching second grade to college. I always told them, "No, you still have to say everything six times!"

Since computers were still fairly new and Bethel wasn't a rich school, I had to supply my own computer when I arrived at Bethel in 1991. It had a dot-matrix printer and there was no internet! In 1996, when I stepped into administration, Bethel finally provided me with a computer.

I immediately recognized one lack in my life. Besides teaching and motherhood, I desperately needed some social outlet in my life. So I gathered some Bethel gals together and started a euchre group. We played two-table progressive euchre each month and took turns hosting and cooking a meal. It was just what I needed apart from my other responsibilities. I continued in that group for several years, and then turned it over to someone else and started another euchre group of just four gals. We ate out to avoid cooking a meal and we played blind euchre. That group has continued for years and still gives me pleasure and entertainment!

Working full-time, being a single mom, taking care of the car and the yard, dealing with insurance, finances, house repairs, cooking, cleaning and laundry, was very difficult. I never had any down time. I remember one very special birthday. We went to Mom's and Dad's for the weekend and Mom watched the girls so I could take a nap! As a single mother, naps were impossible! What a treat!

The girls (six and eight) were so excited to ride a school bus for the first time! They loved their school and made friends quickly. Abbi was very outgoing and didn't know a stranger. Amanda was more reserved and took longer to warm up to people. I had to hire babysitters when I taught night classes, but Bethel graciously helped me avoid as many of those as possible for the first few years, till the girls were old enough to stay alone. They usually managed to keep it to only one night class a week. Abbi continued to accumulate English and was soon speaking like a native. Her only residual mistake was saying "All well," when she meant "oh, well!"

Both girls took piano lessons for several years and Korean lessons for two years. They hated the Korean lessons. But I didn't want them to lose what little Korean they had retained. Unfortunately, the young gal who was teaching them tried to go too fast too quickly so the girls lost interest.

Abbi's hearing seemed to be problematic, so I had her hearing tested. Turned out her hearing was fine, she just didn't listen very well! In fact, she didn't quite hear things correctly (due to being a second language learner, I suppose) and that proved to be quite humorous on numerous occasions.

She loved to sing around the house, but never quite got the words to songs correct. Do you remember the TV ad for Folger's Coffee? The child takes his grandmother a cup of coffee and she finds his toy soldiers in the bottom of the cup. He thought the song said, "The best way to start the day is soldiers in your cup." That could have been Abbi! One day when she was an adult, she had come home after I had surgery and asked what she could get for me. I told her I wanted a Butterfinger malt. What she brought me was a butterscotch malt. It was so runny, I had to drink it! One time, Abbi asked me how Jesus could be born at Christmas and be a grown man by Easter!

Abbi was very entertaining and always the life of the party at family holiday gatherings. She was just delightful and "a hoot"—no other way to put it. Sometimes I was convinced she had blond roots under that black hair! Bless her heart, she was lively and fun! And she didn't know a stranger. She made friends quickly and easily. She was very easy to love.

And Abbi loved to talk! At one point, I suggested we enroll her in Talkers-On-Anon. She was not amused. If I left her notes on the counter of things to do when she got home from school, she never did them. It took me awhile to figure out that although I was a visual learner (I must see things to remember them), she was an auditory learner—she had to hear things. So I switched to telling her things that needed to be done and she remembered and took action, but seeing a note did no good. Very interesting. But the first sign of an auditory learner is that they never stop talking, so it fit!

One day, when she was about nine, Abbi came home from school and proclaimed, "I've fallen in love!" I mentally prepared myself to hear about her newest boyfriend, when she finished by saying, "with meat loaf sandwiches!" Can you tell what I'd fixed for dinner the night before? I chuckled quite a bit over that one.

Since Abbi's two surgeries in Korea for the burns on her arm had not been successful, I took her to Shriner's Hospital in Chicago for more surgery. Again, it did not work. Her skin "rotted." I finally decided to just leave her arm alone since she at least had full use of it, but she still has a bad scar today.

At dinner one night, after Abbi entered sixth grade and moved to the middle school, she complained about the cafeteria food. She didn't like the lunch ticket I bought her. "You mean the balanced lunch plan?" I asked.

She said she wanted to go through the other line because it was better food—they made the food in Elkhart and brought it to her school every day. I knew she meant the "junk" food line but couldn't figure out why she thought it came from Elkhart. I explained that her school had their own kitchen and made their own food. But she insisted it came from Elkhart. I puzzled and puzzled over that through the meal, knowing she wasn't hearing something quite right. Finally, it dawned on me. "You mean the 'a la carte' line? " She had never heard, "a la carte," before and that had no meaning for her, so in trying to make sense of it, she hung its meaning on the closest thing she had in her schema (experience)—Elkhart!

For the rest of the evening, every time I started chuckling to myself, she said, "You're thinking about that Elkhart food again, aren't you?" We have laughed about that "Elkhart food" for years and I used that as a wonderful example to explain "schema" in my Reading Methods classes.

In fact, I used many of the girls' writing samples, LEA projects, and school items as examples in my reading methods classes. They were perfect examples for what I was trying to teach my college students.

I gave my girls an allowance every week, but I automatically put half of it into their banks for savings. From the other half they had to tithe first and then do what they wanted with the rest.

For years, one summer activity we enjoyed was picking blueberries at a ranch near us. The girls loved riding that wagon out to the field, and after we came home with several pounds of blueberries, we made and stuffed ourselves with homemade muffins.

I didn't often have the summers free, but one summer I did, and I planned several surprises for the girls. I never told them what each one was, but about a week beforehand, I told them what to wear or take. Together, we enjoyed a circus, a rodeo (that stretched me!), staying at a Bed and Breakfast with Grma and Grpa, a whole day on the playground, a picnic, and going to Cedar Point in Ohio to meet Jay and Dusty (friends from Korea).

Both girls loved to read (woo-hoo! Don't get me started on the importance of reading to your child, which I did lots of, and how much more successful children will be in life if they are read to and readers! The statistics would probably bore you, but they excite me). One time, when I couldn't find the girls, I searched through the whole house and around the outside of the house. I finally found them laying in the van reading books! It did my heart good.

Reading for fun!

Abbi won a school-wide reading contest in fifth grade by reading over 18,000 pages—more than any other student in the school. Not bad for a kid who didn't speak English just six years before!

Abbi got hooked on Box Car Children books. That was fine, but I wanted to get her into better quality literature, so I got her the Narnia set. One day, when she was in fourth grade, as I was getting ready to go teach my Children's Literature class, Abbi told me she didn't want to finish reading The Lion, The Witch, and The Wardrobe. She wanted me to tell her how it ended. When I asked why, she said it was scary—they were going to kill Aslan and what's more, he was going to LET them! I told her she had to finish reading it herself and that she knew this story. She told me, "No, I've never read this book before." I said I knew that, but if she paid attention, she would find something familiar about the story. She came to me after finishing the book and asked if Aslan was like Jesus! She had made the connection! She had been hearing stories about Jesus at church for years, but I think that book helped her put the pieces of Christianity together. She accepted Christ and was baptized shortly after that! She wanted Grpa DeVon to baptize her, so Grma and Grpa drove up, and he baptized her at the Elkhart Church of Christ (1993). Amanda was baptized at Harris Prairie Church on Easter Sunday, 1995. Then we discovered that Grma and Grpa had been baptized on that exact same date (as Amanda) exactly 60 years before (1935)! Mom and Dad hadn't even realized they had been baptized on the same day as each other! What wonderful discoveries!

In 1995, for their 50th wedding anniversary, I made Mom and Dad a special scrapbook about their marriage and family. My creative attempts

With my precious Grma Faye 1982

Grma Faye at age 90 1991

Mom and Dad's 50th wedding anniversary 1995

were evolving into the scrapbooking fad that became so popular years later. They loved their book. Later, I greatly improved the, "Anecdotes from the Life of DeVon Wilson," book I had made for Dad years before, by changing it into a larger, more colorful and descriptive scrapbook. In later years, I also made both Mom and Dad scrapbooks about their entire lives. They spent hours looking at them.

When each of the girls celebrated their 11th birthdays, I took them (separately) to a fancy restaurant and we had a special talk about making decisions. We talked about how some people really mess up their lives because of poor decisions involving drinking, smoking, drugs and pre-marital sex. Then I asked if they would be willing to sign a contract that they would avoid those harmful things? They both signed willingly and I gave them a bamboo ring on a chain to wear as a "promise" ring. They recommitted to their contracts every year on their birthdays and were to present their ring to their new husband on their wedding night as a symbol of their purity. As they grew and matured, they kept their promises until college. I was quite disappointed that both my girls chose to secretly drink, so without much fuss, I asked for their promise rings back since they had not honored their commitment. But at least we got through those difficult high school years without any of the issues listed in their contracts.

I was quite busy professionally outside of Bethel! I got involved with the Indiana Reading Association and served as an officer for four years. While I was president, we earned honor council status (the first and only time in the group's history) and I flew to California (and took the girls so we could visit Disneyland and Universal Studios) to accept that award. I also participated in community service—Harris Prairie Church of Christ Pre-School board, multi-year judge at the Prairie Vista LearningSphere, Brandywine School Spelling Bee judge, Adoptions Alternative Advisory Board, and the Scholastic Book Clubs advisory panel. I also spoke to several parent groups, spoke at elementary school writing workshops, presented at regional and national conferences, and conducted faculty training sessions at Ancilla College.

In the 1990's, Mom had to move Grma Faye to a nursing home in Wabash, which was less than half a mile from Ralph and Cheri's insurance company. It would have been so easy for Cheri to go visit Grma over lunch break or after work, but she rarely did. She again ignored Grma, which broke Grma's (and Mom's) hearts.

Grma Faye (my last grandparent) died in 1999. Brent and I both gave eulogies at her funeral. What a treasure she was. She influenced her family so graciously and so positively for Christ.

In 2010, Mom was hospitalized for nine months, again within a half mile of Cheri and Ralph's office. They did not visit her, while Brent and I frequently drove four hours to see her. When she finally came home, Dad had installed a handicapped ramp and had to take care of her. He did well!

While in Korea, we had made Sunday night our family game night and continued that in Osceola, but ran into a problem. We found a church we liked—Elkhart Church of Christ, but I also wanted the girls involved in the youth group and our church had so few kids, there was no youth group. So after a couple of years, we changed churches. Harris Prairie had youth group activities during the week. Those valuable Sunday game nights were wonderful for teaching sportsmanship (losing graciously), keeping score, using logic, and best of all, fun family bonding time. We continued them through their high school years. The girls were talented partners in just about every game. They seemed to read each other's minds. It became harder and harder to beat them at any game. They became masterful at euchre. On a Bethel sponsored trip to Chicago's Museum of Science and Industry (I took the girls), two of my Bethel students challenged the girls (eight and ten) to a euchre game, thinking these little girls would be easy prey. They were dumbfounded when the girls trounced them!

Over the years, I took the girls on several trips—to Mammoth Caves in Kentucky, Jamestown, Washington D.C., New York City, the Ozarks, Niagara Falls, the Bahamas, Florida and California. Many times, we traveled with Grma Marcy and Grpa DeVon for extra fun.

The girls adored their Grpa DeVon. They teased him, played games with him, rode on his shoulders, and wrote him funny notes. Brent and I bought Dad a computer and we were quite proud of him when he taught himself how to use it while in his eighties. He never became highly proficient, but managed e-mail and could play games. He never quite got the hang of using a search engine, but he was proud of himself. However, we had to teach him not to believe every phone and e-mail scam he received. He was very gullible. He fell for a few before we could catch them.

The girls had chores and responsibilities. We all three took a week doing laundry and cleaning the litter box. The girls were supposed to work together to cook one night each week. Abbi became quite good at

Lovin' on Grpa DeVon

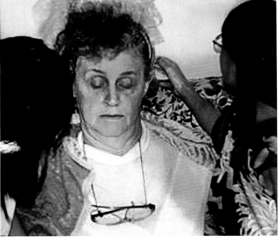

Fixing Grma Marcy's hair

making pies. Amanda made chocolate cake once and it looked wonderful. It tasted awful because she forgot to put in the sugar! Amanda sometimes forgot to move the wet laundry to the dryer. She left it in the washer until it molded. As teenagers, I had them "play adult" one week by writing the checks to pay bills, creating a grocery list, doing the grocery shopping, making sure everyone did their chores, and being "in charge" of the family without being "bossy." It was good training for them.

**Helping mom
around the house**

**Scraping the fence
in their best jewelry**

Roasting marshmallows instead of planting mom's garden!

I began donating blood again in 1991 and soon learned about pheresis donations. So, I switched to donating just platelets, which I could donate every two weeks, instead of five times a year with whole blood. Dad wasn't too happy about that. It meant I would catch up with him in a few years. I got the added benefit of taking a much-needed nap during those two-hour procedures. Then the blood bank got a machine that collected a double product and eventually a triple product. My platelet count was so high I was one of the few people able to donate a triple product. In other words, I had enough platelets in one pint of my blood to help three people. I eventually surpassed Dad's 28 gallons (224 donations). I finally stopped donating blood when I reached 37 ½ gallons (300 pints), when I retired and my health deteriorated.

Amanda's irrational, irritable, angry, explosive, raging, moody behavior and suicidal ideations continued to worsen over the years. Normally children stop crying about everything as they grow older, but Amanda cried constantly. Her first therapy (psychologist) session, when she was eight, was non-productive. All she did was cry and refuse to talk to him. Between 1991 and 2000, I tried various therapists, consulted numerous doctors, psychiatrists, psychologists, and counselors, admitted her to three different psychiatric hospitals (all against her will), and drove her down to Riley's Children's Hospital in Indianapolis for a full evaluation.

I began counseling as well and got started on anti-depressants. One summer things were so bad my entire lawn died because I didn't have time (or energy) to care for it.

During one eight-day stay at Madison Center (after Amanda became suicidal at age 11), they tested her IQ again. It remained in the genius range, and was the same as when she was tested at four years old, so I was relieved that the test, which had been administered so poorly, was indeed accurate.

I received numerous and varied diagnoses for Amanda over the years—dysthymia, major depressive episode, oppositional defiant disorder, parent/child conflict, hypersensitivity, ADD, ADHD, bi-polar disorder, and reactive attachment disorder. I also suspected that she had a touch of autism, since her social skills were poor and she could not identify how she felt about things. She had difficulty identifying with other people's emotions. For each diagnosis, a different medicine was prescribed. Some of them were more effective than others, but getting her to take the meds was a battle, and the periods between med changes were horrible (weaning her off the old and onto the new). Our lives were in chaos. Abbi and I never knew what would set her off. It was usually a small, insignificant thing that triggered her eruptions. It was exhausting to constantly be on guard.

For years, I struggled to figure out if she was willfully misbehaving or if she simply couldn't control herself. I didn't want to punish her bad behavior if she had no control over herself. On the other hand, I didn't want her thinking her behavior was acceptable. It was a "Catch-22." I continued trying every discipline technique in the book and even created a few of my own. Nothing worked.

I dreaded leaving work to go home at night because I knew what I would be facing. I secretly feared Amanda might kill or injure either or both of us when in a rage. I hated what this horrible situation was doing to Abbi, but she learned to leave the house (it was a blessing when she had a car). I didn't have that luxury. Even though I dealt with Amanda in a calm manner, reasoning with her or being rational did no good. She fought me at every turn, even though I was fighting for her. She blamed me for everything.

I feared that by constantly dealing with Amanda, I was neglecting Abbi. I tried so hard to give her the attention she needed and still give her space to be a teenager—much like my parents left me alone while dealing with

Cheri's issues. Abbi spent a lot of time out with her friends and I know that helped her get away from the mess at home.

By the time she was ten, Amanda began getting severe migraine headaches. It seemed she conveniently "used" her migraines to control things which meant I missed several activities, including my college reunion, Nore's master's degree graduation, my aunt's funeral and a wedding because Amanda developed a severe headache at the last minute. I received frequent calls at work to come get her from school. Eventually, the doctors and I figured out that her migraines were self-induced from her anxiety and depression. In later years, she complained that I always seemed to resent having to come get her from school. What I never told her was that I knew she was causing those headaches herself, probably when she felt overwhelmed and couldn't deal with things. It was her way of getting out of situations. I wasn't angry, just frustrated that my job might be in jeopardy if I missed much more work. It was so embarrassing and frustrating to leave meetings I was chairing, to be called out of classes or chapel, to constantly cancel meetings, or to abandon ("stand up") faculty I was scheduled to observe. Trying to reschedule everything became a nightmare.

I had to be emotionally strong at work and at home, but always ended up sobbing my way through church services (where I didn't have to be strong and could let down my guard?) Amanda refused to go to church anymore and eventually began skipping school because she was too depressed to handle it. Her grades went from straight A's to all F's by late middle school. I was frantic to help her, but no one could tell me how to do that.

Eventually, she began twitching and picking at the ends of her hair. I would sometimes find her on the floor curled into a fetal position in a corner. It broke my heart. She stole things from us that disappeared into the jungle of her room. We tried to help her clean it out a few times, but she flew into rages when we did. She simply could not keep things tidy and organized and resented our attempts to help her do that.

Amanda abused us emotionally, mentally and verbally. I suspected she was close to abusing us physically, but she never quite crossed that line. She got so angry with me because I sighed a lot while dealing with her. I recognized that I was sighing to release tension and stress, but she took it as a personal comment against her.

She had the annoying habit of never getting us anything for Christmas or birthdays. She sometimes presented us with a "promise note" inside an empty box, or two rows of a crocheted scarf with the promise to finish it later, or something similar, that never came to fruition. We learned never to expect anything from her. I rarely got gifts from her. But she did surprise me once. During the summer of 2006, while Abbi and I traveled to Peru, Chile and Easter Island, Amanda toured Europe. She purchased a beautiful hand carved nativity set for me in Oberammergau, Germany. I was impressed with her generosity and thoughtfulness.

All through elementary school and into middle school, Amanda was able to "hide" her problem from public view. She was always socially awkward, but it didn't seem to hinder her too much when she was young. She only raged and threw tantrums at home and blamed me for everything. Trying to help her protect her public persona (her wish), I kept my mouth shut about our problems. Her elementary teachers thought she was wonderful. She was able to fool everyone in the outside world. Finally, by eighth grade, she could no longer hide her depression and her friends began to suspect there were issues. She never wanted them to know when she had been admitted to psychiatric hospitals. Her sixth-grade photo clearly showed her depression.

When she was a patient at Oaklawn in Goshen, they recommended electric shock treatments to her brain. I knew I had pneumonia at the time (I'd had it before and recognized the symptoms), but couldn't find the time to go get treatment for myself. Due to constantly dealing with her, I always ended up putting my needs on the back burner. For a few weeks, I got up at four a.m., drove to Goshen, took her for electric shock treatments, took her back to the psychiatric hospital and then got to work by nine or ten. I was the dean then, so my job was stressful as well. It was a bleak time. Those electric shock treatments cost over $50,000.

You can divorce a spouse, but how do you divorce a child? I walked miles around our neighborhood when I got frustrated with her and just had to get out of the house. With each step, I inwardly chanted, "I want her out of my life!" even though at the same time, I knew I really didn't. My head wanted to be free of the terrible stress, but my heart didn't want to give up on her. I dreamed of having the luxury of throwing all her possessions out on the lawn and locking her out of the house. I knew it was my extreme frustration and pain talking, but I began a mental countdown till she turned 18 and I would legally be free of the responsibility of caring for her.

Amanda was a master manipulator. She convinced her doctors that I didn't listen to her. Her definition of "listening" was that I agreed with her. To her, if I didn't agree with what she demanded, I wasn't listening. Over the years, some of her doctors questioned me about abusing her and being a terrible "listener." Many times, while trying to reason with her, I'd start out with one viewpoint, and soon find she had manipulated me to her viewpoint, and I wondered how I had gotten there! Oh, she was good! Being brilliant also contributed to her manipulation skills. I often thought to myself, "Give me a good average child any day!"

Some of her doctors believed her—placing the blame solely on me. So, of course, I began to doubt myself. Was I a terrible mother? My self-concept suffered quite a bit. Two of her doctors at Oaklawn, finally seeing what she was capable of, advised me to contact the Juvenile Justice System and unadopt her—let the "system" take care of her. But I knew in my heart that I couldn't do that to her. I hadn't adopted her to turn her over to someone else if things got bad. I viewed my commitment to her like a wedding vow—for better or worse. And this was definitely the "worse" part.

I was not a perfect parent—there is no such thing. But I was a very good mother, never screamed at her, never lost my temper, and never abused her. I was steady, strong, reasonable, consistent and patient. I had seen good parenting modeled and knew what to do and not do. Unfortunately, none of the "good parenting" principles applied when dealing with Amanda. She was well beyond normal bounds of behavior and was a huge challenge. But I knew my job was to be her mother, not her friend, and I refused to enable her.

The girls had different medical issues. Abbi continued to be short and skinny. At one point, she asked me if she was a midget! I assured her she wasn't, but she continued in the bottom fifth percentile of height and weight charts, even though she ate three times as much as I did. One year she had the audacity to only gain one pound, after the hundreds of good meals I had made for her that year! I decided there is no justice in life. I could barely eat anything without gaining weight and she ate tons and stayed skinny. She entered high school weighing 60 pounds. The school nurse called me to ask if she was anorexic! I assured her she wasn't! Abbi began wearing glasses about age seven and changed to contacts in high school, then got Lasik surgery in college. She developed allergies to several things while in middle school—grass, trees, pollen, cats, dogs, etc. She took allergy shots for a few years because she did not want to give up her precious cats (especially Doogie).

Amanda had to wear braces and she had several head injuries. Her first was a forehead gash when we still lived in Korea. When she was two, she fell down the stairs and had to have several stitches.

That was scary since I had no car and couldn't speak the language well. While in Osceola, she had

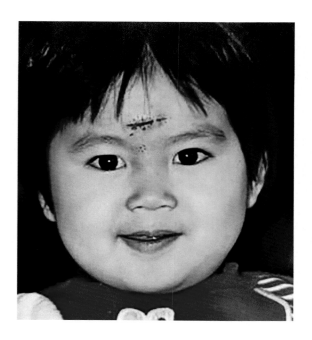

"Doctor changed my head!"

a bike accident and got a bad gash on her chin that required several stitches. Then, one time, she was being obstinate and insisted that she was going to eat some box-mix biscuits we made that didn't rise. They were flat, which told me the mix was old. She ended up in the E.R. over that. Another time she hit her head while at a birthday party and was in the E.R., unresponsive for a couple of hours.

But the worst was when I was driving her to high school one morning (she was late and missed the bus). Just as I pulled up to the school, she told me she had overdosed on a med she was allergic to. I immediately rushed her to the E.R. where they pumped her stomach and called in a psychologist to deal with her attempted suicide (age 14). I firmly believe that she was not trying to kill herself, but trying to kill "the problem."

She was hospitalized for a few days at Oaklawn in Goshen. After she got home, I knew I didn't dare go to sleep, as night-time was when she attempted stupid things and I had to constantly be on my guard. One night, I heard her sneak out of the house and followed her out to the garage, just in time to stop her from stealing Abbi's car. She had stolen Abbi's driver's license too. She later said she didn't know where she was going to drive to. Had she succeeded in stealing the car, I would have filed a report with the police. I was determined not to enable her bad behavior.

I managed to get her, kicking and screaming, back into the house and called the police to help me. She locked herself in her bedroom. Then, while I was talking to the police, she slit the screen in her second story bedroom and jumped out of the window. She landed in a snowbank, so did little damage (other than sore ankles). The police helped me get her into the car so I could drive her back to Oaklawn (after a trip to the E.R. to x-ray her ankles).

When she was released, that time, her doctors advised that I have her live somewhere else for a while, so she lived with the Barnums for a week and then spent a week with the Wolfe family. At one point she also stayed with Dr. Bridges—the President of Bethel! I was so touched that he and his wife (who was a mental health counselor) offered to take her for a few days so I could rest. That meant so much to me.

One year, Cheri and Ralph decided to renew their wedding vows. Cheri told Mom what date they were thinking of doing it but then never mentioned it again. That day, Mom got a snippy call from Cheri wanting to know if they were coming or not. Mom told her she didn't know for sure they were still having it as she'd heard no more about it. So Mom and Dad got dressed quickly and went over. Brent and I were not invited at all.

Another time, Cheri and I decided to share the cost of having a pig butchered and split the meat, since I had a freezer to store it. She said she'd let me know when it would be ready. One Saturday morning, she called and without even saying "hello," abruptly asked, "Well, are you coming to get your meat or what? It is frozen but won't stay that way for long." She had never informed me when it would be coming, so I had not planned on that date. I canceled my plans for the day and we quickly drove down to Wabash to pick up the meat. She was very cool when we got there. I had no idea what she was upset about and didn't ask. We just took our meat and hurried home.

My Bethel classes continued to go well, even though I was so exhausted and preoccupied by the situation with Amanda. In 1995, I was promoted to Associate Professor of Education.

ADMINISTRATION

One day, in early March (1996), Mike Holtgren, the Academic Dean, came to my office. He explained that because Bethel was growing so fast (listed as one of the fastest growing colleges in the U.S.), his job had grown to more than one person could handle, so they were creating a new position—Associate Dean. He wanted me to apply for it. I looked behind me to see who he was talking to! Me? I was dumbfounded. I was the only one he was asking to apply. I spent several weeks mulling and praying. I made several appointments to ask probing questions. I found out that Bethel was working to gradually change the historical practice of men professors making more than female ones (because they were the heads of households—what was I, chopped liver?), that Bethel was gradually evening out salaries for all professors (nursing professors had been earning more than other departments), etc. All in all, I felt I could work with the Bethel administration, and I completely trusted Dr. Holtgren, who would be my immediate supervisor.

Besides my reluctance to leave teaching, my biggest fear was leaving my Director of Student Teaching position. There was no one else to do that job. I took that responsibility seriously and didn't want to leave that up to chance—it was too important for future teachers. Bethel interviewed a new education candidate that spring—Susan Karrer. I liked her right away and walked out of her interview feeling comfortable that I could leave the student teaching job in her hands.

So, I accepted the Associate Dean's position. In June, while I was on vacation with the girls and Mom and Dad, I got a call that another faculty member had applied for the position as well, so they were going to run interviews with both of us. After those were over, the votes were split so they decide to hire both of us in a half-time position. We would continue to teach as the other half of our load. I would be the Associate Dean of Instruction and Dale (who was rather strange) would be the Associate Dean of Curriculum. My salary increased by a mere $3,000—only $2,000 above what my faculty salary increase would have been after the yearly increase. And that was moving to a year-round position! Barb, the secretary in the Education Department office, moved with me to be my secretary in Academic Services. She was a Godsend!

My new job included monitoring all instruction on campus, observing and evaluating faculty, assisting in hiring new faculty, hiring, supervising and evaluating secretaries, revising and managing course evaluations, and overseeing the Registrar's Office (It was the registrar's job to abide by all policies, while it was my job to make exceptions when appropriate—so I listened to lots of appeals). It was also my responsibility to dismiss students who had failed academically, rule on all student appeals for re-admission, and do general problem solving. I worked closely with Dennis Engbrecht, the V.P. for Student Development. We teamed up for several academic/discipline hearings with students, such as plagiarism. I respected Dennis a great deal. I also had the unfortunate task of firing faculty and secretaries. Those were never pleasant situations.

I was also responsible for hosting candidates and their spouses while they were on campus interviewing for a few days. I became the face of Bethel College to them since I met them at the airport, entertained them, sometimes housed them, took them to church, took them out to eat and spent more time with them than any Bethel person. I got to know them quite well, so it was a blessing. My in-depth knowledge of them and insights sometimes made the difference in whether we hired them. I considered hiring good faculty as the most important part of my job.

It was a big job and very demanding. Since it was a new position, it took us awhile to figure out the boundaries between Dale's role and mine. He was to oversee the curricular programs on campus. After four years, Dale moved on to another college and Steve Matteson moved into the Curriculum Associate Dean's position. Steve and I worked very well together.

My immediate supervisor (V.P.), Mike Holtgren, whom I respected a great deal, began losing ground with his health. He finally took a semester off, so Steve and I took on his job as well as our own. Mike finally had to resign, and Bethel brought in a retired interim V.P., Paul Collard. He was wonderful. After he left a year later, Jim Stump took over as V.P for Academic Services. I did not enjoy working with Jim as much. In 1999, my job was changed from half-time administrator and half-time faculty to full-time administrator, while I continued to teach half a load at night, now as an adjunct. So my title changed from Associate Dean to Dean of Instruction. I created several positive things while the Dean. I revamped course evaluations, created the Professor of the Year Award, created an advisor evaluation system, and created the Dean's List Hall of Fame (because I was tired of only athlete's getting acclaim for their achievements).

Tribute to Women Award Nominee 1996

1996   **Bethel Beacon Interview 1996**

As the Dean of Instruction, I learned that dealing with college faculty is like herding cats! I ran into some strange situations. Among other things, my responsibilities included posting job openings, screening applicants, and running interviews for potential faculty. One time I received an application and vitae that looked very good to all those concerned—other administrators, and to the relevant division members. So, I called and invited him to come interview (from a university in Alabama where he had just completed his doctorate). Bethel could only afford to bring one candidate to campus at a time, so I was selective in those invitations. After Dr. Bridges, the President, asked to see his file, he came back and told me the candidate had written his own letters of reference. I was stunned! I had read them carefully and noted nothing to indicate any irregularities, but Dr. Bridges showed me one two-word phrase that appeared in all his letters of recommendation. This was a foreign candidate, so English was not his first language, and the phrase was an awkward one, not one typically used by English speakers, but I had missed it (I suppose due to my familiarity with foreigners). I felt terrible for my oversight. I followed up by calling all his references (which I normally didn't do until after the interviews). They all confirmed that they had not written reference letters for him, would never have done so, and were angry he had used their names on his fake reference letters. I called and uninvited him to interview (that was not a pleasant call!). I received word later, that the Alabama university withdrew his doctorate—dishonesty (reverse plagiarism?) and its consequence in action!

Firing secretaries and faculty was not fun. After I fired Peg, she returned to her office and shredded valuable college documents she had been responsible for in her job. We scrambled to salvage what we could.

Another time, Terri, a faculty member came to me apologizing because she feared her course evaluations might not be too good that semester due to some personal problems she was having. She also reported that she had dropped out of her doctoral classes. I was ordered to fire her because she had not completed her doctorate in the agreed time span. In fact, she was two years past that time limit. I felt terrible because she had come to me expecting support and instead, I had to operate under direct orders to the contrary. However, the general faculty did not realize the decision to release her was not mine and complained I had overstepped my authority. It made for some uncomfortable conversations.

During one fall faculty social gathering, a returning professor, who had butted heads with administration a few times, was chatting with me and a new faculty member. He told the new faculty person to be careful or I would fire him (a totally inappropriate comment for the setting). Sadly, I did have to fire the guy a year later because of suspicious behavior with students.

Kirk, a grumpy professor, whom the president privately referred to as "Eeyore," frequently made emotional, ranting, negative complaints to administration, usually over minute issues. I spent many hours listening to his rages. We were quite relieved when he moved on to another college.

Chris, one faculty member who was internationally famous in his field (he had discovered a new species in Madagascar), began presenting more and more unstable mental behaviors during his time at Bethel. After a probationary period set up by the V.P., during which he took no steps to improve, another administrator fired him, and Chris disappeared overnight. His wife and the police spent weeks looking for him. They finally discovered his frozen body in his truck in northern Michigan. He had written his wife a nasty note blaming her for everything and then killed himself by carbon monoxide poisoning. It was a shock to the whole Bethel community and to those in his chosen field.

Jacob, a wonderful Bible teacher from Africa, and a very gracious man, was issued a great honor. He was invited to be the next Secretary General of the United Nations. He declined. He preferred to teach.

Another strange incident occurred just before spring registration one fall (in the days before online student registration). Students had to come to the Registrar's Office (after meeting with their faculty advisor) to submit paperwork for the classes they wanted. At the time, I was implementing an advisor evaluation system I had created and put forms in the hallway outside the Registrar's Office that students were required to fill out before they could register. One day, the Registrar came to me with a form a student had turned in that evaluated him as an advisee, rather than evaluating his advisor. I looked in the hallway and found the entire stack of forms I had supplied had been replaced with this new form. I immediately suspected Dave, a faculty member who had been quite unhappy with me because I had not given him stellar teaching evaluations in the past. Students fell asleep in his classes because he was so boring and droned on monotonously. He constantly received poor course evaluations from his students, too. He did not like any of my suggestions for ways to improve his teaching, claiming I was not qualified to evaluate him because I knew nothing about his subject matter (history).

This is a common misunderstanding among many professors with doctorates. They think that because they have subject matter knowledge, that automatically makes them a good teacher. They don't recognize the difference between subject matter knowledge and teaching skills. I didn't need knowledge of their subject matter to evaluate their teaching skills and techniques. Many Ph.D.'s also have an inflated ego and do not like to be told they need to improve. In fact, Dave told his daughter, Michelle, who was Abbi's freshman year roommate, that his doctorate was much more valuable and harder to achieve than mine. Colleges and universities recognize that history Ph.D.'s are a dime a dozen, and they certainly aren't the most difficult to earn. But with Dave's inflated ego, he couldn't accept that, so he got a copy of (and read) my dissertation to try to prove that my doctorate was worthless, but since he wasn't successful there, he began a campaign to undermine me.

After I found the fake evaluation form, I called the campus computer technicians and asked them to look through all Dave's "word" files to see if they could find this revised form. They found it. I informed Dr. Bridges (President) of the situation and he said he would handle it. In the meantime, I was dealing with the contamination of my data.

About a week later, I was working at my computer with my back to my office door, when I barely heard someone standing in the doorway quietly say, "Sorry, Becky," and then immediately leave before I could even turn around to see who it was. My secretary told me it was Dave. Evidently, Dr. Bridges had confronted him with his insubordination and insisted that Dave apologize to me. He also had the option of firing Dave, which might have been the wiser move, but he chose to leave it at an apology and a reprimand. It wasn't the first nor the last time Dave would haunt my work in the Dean's office and in my personal life.

Dave was very passive/aggressive—appearing polite in public but undermining me privately. Dave thought he was an expert on everything (just ask him!)—especially education. After all, his wife and daughter were teachers (but not very good ones according to the Bethel standards, and based on our dealings with them in their classrooms), so he figured that made him an expert. He made a habit of attending every Education Division meeting and telling us how we should change the courses and the major. The department chair (Susan) finally went to the Dean to request that Dave be told to stop attending our meetings; he was causing too much trouble. A few years later, Dave was ordered to stop attending all campus department meetings, except his own (even though they were all open to anyone). He was known all over campus for his self-proclaimed "expertise" and knowledge in all majors!

The few Bethel people that knew about my situation with Amanda, were kind, caring and supportive, but Dave chose a different path. Dave and Carol (his wife) took several opportunities to privately tell Amanda that they didn't approve of how I handled things (forcing her to go to doctors and counselors, admitting her to psychiatric hospitals, putting her in a special school), and told Amanda she should come live with them. I learned this from Amanda! She related to me that even she admits many of her behaviors were not acceptable and she couldn't believe Dave and Carol would inject themselves uninvited into her private life and say those things to her. I never confronted them about their actions, but chose to ignore them, giving them the benefit of the doubt, and choosing to believe they were just ignorant of the facts. Perhaps they did not know about Amanda's mental condition, and just assumed it was typical teenage rebellion. I wanted to grab them by the lapels, shake them and scream, "This is none of your business—stay out of it," but I resisted that urge. I dropped out of the euchre group I had started, in part because of Carol. She constantly pelted me with probing questions about Amanda, but I sensed she was just being nosy, not because she cared about me or Amanda. I didn't tell her anything because I didn't want her spreading rumors. In my efforts to follow God's directive that whenever possible, to live peacefully with everyone, I chose to simply avoid Dave and Carol. I had to turn the situation over to God to handle. Today, when I run into them, I am cordial, tell them nothing about Amanda (they always ask) and move on quickly.

As the Dean, one of my summer jobs was approving all graduation applications for May graduation the following year. It was a tedious job and I had to know the requirements for all the majors at Bethel (more than 50), as well as for the numerous catalogs and all those yearly changes. I dared not make mistakes or students would be in college longer to correct any errors in their programs. Most professors/advisors reacted well if I had to send the application back with required changes to the student's program. They worked with me to amend the problem and get the student in the correct classes, but unfortunately Dave did not. I had to reject more graduation applications from him than from any other professor and he did not react well. He claimed that his was the hardest major to advise, but I knew better since I had to understand every major on campus. It seemed his ego would not allow him to admit he had made mistakes in advising students. Unfortunately, it was his students who suffered by his advising mistakes. I couldn't allow that to happen with a clear conscience.

Twice, before their graduation applications reached my desk, two of Dave's student advisees threatened to sue Bethel because his poor advising had cost them an extra year in college (and consequently lots more money). So, I twice ended up with angry parents in my office. I don't remember now how I managed to head off those lawsuits, but Dave was not at all repentant for his bad advising. I suppose that explained his subversive actions regarding my advisor evaluations forms—he didn't want his advisees evaluating him!

A couple of years after I created the Professor of the Year Award, I received a packet nominating Dave. At least five people were required to fill out forms for each nominee. I had specifically designed the award for quality teaching alone—nothing else. I could not give the award to Dave with a clear conscience because he wasn't a good teacher. His observation reports, course evaluations, and student comments supported that. However, a couple of years after I left the Dean's position and returned to the Education Department, Dave was given the award. He was great at attending every student activity, spending lots of time in the coffee house talking to students, and established great relationships with his students, so I assume they gave him the award based on those merits, which missed the whole point of the award entirely. Privately, I wondered how many people Dave had bribed into nominating him.

Another professor, Rod, was a big, lovable, gregarious genius. However, his lack of common sense and serious errors in judgment frequently got him into trouble. His ability to say and do the wrong thing always came back to bite him, so I had to intercede frequently on his behalf, including heading off a lawsuit. Since I helped him so much, he thought we were best buddies and gravitated to me (in a very loud voice) whenever we were in faculty social situations. He was like a puppy following me around. Bless his heart. It was hard to avoid him.

Star, who ran the Educational Resource Lab for education students, considered the materials she managed to be Bethel's most valuable resource and was quite mean to students to protect her materials. It got to the point that students avoided using the lab. It took quite a bit of talking to convince her our students were our most valuable resource (not the lab materials) and to get her to treat students more kindly.

Catherine, a new faculty member, complained that the wife of her department chair was "stalking" her, because she invited Catherine to dinner and tried to make her feel welcome at Bethel. Our investigation showed no solid evidence to support Catherine's grievance, so she left Bethel after one year. I suspect some mental health issues followed her to her next job as well.

Gene, one of our long-term (and highly regarded in his field) professors consistently carried an excessively heavy private tutoring load. Upon investigation, I found he regularly had students private tutor with him to avoid taking one of the prerequisite classes in their major. He earned quite a bit extra that way, but classes did not always "make" due to low enrollment numbers. He was quite angry when we curtailed his private tutoring practices.

One time, I had to secure a restraining order against Sally, an education student, who continually came to campus and caused trouble for the Ed. Department because they had dismissed her from the program. We recognized that she had some mental problems, but we feared what she might do (to a future employer and future students) when we didn't let her finish her degree, which was never going to happen.

One of my advises, Anna, was extremely close to her aunt, who she viewed as a second mother. One day, the aunt stopped at a garage sale, when a total stranger, who was thinking about buying a motorcycle that was for sale, nudged her and asked her if she wanted to take a spin around the block with him. She agreed. Neither of them wore helmets. While circling the block, they had an accident and were both killed. Anna was devastated and I spent a considerable number of sessions counseling her.

One January, on the first day of classes after Christmas break, students came to report that their Spanish professor (an adjunct—a part-time employee), had not shown up for any of his classes. I spent considerable time trying to find Arnoldo. He didn't answer his phone, we did not know of any relatives, and we had no other way to reach him. I finally asked the police to do a welfare check at his home and peek in the windows to see if he was lying dead on the floor! They didn't find him anywhere, so I scrambled to find a substitute to cover all his classes. He showed up two weeks later and said he had been "held up in customs." He had traveled to his home country in South America over break—where time is treated quite differently and being late is acceptable. Being a world traveler myself, I know you don't get "held-up in customs" for two weeks! He just decided he needed a longer break. I fired him on the spot. He couldn't understand why we weren't tolerant of him playing "hooky."

I had loved decorating bulletin boards over the years, especially "interactive" bulletin boards. I continued doing the education department bulletin board even after I moved to the Dean's position. This one says different things as you walk past it. People loved it.

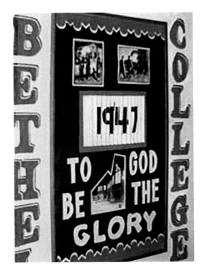 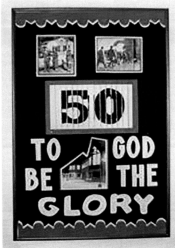 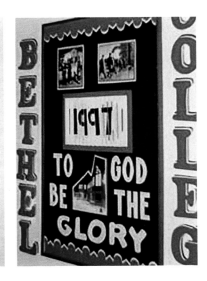

We had a very traumatic summer when Abbi was old enough to get a driver's license. She only weighed 60 pounds and the thought of her in control of a heavy moving vehicle scared me silly. She destroyed three mailboxes that summer. And once, after she was finally allowed to carry a passenger, she and Amanda were on their way to marching band practice. She called me and before she even said anything, I immediately exclaimed, "You had an accident!" She couldn't believe I knew that! She had sideswiped another car and removed the side mirror on both vehicles, but there was no damage otherwise! The other driver (I suspected) was an illegal alien and didn't want to call the police, so Abbi got away with not paying for their damage, but I made her pay for hers. I had bought her an old used car because we simply couldn't survive with only one car anymore. The girls were in too many activities. A few years later, she hit a deer, and then totaled her car in another incident. I think that was the beginning of my gray hairs!

When we lived in Korea in the 1980's, we began planning and saving for an "around the world" trip in 2000 (the year of the Passion Play in

Oberammergau, Germany—or the "Fashion Play" as Abbi kept calling it). The girls faithfully collected their Wahn (Korean currency) for a trip far in the future. By 1998, as the date grew closer, I began to realize I had two problems. First of all, I suspected my name was on a blacklist with the Korean government, due to the strange issue that arose the day we left country. I figured I would not be able to get back into Korea, so I wrote to the new headmaster of SFS and explained my problem. I asked him to have someone check and to let me know how much I owed for the fine incurred. He wrote back that my name was blacklisted, but that SFS had paid my fine! Bless his heart. I was very touched by his generosity.

My second problem dealt with Amanda. Her behavior had become so erratic and extreme that I was afraid to take her. I could never quite figure out if she could control her behavior or not. I continued to try every discipline technique in the book, to no avail. She refused to take her meds, which might have stabilized her. I didn't want to cancel the trip and deny Abbi this fantastic opportunity, when she had done nothing wrong, and we had been anticipating this trip for many years. I considered leaving Amanda at home but figured if I did, she'd punish me for the rest of her life. And who would I leave her with? No one should have to take on that responsibility and I knew I would feel guilty during the whole trip for burdening someone with her. I finally decided I'd have to take her.

In 1997, I had purchased a lot, intending to build a house there, but never quite got to it. I went through several drafts of blueprints (an elder/architect from church was helping me), but due to the cost, I could never quite begin building. In 2000, I sold the lot and used that money to pay for our around-the-world trip.

I had great difficulty planning the trip. I worked with the airlines and learned that for an around the world ticket, you could only utilize two airlines and had to keep the entire trip under 29,500 miles. So I laid out one itinerary after another and consulted numerous times with my friends we planned to visit about potential dates (we had e-mail by then). One time, I had whittled the trip down to bare bones but was still two miles over the limit allowed. The airlines refused to allow that overage, so it was back to the drawing board. Part of the problem was I had to use their "hub" cities, which meant sometimes going "backward" to get back to a hub. That added miles we didn't want or need. It was very frustrating, but

I finally managed to get it solved. Then, I worked to secure all our visas. What a headache! It was quite time consuming.

I had to split the trip into two parts. I planned to withdraw the girls (ages 15 and 17) from their high school for five weeks in March and April and I would home school them as we traveled (The second five-week trip would occur in the summer). Then I would re-enroll them when we returned. That would be easier than having them try to keep up with assignments from their teachers. I secured a home school teaching license. Amanda's teachers were not happy about her being pulled out of school. She had already missed so much school due to her depression and her grades were terrible. I completely understood their frustrations, and agreed with them, but felt stuck between a rock and a hard place. The one teacher who objected the most was her geography teacher. His argument? "She needs to be in my classroom so I can teach her this stuff." I wanted to ask him if he really listened to what he was saying—that she would learn more about geography by sitting in a classroom than by going out and experiencing it? I planned to make copies of the pertinent pages in their texts and work from that. But Amanda insisted on bringing her textbooks, so I let her lug that heavy bag around the world. She rarely used those books.

I took a sabbatical from Bethel. Just delegating my workload to make sure everything was covered while I was gone was a nightmare. The girls were extremely upset with me when I insisted we only pack two pair of pants, four shirts, tennis shoes, sandals, and a jacket. We never checked baggage on any airline, but only used one carry-on bag each. We washed our underwear in sinks and visited laundromats once or twice. I figured it didn't matter if we wore the same clothes every day! We weren't trying to impress anyone, and other than the friends we were visiting, who would completely understand, we knew no one. This trip would be hard work— not a luxurious experience. We would be walking miles every day and I didn't want to be bothered carrying heavy luggage all the time.

In March and April (the first part of the trip), we went completely around the world in five weeks—Italy, Switzerland, Hungary, Turkey, India, Bangladesh, Vietnam, Singapore, Malaysia, China, South Korea, and San Francisco. We visited my friends who had moved on to other countries after Korea, reunited with Nuri in Turkey, visited other overseas schools, saw most of the great art of the world, saw the fabulous landmarks and famous sights we'd heard about all our lives, and I got to share my favorite spots with the girls. I made sure we also included some new countries for me.

In June and July (the second part of the trip), we traveled to Europe and Scandinavia for another five weeks—Ireland, England, Wales, France, Austria, Slovenia, Croatia, Italy, Denmark, Norway and Germany—a total of 22 countries in ten weeks.

While we had some fabulous experiences, there were several times Amanda's behavior was so bad it made us late for flights/buses and she sometimes put us in dangerous situations. I tried to send her home alone a few times. For example, on a street in Copenhagen, she flew into a rage over a city tour ticket I had purchased. She threw a tantrum on the street, and someone called the police, accusing me of abuse. In Hanoi, I jumped into a rick-shaw and spent an afternoon away from her. In Singapore, I sought out an internet café and tried to contact Grma and Grpa, but the message never went through. In Beijing, I called the airlines to book her a flight. Each time, she promised to improve. The stress was unbelievable. I yearned to have the luxury of just walking away from her and leaving her behind.

Since the girls were to have saved up money to spend on this trip, we shopped a lot. I told them it would be like the best shopping trip of their lives. However, in the years preceding the trip, Amanda repeatedly begged me to take her money out of the bank and let her spend it on clothes. After years of her harassment, I finally relented and gave her over $300. She blew it on clothes and then had nothing to spend on the trip. She got so angry every time we saw magnificent things to buy and she couldn't buy anything. I had warned her, so I made her live with the consequences of her actions. She was not a happy camper.

In every country we visited from Bangladesh to Korea, the locals thought my girls were natives of that country and couldn't understand why they didn't speak the language—especially in China (and obviously Korea!). It got to be quite funny. We spent an entire week in Seoul, looking for Abbi's brother and sister. It was miraculous that we finally found them, and it was an extremely emotional reunion. We were all crying so hard we could barely take photos. Her brother and sister wanted her to spend the night with them, which made me very uncomfortable. I had no idea where they were taking her or if they would bring her back. I could tell she was nervous about it, too, but it all worked out well. We got to visit SFS again and reunited with Mrs. Nah. She invited us to her home—a rare opportunity since Koreans do not invite others to their homes like Americans do. It did us all a lot of good to see her again.

One very strange thing happened while we were with Abbi's brother and sister. We were eating at a Korean restaurant (we hired an interpreter for the day) when I mentioned to her sister (Eun Ja) that I was sorry to hear about her husband—he had died six or seven years before. She immediately turned to her son (ten years old) and asked him to go get something. Then she had the interpreter explain to me that Eun Ja had never told her son his dad had died. She told him his father was on an extended business trip. I was dumbfounded. Surely this poor kid thought dad had totally abandoned him—no Christmas presents, no birthday cards, no messages—nothing. I suppose Eun Ja was trying to shield him from the hard facts, but it seemed quite unrealistic and cruel to me to give him false hope that dad would return some day. Another cultural difference? I know it is not unusual for Korean couples to live apart for years while the husband conducts business in another country, but this was the first time I had ever heard of not telling your child his father had died!

We stayed with or visited with several friends—Donita in Italy (friend from Seoul), John and Ann Price in England (I had lived with them while in college), Nikki in England (the exchange teacher who lived with us in Muncie), Nuri and Mine in Turkey (our high school exchange student), the missionary parents of one of my Bethel students in Bangladesh, Edie Eager (friend from Seoul) in China, Mrs. Nah (our old adjumonie), Jonathan and Soon Ok Borden in Seoul, Steve and Phyllis Major in Budapest (friends from Seoul), Dan and Shirley Waters in Vietnam (friends from Seoul), and the Kauffmans in San Francisco (friends from Seoul).

My goal for this trip was to teach the girls to be experienced world travelers—how to manage in airports, navigate strange cities, use different currencies, cope with different languages and be tolerant of differences in cultures and people. As we landed in each new country, I told one of them it was her turn to get us through customs, find us transportation, secure a hotel, and change our money. They also had to use a map to direct us as we wandered through strange cities. They learned fast! Looking back, I realize what a brave undertaking that trip was! We were three females alone, not on a tour, with no reservations anywhere, and traveling with a mentally ill teenager. I must have been out of my mind! But praise God, we got through it.

ODE TO OUR WORLD TRAVELS
March/April and June/July, 2000
by Rebecca Wilson

This spring and summer were really great,
we traveled the world, strange foods we ate
Flew 40,000 miles on 24 flights,
rode dozens of trains and saw all the sights
Spent hours in airports, used a small hand-carry,
after days in the same clothes, we often smelled—very!

Rode rickshaws, gondolas, cyclos, taxis, and
subways underground
On cable cars, wagons, horses, buses, boats, and
camels got around.
Through the Chunnel, rode the Eurail,
tried to see Westminster to no avail.
Used pounds, lire, dollars, shillings, rupees,
and forints—how confusing
Konner and won, the best was
"Two Taka, Two taka!" How amusing!

Too many night trains, played hours of euchre,
ate lots of Nabber Nasi, carried our water.
Walked miles each day, up Mt. Vesuvius with ease,
in an Austrian ice cave, we almost did freeze.
The Little Mermaid, the Eiffel tower,
the London Eye, Beijing's rush hour,

Madame Tussaud's, a double-decker bus,
Wales at sunset, meant lots to us.
From Tower ravens, to the emerald Irish sea,
from Oberammergau, to tunnels under the DMZ,
In Istanbul, saw the center of the world,
waved at Tipperary as through Ireland we swirled,

Riding a cyclo in Vietnam

N. Korean tunnel under the DMZ

Windsor Castle

From Neuschwanstein Castle to the land
of the midnight sun,
learned that Italian ice cream really is fun!
The horrors of Dachau, and King Arthur's round table,
bought Waterford, Bath and Venice glass,
took showers when able.
Lived through a wild taxi ride in India, in Malumgat
ate with our hands,
wore shalwar kameez to blend in,
at Cox's Bazaar walked in the sands

A few hours in Zagreb, thirty seconds in Ljubljana,
mom's country count's at 49, get to 51?—she's gonna.
Pearls in Bangladesh, lace in Venice,
lacquer in Seoul, we became a shopping menace!
No visas for China, a parking ticket in Bath,
Tea and scones at Raffle's, had lots of laughs

In Istanbul, saw where east meets west,
and loved the Var in Budapest
Had sheep on our porch in Norway,
and stepped on rats in the Paris subway.
In London we saw Tony Blair,
in Seoul, met kids with purple hair

Fed pigeons in Trafalgar and San Marco Square,
of many cultures became aware
From the Mona Lisa, the David, and the Sistine,
to the streets of Singapore, pristine
The repainted Last Supper is a marvel to behold,
and the sights of Venice never grow old
The gift of a rainbow that never ends,
reunited with many long-time friends
Beijing's Forbidden City and jungles of Bangladesh,
found we loved Stonehenge the best
Kissed the Blarney Stone, climbed the Great Wall,
drove on the left, saw the Taj Mahal

Eiffel Tower

**Marker at the center
of the world
Istanbul**

Abbi to emergency rooms in Hanoi,
and reunited with siblings in Korea—what joy!
Saw Mrs. Nah, the adjumonie we loved best,
Amanda loved Italy, with key chains was obsessed
We started our travels with ancient Pompeii,
and finished the trip at the Passion Play.

The saying is true, while it's quite nice to roam,
there really is no place quite like home.
In ten weeks of travel, we were very inspired,
but after all those countries, I find I'm quite tired.
God's beautiful earth never fails to entertain me,
but I can't wait for Heaven,
where we'll be plane and train free!

Stonehenge

At the Great Wall

Venice

Roman guards at the Colosseum

In an Irish castle

Taj Mahal

Bangladesh

Dachau Concentration Camp

With Nuri and Mine in Istanbul

Tiananmen Square (Beijing)

Abbi marching in the Rose Bowl Parade

The Penn High School Marching Band was invited to march in the Rose Bowl Parade on New Year's Day, 2000 (not the real first day of the new century—that would be in 2001). Abbi played the flute and Amanda a saxophone and both girls were greatly looking forward to that trip. After we returned from our "Around the World" trip, however, Amanda's behavior continued to escalate. She slept 12-15 hours a day, refused all meds, stayed in her room most of the time, stopped contacting her friends, refused to eat with the family, stayed up all night, and had only functional interactions with us.

I began seeking out schools that could take Amanda full-time. I knew that to save Amanda's life, Abbi's life and my life, I had to place her somewhere she could get continuous care. I simply couldn't do it anymore. I finally found New Horizons School in Marion, Indiana. I spoke to them numerous times and made arrangements to take Amanda there. I knew she would miss marching in the Rose Bowl Parade, but her life was more important. I was afraid she would kill herself (or us) before that. So, in October, 2000, I tricked her into thinking I was taking her to school, stopped and picked up two friends—Carolyn and Michael (a large former Green Bay Packers football player who sat beside her so she wouldn't jump out of the van) and drove down to Marion (two hours away). She was furious and threatened to kill herself again. It was the hardest day of my life. I was heartbroken by what I was doing to her and what felt like my failure as a mother. I loved this child so much and felt I had somehow failed her.

The first thing I noticed when I got home was that there was peace in the house again. It was like the walls were calm again. I spent several days cleaning out her junk-filled room, finding broken glass under the layers of trash, and repairing the damaged walls and screen. I discarded multiple bags of garbage.

My friend, Carolyn and I flew to California and enjoyed the New Year's Day Rose Bowl Parade, even though I grieved that Amanda wasn't there. The band did a splendid job and got to march at Disneyland, too. I was so proud of Abbi.

I was not allowed a parental visit with Amanda for six months and when I did go, it was terrible. She mistreated me again. New Horizons had thought she was ready for it, but she had fooled them. They denied her any more visits until I felt better. They knew I needed time to heal. Even our weekly phone calls were painful, and Amanda's letters were full of rage and frustration. They made her rewrite some of them because she was being "manipulative." That made her even angrier. When we did resume parental visits, they were awkward and emotionally difficult for both of us. She did not earn a home visit for a full year. New Horizons places students on levels and she had to earn the right to move up to each new level. She stayed on the lowest levels for a long time because she refused to cooperate. It made her furious.

I didn't know that New Horizons required Amanda to answer every letter she received. So three months after she began at New Horizons, when I got Amanda's birthday card from Aunt Cheri, I forwarded it to her at school (my bad). She answered it and Cheri noticed the return address was Marion, Ind. She asked Mom about it, but Mom refused to tell her anything and told her she'd have to talk to me. When I discovered what had happened, I immediately guessed what Cheri would assume—that Amanda had gotten pregnant and I "sent her away" like they used to do with pregnant teenage girls. So, I decided I had to be pro-active.

I called Cheri and asked her to meet me in Warsaw. We had an awkward lunch. She confirmed that she guessed Amanda had gotten pregnant. So, I corrected that misconception and finally told her about the hell we had been going through for years with Amanda's mental condition and behavior. Cheri never expressed any sympathy or, "Oh, I'm so sorry you've gone through this," type of statements. Instead, she began telling me all the things I had done wrong and what I should have done (while I gritted my teeth). I wondered when she had dealt with a mentally ill child. I asked her not to contact Amanda anymore and to pray for us. She never called me to check on Amanda after that. I just knew that she was inwardly saying to herself, "See, that proves my kids are better! And I'm a better mother." I really didn't care. I just wanted to stop her from spreading untrue rumors about Amanda. I also made sure New Horizons knew that Amanda was not to correspond with Cheri at all.

Amanda was at New Horizons for two years before they finally figured out the problem—she has Borderline Personality Disorder. They felt all the other diagnoses had been incorrect and I agreed with them. Her behaviors completely fit the checklist for BPD. They suggested I read a book called, I Hate You, Don't Leave Me—Understanding the Borderline Personality Disorder by Kreisman and Stras (1989). I suspect there are more up-to-date books out there now, but I learned so much by reading it and began to understand Amanda's condition better.

Normally students were at New Horizons for 12-18 months, but Amanda was there for three years—she was a hard nut to crack. For the first two years, she manipulated them into thinking she was cooperating and getting better. Once they figured out what she was doing, they were finally able to help her. There is no medication for BPD, no treatment, and no cure. But they were able to help her with her "twisted thinking" and teach her some techniques to help her cope better.

In the meantime, after enrolling Amanda at New Horizons, I had to get out of that house—too many bad memories. And I suddenly had to raise a huge amount of money to pay for Amanda's schooling. The monthly bill at New Horizons was more than I earned in a month! The annual cost was $60,000 and I was only making $57,000.

I enrolled Amanda (15) at New Horizons in Oct, put the house in Osceola on the market in Nov. and it sold in Feb. A couple of interesting things happened while the house was on the market. Abbi was supposed to go to the neighbor's house before potential buyers came, but one day, she got caught. So, she hid under the cloth hanging from my bedside table, and could hear everything they said. First, they wondered where the husband was—he wasn't in any of the pictures hanging on the hallway walls but the mailbox said "Dr. Wilson," so there had to be a man (like a woman couldn't have a doctorate?). Then they opened the refrigerator and saw the kimchi, and commented that these people ate strange food!

I purchased a wooded lot in Mishawaka and designed and had a modular home built. We moved in May, 2001. I put all the money from the sale of the old house towards Amanda's schooling and started fresh with a new mortgage. That broke my heart because I had been close to paying off the old mortgage. That's when I began working four jobs (one full time and three part time) and learned how to use "creative financing"—taking out new credit cards to pay off the old ones (with no interest for a few months) and then repeating the cycle when that grace period was over. I was able to keep ahead of things, but in total, between the New Horizons bills, and all the medical/hospital expenses I had with her beforehand, I was over half a million dollars in debt. It took me many years to pay that off.

New home in Mishawaka, Indiana 2001-present

I put a lot of sweat equity into my new house. I spent the summer (and many subsequent summers) doing hard manual labor in the yard and garden, clearing brush (it was all woods before we moved in), planting plants and trees, laying sidewalk pavers, building planters and hauling dirt and mulch. I also painted and wallpapered the entire house. The physical labor felt good after the emotional years I had survived. I then spent the next 21 years remodeling, replacing windows, replacing flooring, reroofing, tearing out walls, installing new walls, installing two additional kitchens, modifying for rentals and generally maintaining things. It was a labor of love. And it fed that artistic side of my nature.

After placing Amanda at New Horizons, knowing that she was being well cared for, I now needed to care for me, but while trying to heal and regroup, I walked around in a daze. I could hold my emotions in check while concentrating on my job, but if someone said something to me about Amanda or asked how I was doing, the tears surfaced. I was able to do my job at Bethel successfully, but my heart was broken. I was totally "raw" from taking care of Amanda all those years and was a shell of my former self. I felt totally empty. Only God kept me going.

Abbi graduated from Penn High School that year (2001) and in August moved into the dormitory at Bethel, so I finally had an empty nest, which I desperately needed. I needed a respite from motherhood.

Abbi—2001 Senior pictures and Penn High School graduate

That summer, to earn extra income, I volunteered to house three Chinese girls (two high school students and their adult chaperone) for three months. They were interesting, but demanding—I could tell they came from rich families and were used to being waited upon. Interestingly, they had never heard of Tiananmen Square and didn't believe it when I showed them the videos. They also came from families with more than one child and knew nothing about China's "one child" policy—which now seemed to me to apply only to those of the lower class. Clearly both things were evidence that the Chinese government keeps their citizens in the dark about many things.

Besides packing their lunches every day and driving them to and from their English classes daily, they expected me to chauffeur them around town on the weekends. They were amazed by drive-through restaurants. I got frustrated with them at times. They did not like American food, so I ended up cooking 60 pounds of rice in those three months and became quite good at making fried rice! The adult chaperone, Echo, displayed strong signs of being bi-polar (I figured God had a sense of humor to give me such a case right then!). I was happy to see them leave at the end of the summer.

Even though Amanda despised being at New Horizons, her grades were soon back to straight A's. In the summer of 2002, New Horizons felt Amanda was improved enough that she could take a college class at Taylor. I moved her down there just before I drove to Pennsylvania to visit a friend. But then, I got a call that she was having an emotional meltdown at Taylor, and I was too far away to do anything about it, so New Horizons had to go sort it out, withdraw her from the class and take her back to their campus.

One very exciting event took place at Bethel in 2006. President George W. Bush came to speak at Notre Dame and had dinner on Bethel's campus! Security was extremely tight. Every building/office was searched and classes were suspended for the day. You couldn't park anywhere near campus and we all had had our backgrounds checked thoroughly! I worked setting tables in the dining room, but none of us peons were invited to the meal. We got to see Air Force One fly over Bethel on it's way to the airport and he waved to us as he drove through campus. I went to hear him speak at Notre Dame.

Air Force One flying over Bethel's campus

President Bush waving from his limo and as he walked through campus

**Newspaper photo of me helping
to set up for President Bush**

Cheri and Ralph always struggled financially, so I was quite surprised when they decided to completely remodel and expand their house in Roann. I figured Ralph's insurance business must be doing well. It would have been cheaper to tear the old house down and start over, because it was unrecognizable after they were done—none of the old rooms remained. It was several years before I actually got to see it and was amazed at the size and grandeur. It was a huge, 6000-square-foot home! Their boys were grown and had moved out, so I never quite understood their need for such a huge house. To me, it seemed Cheri was trying to prove they were better, had more "class," and could afford a bigger house than the rest of us.

For the many months (a year?) they were remodeling, they lived in Charlotte's house (Ralph's mother), while she lived in Florida. That really surprised me because they did not get along with Ralphs' mother at all (or anyone else in his family). I don't know if they paid Charlotte rent, but I remember Cheri commented once that they didn't pay for the utilities they used while there. And once, when Charlotte was home for Christmas, she wanted to have a party in her own house. Cheri got mad at her for disrupting their lives. After they moved into their remodeled home in 2001, she never invited Charlotte to come see it! I was stunned she would treat her mother-in-law that way after she had let them live in her house for a year! Her excuse? "Charlotte wouldn't understand." We didn't understand, either.

Our family was not invited to see her house, and she did not host any family holidays there. When any of our children were to get married, the two aunts had always hosted a bridal shower. So, Cheri and Nore hosted a bridal shower for Steve and Abbi there at Cheri's in 2008 (probably at Nore's suggestion, that Cheri's house was closer for all of us than holding it at Nore's house in Indy), but otherwise the family was excluded from her home. I got reports later from neighbors that she put in white carpeting and loved showing off her big house to visitors. She greeted guests by telling them to remove their shoes or they'd have to pay to have her carpet cleaned. It put some people off.

Cheri seemed to be building a cage of bitterness around herself—adding another bar for each "offense" she suffered and she definitely kept track! The poison from that bitterness came out in her actions and words toward the family. I am reminded of three sayings.

"If you continuously compete with others, you beco... *bitter,* but if you continuously compete with yourself, you b *me* better" (author unknown).

"You can let your past make you bitter or better" (author unknown).

"You either get bitter or you get better. It's that simple. You either take what's been dealt to you and allow it to make you a better person or you allow it to tear you down. The choice does not belong to fate, it belongs to you." (Josh Shipp)

Cheri constantly competed against us and chose to let her past make her bitter. The only conclusion I could come to was that Cheri felt it was her job to get revenge and punish the family for what she considered offenses instead of letting God handle things. It sometimes felt like Cheri had the form of Christianity, but not the content.

Mom and Cheri were both in the same chapter of P.E.O. I know it embarrassed Mom because Cheri would never attend if the meeting was held at Mom's house, and she ignored Mom at the other meetings. For Cheri, it appeared that being in P.E.O. was a social achievement, rather than possessing the true spirit of the group.

Our church—Harris Prairie Church of Christ—began having problems. One of our elders, a medical doctor, went on a missions trip to South America with our minister, Frank, and a group of our church men. While swimming for recreation, he drowned. We were all devastated. His widow, Teresa (mother of four), began grief counseling with Frank (father of three). Soon, she and Frank began an affair. Frank divorced his wife, married Teresa, and moved to California with her four children. It rocked our congregation and eventually split the church. The church struggled after that, moving from one new minister to another. Eventually the church was sold to another group and the congregants I knew and loved disbanded and moved to other churches.

At that time, churches nationwide began changing their worship music. Hymns were phased out in favor of choruses. Pianos, organs, and choirs became things of the past and guitars and drums were used routinely. I did not relate to this new loud, worldly approach to worship; I had never related to Rock and Roll music. I yearned for hymns. Choruses were lacking the spiritual depth I sought and needed. I often left church feeling like I had just attended a rock concert—not peaceful and spiritually renewed.

By 2005, I began drifting from church to church, seeking one in which I could land. Each Sunday, I'd decide what I needed most that day—the "meat" of hymns, communion, or a good sermon and attend the church that would best feed that need. I could never find one that had all three or preached baptism. Drifting was so unlike me. All my life I had been a steady worshipper and heavily involved in church activities. I had always had a church "home." Now I felt disconnected from church, even though my faith remained as strong as ever, even more so. I finally "settled" on a Missionary Church, but never became deeply involved or thought of it as my church home; I hovered on the edge of the congregation. I also became discouraged by how casual and informal (and to me, disrespectful) church attendees became. Shorts, T-shirts, flip-flops, and jeans became normal attire. Drinking and eating during the service was accepted (and encouraged). Chatting loudly during the song service, showing little respect for others who wanted to worship—these things broke my heart. It felt to me that church was becoming a social event, not a worship service. Even on special church holidays, we no longer sang Christmas hymns or Easter hymns—only the same choruses we sang during the rest of the year, and we sang those to the point of being hypnotized! It dulled my desire to attend church. I tried valiantly to adjust and go with the flow, but my heart was not in it.

Things continued to be tense between the family and Cheri and Ralph. Brent and I frequently spoke on the phone about whose turn it was to call Cheri this time to invite them to an upcoming family gathering, because neither of us wanted to! We never knew what kind of reception we would get. They came to a few gatherings before 2001 and then stopped coming altogether.

In 2002, after my friend, Carolyn, experienced a difficult time in her life, I took her to Ireland with me, where I managed the whole trip, drove on the left and tried to help her recover. She was quite subdued and I'm not sure she was processing everything going on around her. It was a hard trip.

In 2003, New Horizons let me know about an opportunity for Amanda to go on a work/missions trip to the Dominican Republic. She could visit their sister school (Escuela Caribe) in Jarabacoa. So I agreed, and paid for both of us to go. It's a beautiful country, but HOT! We did work for a local church and the school while there and got to see a bit of the country.

Amanda worked hard!   **Downtown Jarabacoa**

Things between us were just O.K. since she had tasks to do while there. We weren't on our own as much and that distracted her from being so unpleasant to me. However, I developed a severe urinary tract infection with vomiting while there, so I was miserable. I got no lovely beach photos since I was sick in the hotel room. I was finally able to get some meds, but Amanda was of no help to me when I was sick in bed or as we went through airports and customs to get home. I was amazed by her inability to "think for someone else," and take charge when I couldn't.

Amanda graduated from New Horizons as the salutatorian, in 2003. She gave the student speech, and I gave the parent speech. She moved home the same day. Within three weeks, she got a used car, a driver's license, a bank account, a credit card, a boyfriend and a job!

The summer was strained with her at home but we managed to get along fairly well. One day a terrible storm was brewing, and tornado warnings had been issued. Amanda wanted to go jogging, but I told her it wasn't safe because of the tornado warning. She decided she was going to prove me wrong and went anyway. She didn't want me telling her what to do. After I realized she had left the house, I drove around the neighborhood looking for her. When I saw her, I ordered her to get in the van. She refused at first, but finally complied. Rain was beating down and the winds were howling, almost blowing her over. I lost three huge trees that day (completely uprooted), but Amanda was adamant she was going to prove she was right, and I was wrong. She moved to the dorm on campus in August, so at least we got through the summer.

Amanda created several problems at Bethel and made some bad choices. I knew she had begun drinking and got a speeding ticket. I suspect she was a "difficult" roommate. I tried to stay out of it and let her handle life on her own. It wasn't easy (her behavior was embarrassing for me as an administrator), but we got through her Bethel years. Her behavior certainly wasn't "normal," but somewhat better, for which I was cautiously thankful.

In 2004, Carolyn, the girls and I accompanied the Bethel Choir to New York City to attend Carnegie Hall, where our choir sang the Messiah. It was wonderful! We also got to see "The Lion King" on Broadway. What a delight to experience those amazing costumes!

**Amanda's Senior pictures and High school graduation
Salutatorian 2003**

The girls had wonderful opportunities at Bethel. Abbi got to travel with the Pacific Rim semester abroad team to Hawaii, China, Australia and New Zealand. She also took part in a missions trip to Alaska and spent time north of the Arctic circle (the locals all thought she was native Alaskan!). Abbi made some life-long friends at Bethel and earned two degrees.

Amanda spent a semester abroad in China (she was the only girl on the team) and worked on a missions team in Mississippi (hurricane relief) and another missions trip back to the D.R. She also got to retrace part of the Lewis and Clark Expedition route for a May Term class.

By 2004, Bethel's enrollment was up to 2000 students, and we were bursting at the seams. We built buildings so fast it was hard to keep up. I was invited to speak in chapel twice while at Bethel. During the first speech, I explained about setting up a life-list. During the second, I spoke about an area of victory in my life. I considered it a privilege and think I did a fairly good job. I hope those addresses spoke to the students.

For Mom and Dad's 60th anniversary in 2005, I made them a quilt with photos of their family. They loved it and Dad faithfully changed the years on it as time went on.

Mom and Dad's 60th anniversary 2005

Abbi—a Bethel "cum laude" graduate 2006

While Abbi was at Bethel, I was her advisor, and she was in some of my classes. It was interesting to see her from a different perspective. Abbi graduated from Bethel in 2006, with honors (Cum Laude) and two degrees—Elementary Education and International Studies (Business). She had added one extra year to her program to earn the second degree. I was privileged to be on the graduation stage to hand her that precious diploma! She was also named to Who's Who in American Colleges and Universities and Bethel's Dean's List Hall of Fame. As part of her graduation gift, I gave her a certificate showing how much debt she had avoided. What a blessing she could earn a degree tuition free! Praise God for that. I paid all her housing and meals, but all in all, I managed to survive the bills.

Right after Abbi graduated from college, I took her to Chile, Peru and Easter Island. Seeing Machu Pichu had long been on my life list. I fell in love with the Moai on Easter Island! When we were there, the island was still fairly non-touristy, and we enjoyed quiet, empty tourist sites. But I hear things have changed now and it is so crowded and busy that the island is having trouble keeping up with the demands. I'm glad we went when we did.

Abbi beside a HUGE moai

Moai are everywhere on Easter Island (Rapa Nui)

Easter Island was like "Wow!"

Abbi is tiny compared to the moai!

Machu Pichu (PERU)had been on my life-list for decades

Shortly after that trip, I began buying Moai for my backyard!

Abbi then surprised me by moving to the east coast to be a nanny for two different families. I had expected her to get a teaching job. Later, she worked for a start-up internet company. She met Steve (her future husband) at the Webbie Awards. He worked for Google and became an executive there after a few more years. Initially she told him she wasn't interested because he smoked, to which he replied that he just quit! They started dating and were engaged within a couple of years.

Amanda kept saying she wanted to go to medical school, but at least twice, she sabotaged her own MCAT exam by not getting her application in on time. I told her if she didn't really want to go to medical school, that was fine; it didn't matter to me. I suspect she knew she wouldn't be able to handle the pressure and missing the application deadline was her way of getting out of the situation.

Amanda graduated from Bethel in 2007, with highest honors (Summa Cum Laude—she had a 3.96 GPA because she got one A-) with a degree in biology and chemistry. Again, just like with Abbi, I was privileged to hand her that precious diploma as she walked across the graduation stage and later presented her with a calculation of how much debt she had avoided by going to Bethel. She was also named to Who's Who in American Colleges and Universities and Bethel's Dean's List Hall of Fame.

Amanda—a Bethel College graduate!
Summa Cum Laude May, 2007

Amanda asked if I was going to take her on a trip, too, after she graduated, like I had with Abbi. I had to explain to her that I had already taken her on a trip—to the D.R. She moved to Lexington, Kentucky to be near her boyfriend, Patrick, who was a great guy. I stood in the garage after they pulled out and with a HUGE sense of relief, praised God that my days of being responsible for her were over! What a sense of freedom! She worked at a shoe store and as a waitress for several years, not really getting anywhere in life. Then she worked as a phlebotomist (drawing blood) at a blood bank.

One time, Patrick and Amanda stayed with me while Amanda was in a friend's wedding. That night, Patrick came home without her. He didn't know where she was—she stayed out all night and when she got a ride home the next morning, she said she didn't know where she'd been all night, but thought she slept on someone's couch. She had been so drunk and unruly at the reception that the police were called. Her ability to ruin someone's wedding concerned me. Patrick (I believe) finally saw the handwriting on the wall (with her behavior) and broke up with Amanda. He was such a nice guy. I felt sorry for him.

BACK TO TEACHING

In 2006, I decided ten years as the Dean of Instruction was enough and I asked to return to the Education Department. I just yearned to teach again. As an administrator, it felt like all I did was solve problems, and the ones I've mentioned here are only a few of the situations I was involved in. My calendar could be completely void of appointments for the day, but I got nothing productive done because I was constantly putting out fires. Some of the situations I dealt with (at a Christian college) astounded me. What must it be like at secular colleges? I felt I had done many good things in administration, but was ready to return to my first love, teaching.

On the day I left the Dean's job, I was touched when four of the gals in the administrative office area (secretaries and Registrar's Office staff) escorted me over to the Education Department as kind of a "royal send-off." They were not happy to see me go and wanted to make sure the Ed Department would be kind to me. The strange thing was that my new office number in the education department was room 108! What an uncanny coincidence that in three of my jobs I was in room 108! In total, during my 25 years at Bethel, I was in five different offices.

In 2006, I was granted tenure after submitting a massive tenure portfolio of all my professional activities since I began teaching in 1972. It was a huge project that took me many weeks to assemble and was over four inches thick. In 2008, I was promoted to full professor. During my ten years in administration, I had been removed from the tenure track and any promotions had been "taken off the table." Now that I was back teaching, and back on tenure track, they belatedly recognized my ten years of teaching half-time as equating to five years full time and promoted me.

Nelson, another tenure track professor, chose not to submit a portfolio. His reasoning was that Bethel knew him and his quality of teaching and his record should stand on its own. He shouldn't have to do all that extra work. In other words, he effectively removed himself from the tenure track by not complying with the protocol. The rule was, either you get tenured or you are dismissed. He couldn't believe it when he was released at the end of the year and claimed he was being mistreated.

Much to our relief, Bethel fired our Ed Dept dean (Candice) in 2008, so I served on a leadership team to run the department for two years. I also had Lasik eye surgery in 2008, but wasn't thrilled with the results and had to have more eye surgery in Indianapolis the next year.

Also in 2008, Carolyn and I took a Women of Faith Cruise to Alaska. It was magnificent being on a ship of all believers over the Fourth of July, where we listened to Sandi Patty sing the national anthem, watched whales breaching and glaciers birthing.

As Carolyn and I began traveling more together, we were quite aware that people assumed we were a gay couple. We did everything we could to dispel that conclusion by conducting ourselves appropriately but it was frustrating.

On an interesting side note—I began seeing two things in the U.S. that I had first encountered in Korea years before—"kyol" (small, easy to peel mandarin oranges) and stink bugs! It seems the stink bugs migrated to the U.S. in cargo shipments. While I was not thrilled to renew my acquaintance with stink bugs, I was delighted to enjoy mandarin oranges again! They are called Clementines in the U.S.

I was still trying to pay off my massive debt when Carolyn and I took a Dave Ramsey course at church called, "Financial Peace University." I loved his phrase about paying "stupid tax" for making bad decisions. It fit so well with my life-list and wanting to do things right the first time. The course was extremely helpful, and I revamped how I was doing some things, which helped me get out of debt sooner.

Abbi married Steve Yap in South Bend on August 23, 2008. Yes, we chuckled that her entire name was now only seven letters long! It was a beautiful wedding and I love Steve. I needed a new hip and had trouble walking Abbi down the aisle, but I managed (I got my first hip replaced that December). Amanda was in the wedding party, but I was so afraid she would ruin Abbi's wedding like she had her friend's, that I arranged for a "bouncer" to remove her at the first sign she was causing a problem. Neither she nor Abbi knew I did that, but I felt it was a necessary precaution. Luckily, the bouncer wasn't needed because Amanda behaved well. Steve and Abbi moved to New York City into Steve's apartment on Wall Street. Later, they moved to Fairfield, Connecticut and Steve commuted two hours each way to his Google office. Having them live so far away was hard. I managed to get out there to visit a few times, but eventually my health prevented that.

Steve and Abbi's wedding   **Aug. 23, 2008**

One day, I got a call from Megan, Grpa Bill's granddaughter in Muncie. I hadn't talked to her for over 15 years and was quite surprised to hear from her. We chatted for a while and then she told me to stop sending e-mails to her grandfather (Grpa Bill). When I asked why, she said he was old and didn't understand the political situation or the controversy about illegal immigrants. She didn't like that Bill and I were on the same page politically and our e-mails sometimes included forwards about illegal immigrants. Turned out, she was dating an illegal immigrant! I questioned why she thought she had the right to restrict her grandfather's e-mails, just because she didn't agree with them (I assume Bill had forwarded them to the family). I told her I would contact Bill and see how he felt about the things I sometimes forwarded to him. I did so and he wanted me to continue, so I did. I didn't tell him about Megan's call. Then I got a letter from Bill's son, Tom, apologizing for Megan's call, saying she really didn't have the right to control her grandfather's communications or demand that I stop sending him things. But then he asked me to comply and stop communicating with Bill, as it was causing family problems. So, this time, I called Bill and explained the situation so he could understand what was going on. I hated to do that, but felt his rights were being violated. He was very angry that his son and granddaughter were making such a fuss about his political views or e-mail contacts. He had a right to his own opinion, as did I!

Then one day, the new V.P. for Academic Services (Dennis Crocker) came to my office (that had never happened before, so my guard was up instantly), sat down and asked if I had been sending "hate" mail. It seems Tom, (Bill's son), had called Bethel to complain that I was spreading discord and hateful ideas. I explained what had happened—it was merely friends exchanging political views with each other. The V.P. was stunned at their audacity to try to limit their grandfather's communications and to register a complaint with my employer. When I asked if I was in trouble, he said "No, it's a dead issue!"

But I continued to receive harassing e-mails from Bill's family, so I consulted an attorney on staff at Bethel. He assured me I had done nothing wrong and that their harassment was illegal. So I let Tom (Bill's son) know that I had consulted an attorney and told him that if they continued to harass me, I would sue them. I never heard any more but was quite saddened by the trouble this had caused poor Bill.

Jason, my nephew, had married Karen (a sweetheart) in 1998, but they had no children for eleven years. Cheri told me that Jason wanted to be more financially secure before having children, but it was evident that Karen was getting more and more depressed by waiting. Cheri told Jason to stop being selfish and have kids now. Personally, I couldn't believe she would insert herself into their private lives and give her unsolicited advice on such a personal topic. It really wasn't any of her business. But I knew she was desperate to have grandchildren and since Pete was divorced, she knew Jason and Karen were the only ones who could give her grandchildren.

Just like Cheri and I are totally different people, we also handle things quite differently. She reacts to everything emotionally, while I react pragmatically and practically. One of my favorited sayings is, "Life is 10% what happens to you and 90% how you react to what happens to you."

In 2005, Cheri was diagnosed with breast cancer. She took the news very badly and wouldn't even say the word, "cancer." She said she had the "C" word. She had a difficult time in her treatments—a double mastectomy, radiation (which literally burned her ribs) and chemo. I felt so sorry for her. She bought a wig to hide her baldness. I sent her cards and flowers, took her some food, and called her to express support.

In March, 2009, while I was at work, I got a call from the Dr. informing me that recent tests showed I had breast cancer. I replied, "Oh, well, praise the

Lord!" and went right back to work. (I remembered those "attitude check" sermons Ralph used to preach to his youth about praising God in every situation). Having cancer never really bothered me, emotionally. Research shows that extreme stress and lack of sleep are risk factors for cancer and since I had both in my life, I wasn't surprised I developed cancer. I also figured it would return at some point.

When I called Cheri to tell her about my cancer, she never expressed sympathy, but just charged right ahead to give me all kinds of advice on what to do and not do. I chose to ignore most of what she told me—especially about needing to have someone with me for every appointment and treatment. I was so used to doing everything by myself, that I disregarded that advice. Cheri did send me one card, but otherwise said and did nothing to support me.

In January of 2009, Steve (Abbi's husband) and I put our heads together to make sure Abbi returned to Korea to visit her brother and sister again. She also needed a chance to introduce Steve to her first culture. We bought airline tickets for July of that year.

After I was diagnosed with breast cancer, I checked with my team of cancer doctors about the advisability of making that long trip to Korea in July. They said it would be o.k. if I felt up to it.

I had a lumpectomy, radiation, and chemo. I was the first person in the county to have the new mammosite radiation from the inside. I had a six-inch long tube sticking out of me, through which they administered the radiation twice a day for ten days. Wearing that tube for three weeks was uncomfortable and irritating, and the open wound seeped constantly. Taking a shower was a nightmare because I had to cover the wound with self-sticking plastic wrap to keep it dry. Using my arm was difficult because it constantly rubbed that tube. One of my radiation nurses was a pure delight though—she worked hard to lighten the mood of her cancer patients. After each treatment, she rewrapped that long tube so it wouldn't be so irritating. After the first time, she commented, "There, I gave you a nice big penis!" We howled over that.

It didn't bother me at all to drive myself to appointments and treatments. I was used to doing everything by myself. Abbi and Amanda each came for one chemo session, but to me, it seemed like such a waste of their time to have them sit there for eight hours. I told them not to bother accompanying me anymore. I never missed any classes (I scheduled my treatments on days I didn't have classes), never bothered with a wig (just wore hats), and taught undergrad and graduate classes while I felt so sick I could hardly think straight. "Chemo brain" (brain fog) is definitely a real thing! And the after-effects were terrible. I ended up driving myself to the Emergency Room the day after every chemo treatment with severe reactions to the chemo or the medicines they put me on. One time, my face was so swollen, you couldn't recognize me. I developed ridges in my fingernails from each chemo treatment. I suppose it was from the trauma of the chemicals they pumped into me.

I swore I would never do chemo again. I am not living for this life, but for the next one, so if my life is shortened by that decision, so be it. I see no reason to make the last few months of my life even more miserable from chemo. I'd rather have a shorter life than a longer, more miserable one.

As predicted, exactly two weeks after my first chemo, my hair came out in handfuls, but not evenly. So, I went across the street and asked my neighbor, Michelle, who owned clippers to cut her boy's hair, to please shave my head. She graciously agreed. Being bald didn't bother me too much—I just wore hats. Losing my eyebrows made me look strange, but I didn't have to shave my legs for months! Luckily my hair began to grow back in by November, before the cold winter weather.

In the spring of 2009, Steve, Abbi and I orchestrated a trip for Dad to visit Wall Street. Dad brought Mom to stay at my house and the day after my first chemo treatment, I took Dad to the airport to fly out to Steve's and Abbi's in New York City (they lived on Wall Street at the time). I don't know what strings they had to pull to get him onto the Wall Street trading floor, but they did! He was so thrilled to finally get to see the place where he had traded for so many years. However, back home, we had a problem. Mom got up in the middle of the night to go to the bathroom and fell trying to get back into bed. I was weak from chemo, so we both struggled to get her back into bed and ended up laughing hysterically because it was such a production.

In July, even though I really didn't feel up to making that long trip to Korea, I decided I was going anyway. So just three days after my last chemo treatment (yes, I was bald and very weak), I flew to Korea by myself. Carolyn later told me she figured she'd never see me alive again! Steve and Abbi met me in Seoul. We spent time with Abbi's brother and sister (and her nieces), showed Steve Seoul Foreign School, reconnected with Mrs. Nah, and I was thrilled to meet Amanda's birth mother! It was an incredibly emotional four days!

Back in January of that year, I had gotten an e-mail from Eastern Child Welfare (through whom I had adopted both my girls). Eastern wanted me to know that Amanda's birth mother was looking for her. I explained that Amanda was absolutely NOT interested in meeting her birth mother (it had been a topic we were not even allowed to mention), but I was! Eastern agreed to coordinate that meeting, so, we set up a time for us to connect at the agency when I'd be in Korea in July. Abbi went with me and we found Amanda's mother to be delightful! She came to the meeting with her two sisters. As a gift for her, I had prepared a scrapbook of Amanda's life and went armed with many questions about Amanda's background, father, health history, etc. She gave me some jewelry to give to Amanda. I found out the birth/family information we had been given at Amanda's adoption was not correct—we had been given someone else's family history! It turned out Amanda's parents were married, but her father was an abusive drunk who beat her mother. Mother finally left him, taking the advice of her family to leave the baby for him to take care of so he would own up to his responsibility. When she went back a few days later to visit little Min Ah, she found out he had turned the baby in to the adoption agency. She was heartbroken. Women have no rights in that culture, so she could not get her baby back without the birth father's approval. Her grief became my joy when I adopted her precious baby.

Amanda's birth mother also told me her father had been married before and had a son by his first wife, so Amanda had a stepbrother! Father was brilliant, but unable to hold a job. He drank and smoked himself to death, dying on August 23, 2008—the same day Abbi got married. Hearing his behavior described, I understood immediately that Amanda had inherited her mental health issues from her birth father. It explained everything. Now I understood. I hadn't been a "bad" mother (like several of her doctors accused me of being) but was dealing with inherited issues over which I had no control. My sense of relief was overwhelming. All the guilt I had carried for so many years began to ebb away. I began to wonder if I had potentially saved Amanda's life. If she had been adopted by someone who didn't understand or know how to work with children, they could very well have abused her in frustration. I know she brought out rage in me that I didn't know I was capable of. I never acted on it, but who knows what someone else would have done? It seems God knew what He was doing when he gave her to me. He knew I wouldn't give up on her, would continue to stand by her and do my best to get her help, even as she resisted all the way and made life miserable for us.

It was a very taxing four days in Korea, and I came home thoroughly exhausted, both physically and emotionally.

That fall, Amanda came home from Kentucky for a visit—which was rare because she never liked coming home. Later, I found out her therapist had recommended the visit to see if she could rebuild some bridges with me. As we sat and talked, I told her that Eastern had contacted me, that her birth mother was looking for her and that she wanted to meet Amanda. I asked if she'd like to meet her birth mother. At first, she was defensive and said, "No." But I told her to think about it overnight. The next morning, she said "Yes," she might like to meet her birth mother. So, I told her I had met her that summer. I gave her the jewelry her birth mother had sent through me. I told her the new information I knew about her birth family and her father and the true story of her adoption. Amanda was absolutely furious. She was so upset I had already met her birth mother before she had that she said she no longer wanted to meet her birth mother. I didn't follow that reasoning. She left for Kentucky in a rage.

I consulted with good friends of mine from Korea—Jim and Mary Pat Fuller. Jim had a doctorate in psychology, and they had also adopted a Korean daughter, Christi. Christi and Amanda were the same age and had been good friends in Korea. After we all left Korea, Jim and Mary Pat eventually settled in Marion, Indiana, where Jim taught at Indiana Wesleyan University. Over the years we consulted frequently, since they were experiencing the very same issues with Christi that I was with Amanda. The similarities were unbelievable. I wanted to know if I had been wrong to meet Amanda's birth mother. Jim and Mary Pat felt, that given the circumstances, I had done nothing wrong. I viewed it as paving a path for Amanda to meet her birth mother. Of course, Amanda didn't see it that way, but at least I felt better having the approval and support of someone experienced in psychology. Jim frequently said he didn't know how I survived the ordeal with Amanda on my own. As a couple, they could rely on one another to take over when one of them had reached their limit. Even having a doctorate in psychology did not help him when dealing with Christi! I had no one else to rely on, never had any down time, and didn't have a degree in psychology to help me figure things out.

Then in November, Amanda insisted I come down to Kentucky to meet with her and her therapist. I had just had eye surgery and really shouldn't have been driving that far, but she didn't care. She was suicidal and wanted me to come. I went, wondering what I was in for.

As we got ready to leave her apartment and go to our appointment, she got on her computer and printed something out. During our conference, she accosted me about many things (again accusing me of being a terrible mother and dredging up all the things I had done wrong.) At one point, the therapist said to her, "Amanda, that's not fair!" I so appreciated his slight support as I had never had it from some of her doctors. She pulled out the computer printout (an e-mail) to "prove" that I had masterminded the entire meeting with her birth mother. She had contacted Eastern, and they confirmed I had met her birth mother, so Amanda assumed that meant I had initiated the contact. We resolved nothing during that session, and she sobbed all the way back to her apartment, because the session had not gone as she had hoped. But she still expected me to stay longer. I had classes to get back to and a seven-hour drive to get home. I was still bald and recovering from the chemo treatments and eye surgery. It took me weeks to recover from that encounter. Soon her "normal" emotional distance resumed.

Later, after seeing a Facebook post where she was sitting with her legs across an Asian woman's lap (who looked like her birth mother), I wrote and asked if she had met her birth mother after all. If so, I told her, I was delighted. She never responded to me and changed her Facebook photo. I never understood why she didn't want me to know she had met her birth mother. I just hope they were able to form the bond that Amanda needed so desperately. I learned later, through a different source, that her birth mother had died. I don't know if Amanda went to Korea for the funeral or what the extent of their relationship was. I'm just glad that poor woman was finally able to meet her daughter and have some closure in her traumatic life. I rest knowing Amanda would never have met her birth mother had I not taken the steps I did. I paved the way for her. But it still saddens me that Amanda doesn't recognize that or want me to know about meeting her birth mother. I was rejoicing with and for her, but that made no difference.

In 2009, I researched, created, and presented a proposal for a new degree at Bethel—the Early Childhood four-year degree. Bethel already had a two-year degree in Early Childhood. My new major was approved with flying colors by the various committees and within three years had 60 majors! I was so pleased. I advised those majors and supervised Early Childhood fieldwork and student teachers in addition to my work with Elementary Education students.

I had one young advisee, Julia, who came from a very conservative background. She wore long skirts and a doily on her pinned-up hair. She had been home-schooled for her entire life, so being in college was a real culture shock to her. And she still lived at home, so she wasn't learning to socialize with other college-aged students or how to exist in the "real world" (even though some students called it the "Bethel Bubble"). Every semester, she brought her father to our academic advising sessions (I'd never had that happen before!) and they came armed with a list of the classes her father wanted her to take next. Unfortunately, he didn't understand what the major required, wanted her to take classes out of sequence, which weren't required for her major, or that had pre-requisites she had not taken. It seemed to me that he selected classes based on what time and day they were offered so it fit her work schedule. I tried tactfully to explain to him why she couldn't take the classes he had selected. He only gave in begrudgingly.

A popular phrase at the time was "helicopter parents," used to describe parents who were always hovering over their children instead of letting them have space to grow up. But the new phrase soon became "velcro parents," to describe parents who were so attached they couldn't "let go" and allow their children any space at all! They were stifling their child! Julia's dad was definitely a "velcro parent."

Finally, after a couple of semesters of this, I talked to her privately and convinced her that she needed to be "driving this wagon," not her father, as part of growing up—that I was her advisor, not her father, who had no training in this area at all. She finally learned to stand on her own two feet and leave dad out of the advising picture. Things smoothed out considerably after that. By the time she was ready for student teaching, she had "loosened up" some, grown up quite a bit, and did a fine job.

In 2011, Becky Smith and I drove down to Sevierville, Tennessee to attend a Women of Faith conference. I called Jason (Cheri's son), who lived in Sevierville, and asked him if we could stay at their house to save a hotel bill. They had a young son, Levi, and we left them money to pay our way. We had a lovely visit with them. But later, I found out that Cheri was not happy we had stayed there or gotten to see her grandson. I was dumbfounded. I could only assume she didn't believe in "shared joy!" Instead, she seemed jealous.

In 2011, Steve and Abbi blessed me with my first grandchild—Logan. He was such a cutie! I spent a week in Connecticut with them.

Logan James Yap born June 26, 2011

I drove out to Connecticut a couple of times, flew out a few times and rode the train out once. But my deteriorating physical condition made those trips harder and harder on me. By 2019, I knew I couldn't get there anymore, so they came to visit me on occasion. But since they were allergic to cats, they had to stay in hotels while here, which made the visits less "homey." I never envisioned being a long-distance grandma—the "other" grandma! I had them call me "Nana," since they called Steve's mother "grandma." I had always wanted to be the Grma they dropped in on frequently, the lap they wanted to climb on, the one they made cookies with, and loved having me read to them. Times of separation from them were long and frustrating. As they grow, I hope they will feel close to me, even if we don't get to see each other very often. I made each of them a book called "My Indiana Nana," with photos of both their families in Connecticut and Indiana.

It was a joy for me to watch from afar as Steve and Abbi grew in their faith. Their church involvement, Bible studies, teaching teens, and small group involvements were gifts to my heart.

By now the three of us siblings each had grandchildren. Brent and I always listened to Cheri brag about hers, but she showed no interest in ours. She always changed the subject if we mentioned anything about our families. She also mentioned a few times that her children and grandchildren were "better" than ours. What does one say to that? Any response on our part would only have made the situation worse.

It appears that in Dad's branch of the Wilson family, the Wilson name will die out with our grandchildren's generation. Chad, the only male with the Wilson name, has no sons. The rest of the grandchildren's family names have become Frank, Yap, or Shipman.

After moving into my new house in 2001, I rented out the basement to Bethel students for a few years. Then, I hosted guests through the Notre Dame Bed and Breakfast program for six years. That was a LOT of work! It was also during this time that I worked four jobs—Deaning full time at Bethel, teaching an additional half-time load at night, teaching eight hours on Saturdays for Indiana Wesleyan's graduate program, and hosting weekend guests with the Notre Dame Bed and Breakfast program, which included fixing two fancy breakfasts (with cloth napkins, not paper!). I was trying desperately to climb out of the financial hole Amanda's care had thrust me into. But praise God, I eventually got myself out of debt. Whew! It was a long, hard struggle and between that and dealing with Amanda over the years, it took a big toll on my health, which began failing.

Between 2008 and 2023, I had 24 surgeries. I became a "frequent flier" at Memorial Hospital! All those years of extreme stress with Amanda severely affected my health and played out in major ailments and weight gain. I tried every diet available, to no avail. I was even rejected for bariatric surgery. They claimed I had a stomach problem, of which I was not aware and I've had no problems. My legs became weaker and weaker. While Brent inherited Dad's shaking hands, I inherited Mom's weak legs. I'm just thankful I traveled and saw the world while I was young and healthy!

My blood pressure was quite high from the years of stress. It took several years after I was no longer responsible for Amanda for me to get off my blood pressure meds and off the anti-depressants. But I finally managed both. My blood pressure is normal now.

On July 7, 2012, I managed to get the whole family together for a family photo while Mom and Dad were still with us. Since our extended family lived in so many states and I had so many schedules to work around, it was a difficult undertaking. This ended up being the first and last time we were all able to get together in one place. Cheri insisted we do it at her house (the first time we had been invited there—I knew she wanted to show off her beautiful house) and she wanted Jason to take the photos. They turned out well and Mom and Dad were so pleased with the outcome. The last four great-grandchildren had not yet been born.

Amanda, Steve and Abbi stayed with me the weekend of that family photo. I feared Amanda wouldn't be able to "hold it together" for the whole weekend. She did pretty well on Saturday, but on Sunday morning as we were trying to get to church, she exploded over the way Abbi was loading the dishwasher. I told her calmly, "Amanda, I don't have to put up with this

The entire Wilson family 2012

Four generations 2012

behavior anymore. You are an adult now. I'm going to give you two choices. You can either 'get happy' (a phrase I used to use with her when she was young—she would go to her room till she could be pleasant) or you can leave." She chose to leave in a rage. Poor Steve had never seen this side of her and I'm sure he was in disbelief. She made sure to tell everyone I had kicked her out of the house, even though she had made the decision to leave.

After the photo session, I wrote Cheri a follow- up thank you note (see **Appendix A**).

Cheri responded several weeks later. Her letter is presented (in **Appendix B**) exactly as she wrote it.

It took me quite a while to compose a response to Cheri, to make it as tactful and non-threatening as possible and to address all the items she had brought up. I made sure I had Carolyn edit it for me. Actually, I felt like Mom writing Cheri those long letters while she was in college! I finally sent her the response found in **Appendix C**. These letters are included "as is" merely to present facts accurately, not to make it appear judgmental or that my way of handling life pragmatically is better than her way of handling life emotionally. Our two ways were quite different. I suspect that difference was at the root of our conflicts.

Cheri never responded to that letter. So, no further attempts were made to reconcile with her. We resumed our strained and distant relationship.

In 2013, Mom and Dad had an estate auction, which was very painful for them. Brent and I went beforehand to help them (and my friend, Becky, came too and helped clean out cupboards!). Cheri came to help once, stayed an hour, found a few things she wanted, and left. She claimed she had to work. Like Brent and I didn't? She did not attend the auction, or even contact Mom and Dad. Then they moved to Peabody Retirement Community in North Manchester, Indiana, where they rented a double apartment. I was delighted they had "landed" so well and could afford that bit of luxury, since they had scrimped and saved all their lives. Brent and I made monthly visits to see them, while Cheri went to see them only a few times. Mom and Dad reported that sometimes Cheri was somewhat friendly and other times she was curt and cool.

Then I rejoiced again when Steve and Abbi gave me a granddaughter, (Devon) in 2014, and named her after Dad. He was thrilled, of course! Her birthday was just 2 days after his.

Devon Kim Yap born March 11, 2014

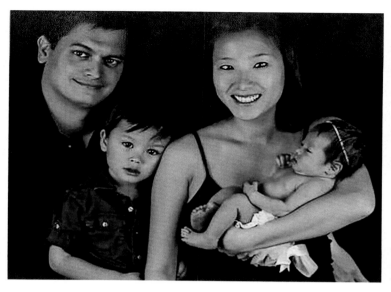

Steve, Logan (3), Abbi, and Devon 2014

Logan

Amanda with her nephew Logan

Logan with his new baby sister, Devon 2014

Devon

**Grma Marcy with two of
her great-grandchildren**

**Grpa DeVon with
his namesake**

Devon

Logan 5, Devon 2, 2016

One time, Cheri's son, Jason, his wife, Karen and their two boys traveled to Indiana (from Tennessee) to visit Cheri and Ralph. Mom and Dad wanted to see them, too, but Cheri said they didn't have time to drive up to N. Manchester to see their grandparents, so if Mom and Dad wanted to see them, they'd have to come to Cheri's house. Mom was in a wheelchair by then, but Dad loaded her into his van and drove to Cheri's house—not an easy task for a man in his 90's. When they got there, Cheri met them at the door and said, "We have a lot to do, so you can only stay for half an hour." Mom was devastated to be treated so shabbily, but said nothing, knowing it would do no good. They left on time, as ordered. I often wondered if Jason and Karen (who were always kind to Grma and Grpa) knew how Cheri treated her parents. I suspect she spoke badly of us, but not hearing our side of things meant Pete and Jason never fully understood the tensions in the family. All they ever heard was Cheri's emotional complaints, even as they witnessed Grma and Grpa being nothing but kind to Cheri and Ralph. I hope they realized there was more to the story.

A couple of times over the years, Amanda called and said she wanted us to call each other more often and be on better terms, but then she harassed me all over again. I agreed to call her more often, but I set some emotional boundaries. I had previously stopped calling her because she gave me one-word answers and made it clear she didn't want to talk to me. This time, I told her I would hang up if she abused me verbally. And I told her I didn't want to be the one always initiating the calls. She had to do her share, too. It worked for about a month and then, after she stopped calling me, I discontinued the attempt. I assume her therapist had suggested it, but she couldn't follow through and I knew I couldn't take the emotional abuse anymore.

My relationship with Amanda varied from time to time over the subsequent years. Sometimes she acted like she wanted to have a relationship with me and sometimes not. If I called her and got one-word answers, I gave up. Other times she might be willing to talk to me. I finally left it that she could call me when she wanted to. I did hear from her a couple of times a year, but rarely did she remember my birthday or Mother's Day. Sometimes, not even Christmas.

These quotes speak to me:

"Train up a child in the way he should go and when he is old he will not depart from it." (Proverbs 22:6) Hopefully the training I gave Amanda will someday pull her back to God and me.

"You can love them, forgive them, want good things for them. . . but still move on without them." (Mandy Hale). I finally got to the point, where I had to move on without Amanda. That is NOT saying I abandoned her, just that I left her in God's hands and moved on with my life.

"One of the hardest things you will ever do is grieve the loss of a person who is still alive." (Anna Grace Taylor) I do grieve the (hopefully temporary) loss of Amanda, and pray that she will someday be restored to me.

"Not everyone you lose is a loss." (Dr. Phil). I don't view my experience with Amanda as a loss, but as a learning experience. Me adopting her was a gain for her.

As painful as the realization was, I came to see that I had been given Amanda for a reason and a season. The reason was to raise her in a Christian home and make sure she got the mental/medical help she so desperately needed, while the season was till she reached adulthood. Not all adoptive parents would have endured so long with her or tried so frantically to solve the mystery of her condition. I think God gave her to me knowing I wouldn't give up on her—that I wouldn't unadopt her, like a couple of her doctors advised, that I would stick with her through thick and thin, no matter how badly she treated us. It was my job to be faithful. I can honestly say I did the very best I could for her. What she chooses to do with that is up to her.

In 2012, I began to "catify" my house—gradually installing a "cat run" up high near the ceiling of four back rooms (not visible to visitors), including cat doors in the walls so they could pass through to the other rooms. It took me five years to finish it, but the cats love it and frequently spend half their day up there. They love sitting above me "supervising," when I am at my computer writing.

My life story would not be complete without mentioning the plethora of cats I've loved over the years—what joy they provided. But, no, my house didn't smell like a litter box! I refused to live with that odor and cleaned the litter box every day. Most visitors commented they couldn't even tell I had cats since my house didn't smell. Over the years, I've learned that I LOVE black cats! They look so regal and dignified.

My favorites cats were Doogie and Benji (but don't tell the others!) because they were the best cuddlers, letting me hold them on their backs in my arms like a baby. I usually adopted shelter cats, but bought two pedigreed cats when I retired. Biscuit and Moki are Ragdolls, specially bred for their calm, easy-going, laid-back demeanor. I've never heard them hiss or growl. Cats practically take care of themselves and you don't have to take them out for walks! One morning, after COVID broke out, as I emerged from a deep sleep, I realized I couldn't breathe. I subconsciously thought to myself, "Oh, no, I have COVID!" Then, as I rose more fully out of my sleep, I realized I had the Ragdoll cats sleeping on my throat and chest. They weigh 16 ½ pounds each, so of course I couldn't breathe very well with 34 pounds on my chest!

"Until one has loved an animal, a part of one's soul remains unawakened." (Anatole France)

Abbi and Nutmeg

Amanda and Max

Button, Max and Doogie

Nutmeg helping Abbi practice!

Just begging for a belly rub!

Reuben and Moses

Moses, Tanner, Reuben, Feather and Chloe

Moki (Ragdoll), beautiful blue eyes   **My beloved Benji is so delicious**

He always puts one paw over his eyes   **Fred, the squirrel, teasing Shadow**   **Biscuit (Ragdoll)**

Feeling frisky   **Shadow follows me from room to room**   **Baby**

Baby, Moki, and Benji

Up on the cat run

Moki, Biscuit and Baby at the top of the stairs—two stories up!

In 2014, Carolyn and I met in Costa Rica to experience that wonderful jungle setting (she had moved to California in 2013). The highlight of that trip happened while we were boating down a jungle river and two capuchin monkeys jumped into the boat, climbed up my arm and sat on my head! Then in 2016, we took a cruise through the Panama Canal and visited a total of seven countries—Bahamas, Colombia, Panama, Costa Rica, Nicaragua, Guatemala, and Mexico. The Panama Canal was extremely impressive!

I love collecting funny things kids say and my brother's granddaughter, Maya, provided another one. In her preschool one day, the teacher asked the kids if any of them could spell their daddy's name. Maya (four) raised her hand and then began calling our letter names at random (she couldn't read yet, but knew letter names). "S, T, U, D." Chad, her dad, said that was about right.

After a few years, Amanda started nursing school at the University of Kentucky. She had always talked about becoming a doctor, so it really surprised me that she chose nursing, because her people skills were not wonderful. Nursing requires good bedside manner and good people skills. The university paid for her schooling if she agreed to work there for two years after completing the program. She stayed there for four years, working 12-hour night shifts in the Emergency Room. I know that must have been difficult and that she saw and handled many unpleasant situations. But, finally, her career choice made sense to me—the constant adrenaline rush from working in the E.R. made her feel better and she didn't ever have to see the patients again. So, her people skills weren't as necessary as they would have been for in-patient nurses.

Then in 2021, Amanda began work as a traveling nurse. I was proud of her for taking the initiative to get a nursing degree and she seemed to do well. Now she was willing to step out and try something new. She has come a long way! I praise God that she is self-supporting and successful. I can't quite figure out where she got it (☺!), but Amanda loves to travel internationally. She spent time in a yurt in Mongolia, climbed Mount Kilimanjaro (Tanzania) and has taken several other excursions. She has definitely applied those lessons she learned on our around the world trip!

It took me years to heal emotionally (I still haven't fully arrived), and I still suffer many physical problems from all the years of extreme stress, which does terrible things to your body. But my health was a small price to pay if Amanda has her act together enough to support herself and help others.

Cheri developed cancer again in the spring of 2014. Even though I had no reason to drive to Wabash anymore (an hour and a half away), I made a point of driving down there to take them food and visit her once in a while. One time, I took them a nice $80 Heavenly Ham (which I couldn't afford). She asked if Bethel had given it to me. I was so insulted that she accused me of regifting, that I wanted to throw the ham at her, but all I said was, "No, I bought this just for you." When I visited her at Christmas, 2014, she looked bad. Pete was there visiting so I got to see him, too. I didn't stay long because I sensed she didn't want me to. That was the last time I ever saw her.

On January 19, 2015, as I was getting ready to leave for work, I got a call from Ralph, who had NEVER called me before. I immediately knew it was bad news. He said Cheri (67) had passed away in the early morning hours, probably from a blood clot. It was difficult attending her funeral, trying to present a pleasant face to those who praised her for her kindness to them. I was just glad she had been kind to someone, since it wasn't to her family.

A few weeks later, when I was visiting Mom and Dad, Mom made the comment that she was sorry Cheri had passed away, but she had never shed a tear. I told her I hadn't either. How sad. Even though, over the years, Mom and Dad and I had made numerous attempts to reconcile with Cheri, she remained defensive and stubborn. Mom and Dad were heartbroken, not just because of the way she had treated them, but because they didn't understand the reasons behind her behavior. She remained an unsolved mystery and heartbreak for the whole family.

In 2015, Carolyn and I visited the fabulous Grand Canyon. In 2017, I got to see the Ark Encounter (Noah's Ark recreation) in Kentucky—amazing. It was built by Leroy Troyer, the guy who built so many of Bethel's buildings.

I made some fantastic friends at Bethel, but the one that had the biggest impact on my life was Carolyn. She began at Bethel in 1996, when I was going through hell with Amanda. She listened, let me cry, sympathized, gave advice (she had a psychology degree), and stood by me through thick and thin. I owe her so much for all the wonderful things she did and does for me. We took numerous trips together, played euchre, talked for hours, and laughed and cried together. When she retired in 2010 and moved to California in 2013 (to take care of her mother), we continued our friendship long distance, visiting, e-mailing and calling to catch up. We have the kind of relationship where we can be brutally honest with each other about our faults and sins. We hold each other accountable for our actions. We give and seek advice from each other. I think she is one of those people God put in my life when I most needed it. She helped me maintain my sanity through the worst days of my life and continues to help me with my health issues. I also helped her through some of her tough health issues and life problems. In other words, we were friends in good times and bad. A day is not complete for me if I don't hear from her via e-mail. And now she serves as my editor as I write books!

As I neared retirement, I decided I wanted to audit some Bethel classes to learn things in areas I wasn't well versed in. The first class I signed up for was Dr. Bob's Old Testament class. To audit a class, I had sit in on the class, but not participate or do any assignments. I just listened and learned. I loved it. Dr. Bob had a fantastic reputation and I learned so much.

Unfortunately, one day as I sat in his early morning class, someone broke into my home and stole all the jewelry I had accumulated from around the world. It appears they were interrupted because they dropped a lot of other items they had piled up to take as well. They left all my house doors standing wide open and since this was in February, the house cooled down quickly. It took hours to reheat it. I am so fortunate none of my cats escaped. A neighbor saw the open doors and called the police. None of my jewelry was ever recovered and they never caught the thief. I decided to look at the jewelry I lost as "just stuff." Even though it meant a lot to me, my life would go on and would not be affected negatively. It wasn't the end of the world for me. I didn't think it was worth getting all steamed up over.

Even though I had planned to teach a few more years, in December, 2014, I decided I wanted to retire the following May. Suddenly, I had had enough. I was tired. I left Bethel making $65,000 a year. Even during my ten years as the Dean, my salary had not been any higher than that. When I returned to teaching in 2006, my salary dropped again, and I spent the last ten years of teaching getting it back up to $65,000.

Along the way, two of my former Bethel students earned their doctorates. They eventually came back to teach at Bethel, replacing me when I retired! How rewarding that was!

Bethel graciously gave me a nice send off. Between Joyce, Susan and I (we all retired the same day), we almost wiped out the Education Department! I did teach one extra semester as an adjunct professor (art) but didn't enjoy it and have not been back to the Ed. Department since. I had been "in school" since I was six years old—I wanted and needed a complete break. Susan continued to supervise student teachers, but I wasn't interested. After doing for others all my life, I wanted some time to do for myself. And I didn't ever want to attend another meeting or pack my lunch again! Forty-five years of that was enough! Although I loved Bethel, I was more than ready to vacate this room in my life.

CHAPTER NINE
ATTIC
RETIREMENT
(Mishawaka, Indiana)
2015 - Present

I view retirement as the attic of my "house." I hadn't had time to properly peruse some things while teaching for 45 years, but had merely stored them away in an old trunk for later. Now, I was free to spend peaceful time there, amidst all the detritus of my life, digging things out and taking pleasure in reliving old memories, sorting out things, seeing things more clearly in retrospect, even if they were dusty and not organized in that big attic of life.

Settling into a new routine was not hard. I LOVED sitting at my kitchen table or out in my pavilion each morning communing with God in my own personal Garden of Eden. What a precious way to start each day.

I finally got to spend time the way I wanted—reading voraciously, writing books, scrapbooking, working puzzles, visiting with friends. Such

My own personal Garden of Eden!

a relief after a stressful lifetime of teaching and taking care of others. Now I could take care of me.

My health problems worsened during my last ten years of teaching and got even worse after retirement. Twenty-five years of extreme stress took a huge toll on my body. In 2016, I had my left hip replaced and then seven weeks later had a total hysterectomy because I was diagnosed with uterine cancer. Two major surgeries in such a short time took a big toll on me. Then, in 2017, I fought my third bout with cancer (breast again). I went through surgery and let them convince me to undergo seven weeks of radiation, and suffered from severe radiation burns. But I refused chemo. Will my cancer return at some point? Of course, it will, but it doesn't worry me.

Then, I had nine more kidney stone surgeries and cataract eye surgery in 2019. In 2020, I had my tenth and eleventh (but first invasive) surgeries in Indianapolis to remove kidney stones too large to pass. In 2022, I spent five weeks in the hospital/rehab with a severe spinal infection that started from a kidney stone and morphed into a UTI and blood infection. Then in 2023, I had two hand surgeries.

The first thing I did after retirement was to remodel an annex of my bedroom to create a separate office. I needed a place to work, write and scrapbook. I designed it so the cats could sit above me on their cat run, but couldn't get down into the office to disturb my projects. They loved sitting on the cabinets above me, watching and supervising!

I have long known that I am happiest when "creating" something—a new course, sewing, designing my house, decorating a room, designing my new studio kitchenette or my new bathroom, writing books, painting, wallpapering, scrapbooking, etc. So retirement gave me time to indulge myself in those things. What joy that gave me! I can't begin to imagine the joy God experienced while creating the universe, especially the wide variety of animals! What fun He must have had thinking up the giraffe, the cat, the elephant, etc. Such wondrous variety and clever ideas He had.

After the girls and I had traveled around the world in 2000, and had all our pictures developed, I refused to let them take any of the photos, because I knew "someday" I wanted to make a scrapbook of our trip. So that was one of my first projects. We had each taken our own photos, so I had three versions of our travels to winnow through. It took me four months and four scrapbooks to put together that trip, but what a delightful project to finally relive the whole trip. Sure, it was 15 years late, but what a treat! I kept the hard copies and sent the girls discs of the scrapbooks, per their requests.

Then I made scrapbooks of the girls' school years. I had saved lots of items from each grade and included their signatures as they aged. They turned out so nicely! Every once in a while, I browse through them again to relive their precious childhood years.

After that, I spent two years writing my two books about my cultural and adoption experiences in Seoul—*Seoul Searching* (published by Xulon Press in 2019) and *Re-Searching Seoul* (published in 2020). To protect Amanda's identity, I changed her name in both books to her middle name, Faye. I kept Abbi's name the same in the books because she was now married and had a different last name. I also changed my friends' names to protect their identities and didn't use many last names.

I had first begun writing drafts of those books back in 1987, when Amanda was little. Then I improved the drafts during the summer of 1995.

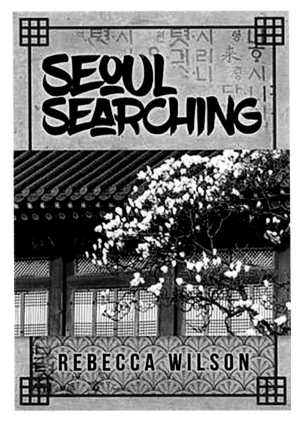

Published 2019   **Published 2020**

But life was too busy, and I wasn't able to complete them then. Now I dug deeply into my records (thank goodness I kept copious notes!) and wrote my two books, for which I praise God. I wanted my girls to have a detailed description of their adoption story. They had heard bits and pieces over the years, but never the whole story in some logical sequence. I added lots of photos to help the reader understand the Korean culture and our story. Carolyn served as my editor. I got extremely frustrated with my publisher (Xulon Press), who kept creating new errors every time I sent them a list of old errors to fix. They eventually said they were going to charge me more if I made any more changes, even though the corrections I was trying to make were their mistakes. I finally gave up, so my books do have a few clerical and grammatical errors, but the gist of the story is there. I've had lots of people tell me they enjoy reading them! I sent copies to both girls, but I suspect Amanda never read hers and likely won't in the future.

Then, quite by accident, I began helping my friend, Dusty, write her life story. She was a missionary kid, born in China, and was a prisoner of war in a Japanese prison camp during W.W. II. It took us about a year and a half to

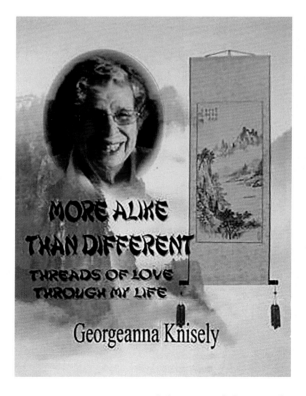

Two autobiographies I ghost wrote/edited for others

write her story and it was especially hard doing it long distance between Indiana and Pennsylvania. She was 86 and wasn't well versed in computer technology (neither am I, but I manage) so we spent a lot of time on the phone. I had to teach her how to word process and attach files to e-mails. We finally got the first draft completed in November, 2019, when I got a call from her son, Steve. Dusty had passed away suddenly; I was devastated. After taking time to think about it, Steve and his wife, Karen (whom I knew from Korea), decided they wanted me to finish Dusty's book. So between frequent e-mails and phone conferences with them, I managed to finish that book and they published it in 2020.

Then in the fall of 2020, I got a call from a total stranger, LaDonna, who had been told I could help her write her autobiography. She had had a tragic childhood but overcame many obstacles through her faith in Christ. I spent several months writing and editing on her book. She spent another year getting it published and I finally got a copy in 2022.

My next project was to write my autobiography—this book! Who knows what I'll tackle after that?

After I turned 65, I decided my brother Brent had gone around me in age and was now older than I was, so we joked about that for years and traded many insulting barbs. Our disparaging comments were fun and lighthearted, something we both needed while dealing with Mom and Dad. I was always teasing him for being older and he teased me about being confused and senile. He called me "Hilary" several times ("If you say something enough times, people start to believe it"), and then Biden (weak and ineffective).

My income from Social Security was not good. I had not paid into S.S. until I stared at Bethel. Ohio had their own retirement system and while in Korea I paid into a retirement plan, but nothing into S.S. until 1991. So in retirement, those monthly payments were quite small. Luckily I did get monthly checks from my Edward Jones account. But I knew I needed more to live on, hence I rented out part of my home.

I continued hosting guests in my basement apartment. I had one family from North Dakota that came back year after year for Notre Dame football games, starting in 2006. They started out a group of six brothers, but after some passed away, the group size dwindled. I also hosted other repeat guests, but none as long or as frequent as the Nikolas "boys." One time, they sadly said they couldn't stay with me anymore. When I asked why,

Euchre Pals!

I continue playing euchre with my friends: Carolyn Arthur, Susan Karrer, and Becky Smith. We trash talk a lot and rib each other constantly. What a good time we have!

they jokingly said they always figured they were God's favorite until they saw the plate on my car that read, "Jesus loves you, but I'm His favorite!"

Then the Notre Dame Bed and Breakfast folded because they were losing business due to the increasing popularity of Airbnb. I rented to students again for a while, then, I posted the basement apartment on Airbnb and VRBO (Vacation Rental by Owner). I had both some great people and some terrible guests. It was still a lot of work, but at least I didn't have to fix a fancy breakfast like I had with the Notre Dame program. I just had to wash tons of sheets/towels and clean up after people! I am amazed what people will do in someone else's home.

In 2016, at age 92, Dad was diagnosed with bladder cancer, so Brent, Nore and I increased our trips to visit them (two hours each way) to help Dad (who needed transport to the Fort Wayne hospital for four or five surgeries) and to keep an eye on Mom. Dad also had radiation treatments in Warsaw. He held up pretty well for his age.

After each surgery, where the Dr. scraped the lining of his bladder, Dad's bleeding would stop for a while. Each time it began again, we took him for more surgery until finally they couldn't operate any more. I was quite surprised he lasted for four years with his cancer.

Each time we visited Mom and Dad, we usually played euchre. I was amazed that their thinking was still clear enough to play. Then Mom stopped playing; I suspect she couldn't think clearly enough anymore. But Dad remained fairly clear-headed till the end.

Dad had invested in the stock market for years and had done extremely well and he had amassed a nice nest egg. But one thing bothered Brent and me. Dad loaned almost half a million dollars to a guy named Gary Dolbery to drill oil wells in Texas. That was completely different than investing in the stock market. We had been talking to Dad for years about this questionable investment because he saw no return on his money and Gary kept making excuses why he couldn't drill yet. Dad kept giving him more money to "keep the office open." To us, it sounded like a scam, but Dad insisted he would eventually see a nice income from those personal loans.

We got Steve and Abbi to talk to Dad since Dad respected Steve as a businessman, but he wouldn't believe them, either. Finally, we hired a private detective to investigate Gary. Turns out, we were right. We confronted Dad but he did not take it well. He was upset we hired someone to snoop in his business. I don't think Dad ever had a credit card, so I showed him what a credit score was, how high mine was and how low Gary's was so he would understand that giving Gary money was a huge risk, but he still refused to believe it. I don't think he ever forgave us for going behind his back. I tried to explain to him that when you find yourself in a hole, the first rule is to stop digging. He felt he had to keep giving Gary money to protect his investment. He never got that money back, but at least he stopped giving Gary any more money.

Dad also loaned a lot of money to a guy named Shannon. Brent is still trying to get that money back. We discussed suing both Gary and Shannon for elder abuse even though the statute of limitations had run out.

Dad trusted everyone and was very gullible. Over the years, we had learned to watch out for his best interest. We dealt with a few other situations, as well, but he kept falling for scams. It was a mess. He had created an idea for a shelf and sent it to a business to make a prototype, so he could apply for a patent, but when nothing came of it, he feared they had stolen his idea. He insisted I get the police there to take down the information and then go to the factory to see if they could get the drawings and prototype back. We got it slightly resolved, but never fully solved. Brent and I knew his idea was never going to be patented or go anywhere, because society's inventions had moved beyond his idea, but we didn't tell him that.

In 2017, I bought a used yellow Jeep! I didn't care what kind of car I had, I just loved that it was yellow. It seemed so boring to me that everyone else was buying black, silver or white vehicles. I now have no trouble locating my car in a large parking lot! At the time, I didn't think too much about it, but later questioned why I bucked doing what everyone else did. That same old theme from my childhood—I didn't want to be like everyone else. Interesting.

In 2005, I hosted a reunion with my college friends from 1971. We had a wonderful time catching up with each other's lives.

2005 Reunion with my college friends
Left to right: me, Jonni, Lynn, Kathi, Linda and Barb

My third Korea reunion (2018) with my Korea friends—Left to right: Betty, Dusty, Jim and Mary Pat, me, Mark, Gaila, Lois, Gwen and John

In 2018, I hosted my third Korea reunion (the other two were in 2004 and 2007) for my special friends from Korea. I was so honored that Dusty (85) and Gaila (89) made the effort to fly here. The eleven of us had a delightful time laughing and reconnecting again, knowing that most of us would never see each other again. I also flew to California that year to visit Carolyn and we got to attend the taping of a Dr. Phil show.

By 2018, Brent and I began visiting Mom and Dad once or twice a week, sometimes taking turns so we could still meet our other life commitments. Brent finally took Dad's driver's license away from him and sold his van in January, 2019, which infuriated Dad. We did pray that God would take Dad first, because we knew Mom would be much easier to deal with. Dad was going to be "difficult" if Mom passed away first. Dad once had a "vision" of someone coming in and sitting on his headboard at night. When he turned to look at them, they disappeared. We wondered if he was seeing an angel?

will." That's how Mom learned Grma knew about the affair, but Grma would never talk about it. How sad that she couldn't bring herself to talk about it with her own daughter. It might have given Mom some much-needed emotional support.

I began to wonder if all those years of private pessimistic comments from Mom were actually a subconscious reaction to Dad's affairs. She felt she couldn't tell anyone, so the frustration came out in negativity regarding other things. Basically, Mom was a positive, cheerful, gentle and kind person, so my interpretation of her transference of the trauma in her life made sense to me.

Mom continued to get worse (physically and mentally), and we moved her to the Health Care Unit in May, 2019. I called on Hospice in June and we worked closely with them. Mom and Dad celebrated their 74th anniversary June 12, 2019. We hoped they would make it to their 75th, but it was not to be.

While Mom accepted the state of things and was a compliant and pleasant patient (the nurses loved her), Dad was not. Brent and I found ourselves putting out "fires" Dad created by seriously offending people— several people at Peabody, Hospice, his doctors, etc. It seemed to be non-stop turmoil, and was exhausting and frustrating, especially trying to deal with things from a distance. Dad got very angry with us several times, especially when we had to be blunt with him about his behavior. I know he was frantic about Mom and about losing control of his life, but he took it out on others until it was very embarrassing for us. He was known as a "difficult" resident/patient.

My hardest conversation with Dad was about three months before Mom passed away. I told him he was my father, and I would always love him, but that I struggled to respect him. Then I confronted him gently about his many affairs, letting him know that the whole family knew about them, too. (He thought he had gotten away with it because no one knew.) I told him I had figured out two of his affairs so that meant there were probably more. (Mom said there were seven or eight—but I didn't tell him that). I told him Mom had kept her mouth shut and suffered in silence all those years, while it ate away at her. He was surprised I knew. But his only response was, "You have no proof."

"I don't need proof," I replied gently. "That's not why I'm talking to you. You hurt Mom deeply and you need to do three things—apologize to her, ask for her forgiveness, and ask God's forgiveness." Mom thinks you are sorry, but you've never said those words to her or asked for her forgiveness and you need to do that before she passes away." Dad said he asks for God's forgiveness for all his sins every day but just assumed Mom understood. I told him that wasn't enough. I reminded him he shouldn't appear before the throne of God carrying those unrepented sins. He needed to make it right with Mom and with God.

My own personal reasoning is that Dad had affairs over the years because he craved the attention women gave him. After a childhood of feeling ignored, he thrived on any attention he got, even though Mom did her best to feed his ego, never told him "no," or ignored him in any way. He simply had a bottomless void that he couldn't fill. That also explained all his church activities where he was constantly up in front of people. He loved that attention.

I never followed up on that conversation with Dad or checked to see if he had taken any action. I felt God nudged me to confront him about it but what he did with that was between him and God. I hope and pray he took action—poor Mom deserved that much, at least. She was a strong woman who bore her grief privately. I admired her for that but wept for the burden she had carried silently and for so long. When I told her I had spoken to Dad about his affairs, telling him he should make it right with her, she weakly whispered, "Thank you."

When Dad was a kid, his own father, Allen, had had an affair with someone on his mail route. When Grma Charlotte found out, she made Allen tell his children what he had done. Dad remembers that incident. I also strongly suspect that Grpa Ora once had an affair with Lola, a woman at church, because that is the only person Grma Faye ever expressed any animosity toward, and then only through a slight indication of disapproval. But it stood out a mile, because she always refused to bad mouth anyone. Mom confirmed that she suspected Grpa Ora's affair as well, but never talked to Grma about it.

So, it seemed marital affairs were in our family background, which really saddened me. What amazed me is that Dad would do the same thing to his wife, after witnessing the pain it had caused his mother. I wanted this generational sin to stop. I made Brent aware and let him make the decision whether or not to tell his children. I told Abbi and Steve. They had named their daughter, Devon, after Grpa DeVon, before they knew about his affairs. I have since wondered if they would have named her after Dad had they known of his indiscretions. What a sad legacy for Dad to leave his family. It definitely tarnished our respect for him.

Over that summer (2019), Mom gradually worsened till she was finally unconscious. I sometimes sat by her bed singing hymns to her or playing Christian music or spent the night sitting in a recliner by her bed. In August, I took a picture of Dad as he sat faithfully by her bed, not knowing she would pass an hour later. I told Dad to take a break, so he went back to his apartment. As I sat by Mom's side, I heard her breathing change and a few minutes later, she stopped breathing altogether. I had a nurse come to verify that Mom had passed away. But I couldn't get ahold of Dad in his apartment. Finally, one of the staff workers found him in the laundry room. He came and I got another touching photo of him holding Mom's hand an hour after she passed away. I know he loved her. Then we called the funeral home and I held his hand as we sat and watched them take her away. She was 95.

My precious mother 2015   **Shortly before she died 2019**

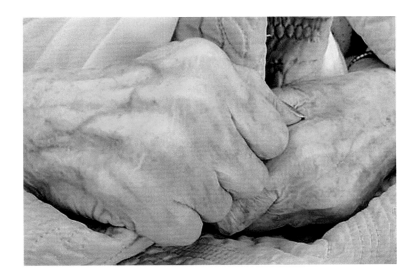

Mom's precious hands that served so many

I planned Mom's funeral and we got through it fairly well, but I missed my best friend in life. Dad (96) held up better than I thought he would, but neither Brent nor I thought he would last long after Mom passed away.

Surprisingly, he lasted another six months. Within a few weeks after she passed, he began having anxiety attacks (calling us at night saying he was going to die that night) and we hospitalized him for tests. He began meds for anxiety, but his bladder cancer continued to worsen, causing major bleeding episodes. He was able to stay in his larger apartment for a while, with Hospice monitoring him. Then we moved him to a smaller apartment in October. We had to separate their belongings into what went to the new apartment, what to toss and what to give away. Dad was NOT happy with us for wanting to just give things away (he was convinced it could be sold) and became quite upset with us a few times. I figured that was a reaction to losing control of his life.

In January, there was an outbreak of scabies in the retirement home and Dad had to be isolated for a few weeks. It was hard on him and on us. Finally, due to his worsening cancer, Peabody and I had to move him (against his will and protesting loudly) to the Health Care Unit on February 13, 2020. His bladder cancer bleeding had gotten so bad they had to insert a catheter. He was very angry at being moved and at having the catheter. After we got him settled in, I told him I'd be back to see him four days later (on Monday), but on Sunday morning (Feb. 16) they called to report that he had passed away. I felt terrible no one was there with him when he passed. Hospice had thought he still had a couple more weeks.

Dad was always so proud of his family and frequently commented how lucky we were to have such a nice family. He elevated us in his mind and was convinced I ran Bethel College, Nore ran her hospital, and Steve ran Google. He was so proud that we were all clean, well-adjusted adults and that his grandchildren were well adjusted, productive members of society and had good values. We had no smoking or drug use in our family (that we knew of) and only one divorce (Pete), although they were concerned that Pete had tattoos and stretched his ear lobes to abnormal sizes and was starting to look "scruffy." While I am very disappointed that Abbi and Amanda choose to drink, I'm not sure Mom and Dad ever knew they did.

In the last few years, Brent and I had divided up the responsibilities for taking care of Mom and Dad. In many ways we were glad we didn't have to deal with Cheri in this process, too, since she would have caused problems at every action we wanted to take. Brent dealt with Dad's finances and I took care of everything else. We were both exhausted from the months of frequent driving to and from N. Manchester but had to clear out the apartment in short order and arrange Dad's funeral. We held the funeral just before the COVID shutdown occurred. What a blessing to know Mom and Dad didn't have to be isolated for COVID. They would not have understood or tolerated it very well. That was one less thing for them to deal with. Normally Brent, Nore and I would only see each other once or twice a year but since we'd spent so much time at Mom and Dad's, seeing them a lot was a real blessing to me. I missed seeing them after both our parents passed away.

I remember what a traumatic weekend it was when Dad died. I had moved Dad to the health care wing on Thursday (Brent wasn't available); on Friday my e-mail crashed and Nore called to tell me she had discovered Pete was in jail (in North Carolina). On Saturday, Ralph called to let me know he had remarried (a year before, but hadn't told us) and that my nephew, Pete, was incarcerated for sexual misconduct with his middle school students. Brent and I toyed with whether to tell Dad about Pete. But we never had time to tell him because Dad died on Sunday (and I had no e-mail to communicate with the funeral home). On Monday, after I finally got my e-mail working again, Nuri, let me know he was coming from Istanbul, Turkey for the funeral, and on Tuesday we cleaned out

Dad's apartment. Later that week, we held Dad's funeral. I mulled over what to do if Nancy showed up for the funeral. Should I escort her out immediately, or just ignore her presence? Luckily, she didn't show.

My friend, Becky, volunteered (bless her heart!) to go down and help us clean out the apartment. What a job! Having "down-sized" them a few times already really helped, but there was still a lot of stuff to sort through. One thing we found was Dad's old toothbrush, and I do mean "old." He had insisted on using the same one for years. It was so filthy, it gave me the creeps! And we stabbed our fingers on all the toothpicks we found in every suit pocket—Dad was never without a toothpick.

There was one thing I was quite relieved about. I consider it a true blessing that neither Cheri, Mom nor Dad ever knew about Pete's incarceration. It would have destroyed Cheri to think her son was in such trouble and Mom and Dad would have been heartbroken. Thank you, Jesus, for sparing them that.

After Dad's funeral, I was beyond exhausted, but still couldn't "crash" because Nuri was staying at my house and I had to clean, cook, and entertain him for a week. I got very sick just before he left and I was down for seven weeks. Nuri got home to Turkey just before the COVID pandemic isolation took effect.

I had called Mom and Dad every Friday night for 30 years, so it was an adjustment not to talk to them frequently. Even now, I get the urge to call them on Fridays and have to remind myself that they are gone.

I was so glad my parents had avoided the pandemic. They would have struggled with the isolation, which didn't bother or inconvenience me as it did so many others. I was lucky to be retired, so I didn't have to deal with online teaching. I was quite used to staying home and putzing on my own, so that lack of social stimulation didn't bother me. In fact, I loved being home alone after all my years of dealing with life on a global scale. I was content to withdraw from the world a bit. I managed to avoid COVID, wore my mask, and got the COVID shots as soon as they came out in spring, 2021.

Brent took care of the lengthy and messy process of settling Dad's estate, thank goodness. Had it been up to me, I would have had no idea where to start. But his CPA background and understanding of Dad's affairs were a real blessing. He struggled to get paid back from either Gary or Shannon, both of whom still owed Dad money. He couldn't close Dad's IRA account because there was a delay sending Pete his share of the inheritance, but no one would tell Brent why. So, things were hung up for over a year and a half. He finally settled the estate without that loose end tied up.

After Ralph remarried, he moved to the Cincinnati area with his new wife (also named Sheri), and he had inherited his mother's place in Florida. On the internet, I found that huge house they had built in Roann on the market for $600,000, but Ralph had to keep reducing the price because it did not sell. Such a huge home in the little town of Roann was not in great demand. Homes in that area were usually selling for less than $100,000. It finally sold for $400,000 after more than a year (or two?) on the market.

Even though the blood bank always screened my blood carefully and said my blood was safe to give to sick patients with no risk, due to my health issues, I was content to stop donating blood after I had donated 300 pints of blood—37 ½ gallons. I calculated that with my triple donations, I had donated enough blood over those 45 years to help 500 very sick people. My mom always told me to do something nice for someone every day without them finding out who did it. I liked the anonymity of donating blood, but it was time to stop.

I heard a devotional at church one time that really struck home with me. The speaker said he had been the recipient of a blood donation and that he personally knew the donor. That intrigued me since donor information is never divulged to recipients. Then he said his blood donor was Jesus. What a wonderful new way to look at what Jesus did for us on the cross! Jesus is my blood donor!

I began reconnecting with my high school friends a couple of times a year when we all met in Warsaw for lunch. What treasures they are to me!

In May, 2020, I got a request from a traveling nurse to rent my upstairs bedroom for a thirteen-week stint (the basement was already rented out). Kelly shared my kitchen space, which drove me crazy! But we got along well, and she kept extending her contract.

So, like so many others during the pandemic, I remodeled! Construction companies were overloaded with business, but I was fortunate to get a new kitchenette installed in what had been the upstairs bedroom closet to create a studio apartment.

Kelly stayed in that upstairs bedroom until September and then moved to the basement apartment, along with her friend, Rose (a friend she was

High school friends: Sue (Hartong) Behrends, Sally (Hipskind) Gerard, Becky (Eiler) Cordes, Jenny (Wilcox) Chapman—2019

introducing to being a traveling nurse), so I could install that kitchenette. That major project took three months and left my house a mess. But it turned out to be adorable! Rose moved up to the new studio apartment in November, when Kelly resigned her position and moved on. Rose stayed through March, 2021, and we got to be good friends—another blessing.

In April, I posted the studio apartment on both Airbnb and VRBO and quickly had several bookings. So now I manage two rentals! Between the rentals and writing, I keep quite busy. I've now switched to hostessing just traveling nurses, because they stay for 13 weeks, which makes the constant laundry and cleaning duties easier for me. So far, I've met some great people! God has been so generous to give me this house that helps me with my retirement income.

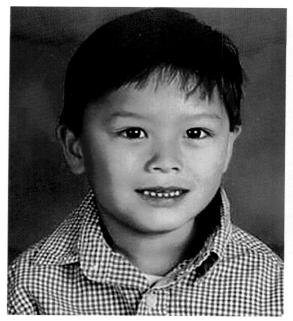

Logan (3) 2014   **Devon (4) 2018**

I have the cutest grandkids in the world! My prayer is that they will grow up to be Christ followers, have kind hearts, and live a life of integrity.

At Steve and Abbi's bridal shower I gave Abbi a Korean chest full of things from Korea and from her childhood. She could still fit into the Chinese jacket she wore when she was four! Now Devon wears it!

Steve, Devon, and Logan

Nana Becky caught a groundhog!

Quite a golfer!

**Left to right:
Abbi, Logan (10),
Steve and Devon (7)
2021**

Logan (9) 2020

Devon (6) 2020

Logan (10) 2021

Devon (7) 2021

During the spring of 2022, I had a catio (cat patio) built and installed. The cats access it through a cat door in my kitchen wall. They LOVE being outside to watch the squirrels, chipmunks and birds after I feed them each morning. In 2023, I expanded the catio, adding tunnels to the side and front of the deck. What a hoot!

In the last few years, Brent, had developed a severe shaking in his hands (essential tremors)—a condition he inherited from Dad who had inherited it from Grma Charlotte before that. Poor Brent couldn't write any more, hold a plate in a buffet line, cut his meat, sign checks or anything that required a steady hand. His doctor put him on some meds that helped a little, but he was told he would be best served by brain surgery. He debated about it for a couple of years. Trying to help him look on the bright side, I told him, "You know, there is one good thing that could come from this surgery. While they are in there messing around with your brain, maybe they can fix your personality!"

"No, the Dr. says my personality is perfect," he exclaimed. I told him to get a new doctor! Then I said if the implants didn't work and his hands started shaking again, he could accidentally hit Nore. If so, she could just smack him in the chest where the battery was. But he replied she was too short to reach it. Besides, she was still on probation. When I asked what he meant, he replied, "We've only been married 48 years, so she still has two more years on probation.

We have laughed over such things numerous times. What joy to have a sibling I can joke around with! Since hospitals shut down elective surgeries due to the COVID pandemic, he waited for quite a while. He finally had the first brain surgery in March, 2022. He was to have the second surgery a week later to implant the battery in his chest, but he'd had a slight stroke, so they performed a second brain surgery to remove the implants instead. His shaking hands returned. He struggled with a long-term brain infection, C-Diff (like colitis), physical therapy, occupational therapy and speech therapy for weeks afterward. He was finally moved to a rehab facility and then a sub-acute facility and was able to go home two months later, but still struggled with frequent fevers. Finally, after three months, his brain infection cleared and his kidneys were fully functioning. His incredible wife, Nore, was with him through thick and thin. Her nursing skills and his son Chad's physical therapy background were very helpful to him. In a few months, they may revisit the options to solve his essential tremors, but I doubt he will be willing to undergo brain surgery again.

My nephew, Pete, was in jail for two and a half years before his trial was held. The courts all shut down due to COVID. During those 2 ½ years, he had two trial dates set, but both were cancelled at the last minute, which prolonged his frustration. Brent, Nore, Abbi and I sent him books and deposited money to his account, so he could buy things he needed. I wrote to him quite a bit and he gladly responded. He was so lonely and depressed. His trial was finally held in May, 2022. Ralph and Jason were there to support Pete, who was found guilty. We were all devastated. He had been the first grandchild, the first great-grandchild, my first nephew, and I had spent hours babysitting for him. He used to ride up on my shoulders while holding onto my braids. He was very special to the whole family. At his sentencing three weeks later, he was given a 50-61 year sentence, which didn't make sense to us. There was no rape or murder involved and many criminals who perform both those horrific crimes receive much less severe sentences. We were heartbroken for him and the victims involved. We all grieved this tragedy.

At this time, I was also helping my friend, Carolyn, find a condo, and move back to Indiana (after 12 years in California). She stayed in my basement and stored all her furniture in my garage while waiting for the closing on her condo. Then we painted before moving her furniture in.

Between Brent and Pete it was a frustrating and discouraging time. Carolyn's move added to the stress, although I was quite glad to have her close by again.

I've always known that God's timing is perfect, and that was proven once again in August, 2022, just three months after Carolyn moved back to Indiana. I suddenly found myself in the hospital for two weeks and then a rehab facility for three weeks after developing a severe bone infection in my spine. Carolyn stepped in and took over my life, feeding my cats, paying my bills, managing my rentals, and generally taking care of all my responsibilities. What a comfort that was to me! Praise God he brought her back to Indiana when He did!

On a side note, out of the three siblings in our family, I was the only one who remained single for life. Looking back, I doubt if either my brother or my sister could have successfully handled being single, either financially or emotionally. They would have been miserable going to church or restaurants alone, and would have struggled to make it financially by themselves. They both emotionally "needed" someone else to complete them. It seems God gave me enough determination to make my own way, enough ability to do it, and enough grit to deal with life issues alone. For those blessings, I am truly grateful. If one of us had to be single, I'm glad it was me. I learned to sum up situations and make decisions on my own. For me, being single was a blessing, not a curse. I would not have been able to do the things I've done in life had I needed to work around/with a husband whose path in life might have been in a different direction.

I claim this verse: "I can do all things through Christ." (Philippians 4:13) But I certainly have the scars from my battles. "A really strong woman accepts the war she went through and is enabled by her scars." (Carly Simon)

But approaching life alone was not easy. I have a framed quote in my office that says,

I'm a strong woman. I've dealt with everything that's hit me in life.
I've cried myself to sleep, picked myself up and wiped my tears.
I've grown from things that were meant to break me.
I get stronger by the day, and I have God to thank for that.
(Positive Tree)

One thing I have never been able to figure out is why Amanda, who had a wonderful, warm, secure, loving childhood, had so much trauma in life and so many problems, while Abbi, who had a terrible start in life (lived in a cardboard shack on the streets of Korea, had a burn scar, suffered from malnutrition and TB, and experienced the death of both parents) turned out to be a cheerful, happy well-adjusted adult. The only thing I can figure out is that God gave me Amanda so her life wouldn't turn out much worse than it did. I assume that adopting both girls was why He directed me to teach in Korea. Today, I have a positive relationship with Abbi, but a strained one with Amanda. She has begun informing me more often of where she is living and she both called and sent a Mother's Day card this year! That was a welcome change! Perhaps sometime in the future, God will bring about a better relationship with Amanda. I pray so. I love her so much.

I have made a plethora of friends in life. So many, that I sometimes must stop and think which "room" I know people from. My sincere thanks to these dear friends for their contributions to my life:

- my high school "room"—Jenny Wilcox, Sue Hartong, Sally Hipskind, Becky Eiler, Linda Dale, and Nuri Cakan;
- my college "room"—Kathi Oosting, Linda Filbrun, Jonni Harstick, Lynn Dudek, and Gayle Webb;
- my Ohio "room"—Chris Cope, Barb Church, Cheryl Nungesser, Stephanie Pentiuk, Sandy Boylan, Julie Beery, Annamary Gardella, Pat and Paul Gale, Rob Libbee, Howard and Martha Brammer, and Brenda Hoff (who became the famous Christian author B.J. Hoff);
- my Korea "room"—Becky Anderson, Donita Johnson, Dean and Gaila Kauffman, Jim and Mary Pat Fuller, Jay and Dusty Knisely, John and Gwen Johnson, Mark and Lois Zollinhofer, Barry and Evy Jenkins, Pam Dedricks, George and Lois Blanks, Soon-Ok Borden, Wanda Ward, Carol Taylor, Edie Eager, Ross and Betty Partington, Mrs. Yoon, Nancy Pearson, Steve and Phyllis Major, Dan and Shirley Waters, and Kim and Nancy Greene;
- my grad school "room"—Jon Leonard, Young-Chi Ni, Merribeth Bruning, Bill and Carol Hirons , and Sue Drake (my dissertation chair);
- my Bethel "room"— Carolyn Arthur, Becky Smith, Susan Karrer (who taught in Korea when I did, but we never met until at Bethel),

Liz Hossler, Leslie Greising, Bob and Joyce Laurent, Barb Rodgers, Bob Ham, Mike and Judy Holtgren, Hutch Ury, Tom and Alice Terry, Steve Matteson, Jayne Hammontree, Jody and Sonya Martinez, Dennis Engbrecht, Deborah Brackley, Diane Osborne, Nan Hussey, and Claudine Cortier.

What a blessing friends are! The world is full of wonderful people, and I've been privileged to share life with them. One thing I discovered about living overseas was that you make friends easier, quicker and more deeply than with your stateside friends. I suppose we all knew we only had a short time together, were all in the same boat with cultural struggles, and had something quite strong in common—the desire to live overseas, a trait not shared by everyone! Those precious overseas people remain some of my dearest friends.

While I have many dear friends, I have one "stand-out" best friend from each room of life. Sue in high school, Kathi in college, Chris in Ohio, several in Seoul, Jon in grad school, and Carolyn at Bethel. God is good to provide rich companionship for us.

I have been blessed to have amazing experiences in life. God has been so good to me. Please do not read this list as me bragging, because I have no cause to brag in anything except that I have been redeemed by Jesus. I only include this list because of my amazement over what God has allowed to transpire in my life. I stand amazed at the things God was able to achieve through such an average person as me. He is wondrous and greatly to be praised. Through HIS grace, I've:

- been loved and redeemed by Jesus
- had wonderful parents and a great childhood
- expanded my horizons and expertise with three degrees (earning my master's degree in a foreign country)
- lived and taught in two foreign countries (England and Korea)
- been to 57 countries (many of them more than once)
- twice traveled around the world
- attended the 1988 Seoul Olympics
- been stung by jellyfish in the South China Sea
- attended church with Queen Elizabeth in Scotland
- boated on Lock Ness in Scotland

- been behind the Iron Curtain in E. Germany (when it was still divided) and into communist North Korea.
- twice climbed around inside Mt. Vesuvius (a live, but not active, volcano in Italy) and explored the destroyed city of Pompeii
- twice climbed the Great Wall of China
- marveled at the life-sized terra cotta statues in Xian, China
- been awed by the Taj Mahal
- bought beautiful rugs in Nepal, Bahrain and India
- driven on the left in Ireland, England, and Wales
- been through the Panama Canal
- gone trekking in the Himalayas
- ridden a camel around the pyramids in Egypt and crawled inside a pyramid
- ridden elephants through the jungles of Thailand and later Nepal
- slept in tents while on safari in Kenya
- ridden camels, gondolas, cyclos, elephants, horses, rickshaws, taxis, subways, cable cars, the Japanese Shinkansen (bullet train), the London Eye, the chunnel and Eurail, etc
- attended the Passion Play in Oberammergau, Germany
- twice witnessed the horrors of Dachau Concentration Camp in Germany
- stood where Paul preached in Corinth
- floated down the Ganges River at dawn in India
- wore a python around my neck on Christmas Day in Bangkok
- visited the sobering Hiroshima Museum in Japan
- had two wild monkeys climb up and sit on my head in the jungles of Costa Rica
- visited Stonehenge (my favorite!) three times
- thrilled to see the Moai on Easter Island and Machu Pichu in Peru
- seen most of the world's great art—including the Sistine Chapel and the Mona Lisa twice.
- eaten things you would not believe
- escorted 12 Korean babies to the U.S. on two orphan flights
- saved many lives by donating 300 pints of blood
- raised two daughters by myself

- personally handed my daughters their college diplomas
- furnished my home with souvenirs from all over the world
- survived cancer three times
- worked in positions of both service and authority
- written eight books (including three #1 selling textbooks in a foreign country)
- fought and won (!) four legal battles against the Korean government (without an attorney)
- taught for 45 fulfilling years—at every level from pre-school through graduate school
- influenced hundreds of future teachers
- never been fired. I always moved on while things were going well for me both professionally and personally.
- loved making friends all over the world
- worked hard to climb out of a deep financial hole and am now debt free!
- rejoiced at having two beautiful, successful daughters, two wonderful grandchildren and a lovely home.
- lived in the same house now for 22 years—a rare privilege since I have moved 21 times!

Despite all these blessings (and, yes, cancer was a blessing, too), I also had some terrible, stressful times in my life. But God used those bad times to build my character. He didn't let me "waste" those experiences (thanks, Grma Faye!). I grew and learned hard lessons. I learned to depend on God more and myself less. Probably the most useful lesson was to become better, not bitter. I learned through struggles, mistreatment and misguided social expectations. Dad, Cheri, Amanda, and Dave were all difficult experiences, but great learning opportunities for me. I am still "healing" from some of those hurts, but God is my comfort and strength.

What a blessing life has been! I have no idea why God should allow me these privileges. God has been faithful to me, and I've tried to be faithful to Him. I want this book to stand as my testimony that God is my strength and courage.

I am extremely grateful and count my life a good day's work.

The Wilson Family Through the Years

1954

1955

1961

1966 (Yes, I'm the one with the cat!)

1982

1983

1984

1986

1987

1988

1989

At Grma Faye's 90th birthday party in 1991

2012, The last four great-grandchildren were not yet born.

EPILOGUE

In retirement, my vision changed from looking forward to the next phase, project, or activity to looking back over my past, to review what had taken place.

I have been blessed to live a long life. But was it a worthy life? In these, my twilight years, as I look back on my life and my career, I ask myself some important questions. Was I a responsible and decent human being? Did my life honor Christ? Was I a good mother, teacher, and friend? Did I effectively use or waste the gifts/talents God gave me? Did I make a positive difference in other's lives? Did I bring anyone to Christ? In the great scheme of life, was I a blessing or a burden? Is the world a better place because I existed?

I recently spent considerable time going through old files. What fun it was to peruse my placement files, consider reference letters people wrote for me, review my transcripts, traverse my tenure portfolio, reread 45-years worth of teaching and course evaluations , and enjoy looking through all the scrapbooks I had made! I reread the hundreds of thank you notes and letters people sent me. What a blessing to step back at the end of life and view the products of my existence. It clarified for me that perhaps I did touch lives and influence future teachers. Just recently I had the privilege of having a former college student over for dinner. He had just written a book and in the conclusion had mentioned that he started writing because a college professor encouraged him to do so. I asked him if it was Maralee, one of his English Department professors (his major area). He said, "No, it was you!" I was surprised, because I didn't remember doing that, but I was very touched!

I hope I made a positive difference in the lives of those 3000 students I taught over a 45-year span. I continue to hear from some of them and they are always complimentary about my impact on their lives. The Bethel Alumni Office recently told me that when they canvas former students about which person at Bethel had the biggest impact on their lives, they sometimes hear my name. I run into former students in the community who are now teaching and impacting their students and it is a joy to know I somehow had a part in that.

I know I made a difference to those 500 people who received my donated blood. And since I will be an organ donor, there may be future patients who benefit from some of my organs.

I made a huge difference in the lives of my daughters. While the years were rocky and challenging, I know I shaped their lives in positive ways. Abbi would have died of TB had I not adopted her. Her birth mother died of tuberculosis in a country where TB medicine is free. All they had to do was go get it. So, I know she would not have been treated, either. She was born into the lower class, raised in the middle class, and married into the upper class of society. She survived and her life has drastically changed because I adopted her. Had I not been faithful in sticking by Amanda and getting her help, she would probably have ended up in "deep kimchi"—abandoned, abused, severely traumatized, or dead. She probably would have committed suicide, like she attempted to do and like so many others with her condition have attempted. Instead, she is a fully functioning member of society serving others through nursing! Perhaps someday, she will realize how her life changed for the better because I adopted her. And I rest in the knowledge that I did not cause her inherited problems, but was the one chosen by God to help her deal with them. If not having a wonderful relationship with her is the price I must pay to make sure she made it this far in life, then so be it. It is a valid trade-off. I am content.

Most importantly, I introduced my girls to Jesus. I gave my daughters roots and God gave them wings.

Yes, I sacrificed greatly to raise my girls. I sacrificed my time, my finances, and my health. I don't see myself as a martyr and don't seek praise or sympathy—just understanding about the impossible situation I chose and was dealing with. My close friends were very helpful and supportive.

So, in hindsight, yes, I think I made a positive impact on the world. I did my best in my little corner of life to help others. I am confident I was a valuable member of society. But was I working within God's plan for my life?

Years ago, I took a test and learned that my three spiritual gifts are teaching, leadership/administration, and service/giving. I think I used all three effectively. So, following God's plan for my life through my life list worked! Praise God!

I recognize there were times I made foolish mistakes. I humbly confess that there were times I said and did things that hurt people. Sometimes, I wasn't as kind or patient as I should have been. Even though I was blessed with a great deal of common sense, my human limitations naturally resulted in sin and errors in judgment. I have tried to apologize and make amends when I could. And, praise God, through Christ, I am forgiven! God has wiped away the totality of my sins. I will leave this life knowing I did my best and was an instrument God used to help others. Like the Apostle Paul, I can say, "I have fought the good fight, I have finished the race, I have kept the faith. Now there is in store for me the crown of righteousness, which the Lord, the righteous Judge, will award to me on that day" (2 Timothy 4: 7-8).

These words from the hymn "In Christ Alone" (Townsend and Getty, 2011) sum it up well:

No guilt in life, no fear in death, this is the power of Christ in me.
From life's first cry to final breath, Jesus commands my destiny.
No power of hell, no scheme of man, could ever pluck me from his hand.
Til He returns or calls me home, here in the power of Christ I stand.

While each of the "rooms" of my life were important in shaping my character, my next abode—Heaven—won't just be another room, but will be my "HOME." What joy it gives me to know that!

Thank you, Jesus! I can't wait to meet you face to face!

APPENDIX A

July 17, 2012

Dear Cheri,

Thanks again for hosting our family photo session. I really appreciate you opening your home to us. I thought it was great and everyone seemed to enjoy themselves. Mom and Dad have mentioned to me several times how much they enjoyed it and how blessed they are to have four generations of such a wonderful family.

Cheri, I made a mistake several years ago when I was young and stupid. I sent you a letter (with the best of intentions) that didn't go over well. I want to apologize and explain. My friends and I have always had open and honest relationships where we hold each other accountable for behaviors, faults, sins, etc. Since you had pointed out some of my faults over the years (which I tried to grow from), I just assumed we had that same kind of relationship and I acted accordingly. As soon as I got your response and realized how hurt you were, I dropped the matter rather than respond and make things worse. In the intervening years I've tried to maintain a relationship with you and show you I care, but I never know what kind of response I'm going to get. Sometimes you seem receptive and sometimes not.

You are my only sister and I want a relationship with you. Therefore, God laid it on my heart to apologize to you and ask if we can start afresh. Please forgive me. I look forward to hearing from you.

Love, Becky

APPENDIX B

August 30, 2012

Dear Becky,

Sometimes when a person reads a letter they put inflections in there. That is not the case here. I'm just stating things, not putting any inflection in my voice, so don't put it there.

If you want to let bygones be bygones, I have to clear up a few issues.

First, the LETTER—you waited 30 years to apologize. That tells me that your pride has been in the way for way too long. My children have turned out great. In fact, my 2 are the only grandchildren that don't drink alcohol or waste money on elaborate trips, etc. They are both very giving to others. Your opinion was out of line, and you didn't even have children. I pray that you will keep your opinion to yourself, unless asked for.

The AIRPLANE RIDE—You were sneaky and tricky to get me into the plane because you knew I wouldn't want my boys to know of my fear. Just because you like something doesn't mean everybody else. I like lots of things that wouldn't interest you, but you have always you that your likes were to be imposed upon others. Sneakiness and trickery are not very good qualities to have. I have my walls up around you because the trust isn't there for this very reason.

Every time I talk to you, you say something that hurts me, and I end up crying after it's done. Two quick examples, and then I won't mention any others. When we did our deck at the house when we first moved there, you came and said, "It doesn't even look finished to me." We had planned and spent what we could on that and I cried and cried after you left. Here again you gave your opinion when nobody asked for it. Everyone that saw it said it was great, but your sentence hurt so bad. I realize that you don't have a husband that tells you when you get home, that maybe something you said was hurtful. My sweet husband and I do that for each other. And I will tell you you can't have pride and be married. You blurt out so many things that the rest of us wouldn't do because we've learned over the years from our spouse to keep quiet. The other example was when we remodeled this time, you came in and said, "That isn't white carpet." Oh, yes, it is. The name is Ice and I don't care what you think. But again, you stab me with your opinion. So, yes, my walls are up and don't come down easily. You can criticize me for being too sensitive. Sorry, that's the way God made me, and just because I'm not like you doesn't make me wrong or bad. I lived too many years feeling like the odd one in the family. It has taken me time to realize that each person has value and is different. I'm glad I'm not like any of the rest of you. You are so proud of being a college professor that it's arrogant. I know janitors who are nicer than you and do their job well and that's what is expected of each of us. All jobs are worthwhile, and it shouldn't get in the way of friendship or attitudes.

You have a way of just taking over and controlling things. The MATTRESS is a good example. You didn't ask for my opinion, you just bought a very expensive one and expected the rest of us to go along with it. I was shocked to see that Mom's Lenox and silverware were gone. You again took over. I have seen many things at your house that were Grandma's I would have loved to have a few things of hers, but between you and Mom, I wasn't asked about any of it. Of course, that was when the family decided that my precious husband wasn't good enough for all of you. He is a bigger person that any of you will ever be. There is no excuse for the way we were treated.

I have forgiven you—I have to. My relationship with Jesus means more that the hurt. But it's hard to forget them. When I start to think about all the different things you've said that hurt, I'm usually down for days. Well, I won't let that happen again. I will say that the last year has been better when we talk, but that's only because you're treading on eggs around me. And I guess that's OK. Maybe you've learned that we all have feelings and you better tread lightly. I sometimes feel like maybe you've realized Mom and Dad aren't going to be here to much longer and selfishly, you want to have a relationship with your only sister. As I said, I have to get this off my chest, so I hope the truth doesn't hurt you too badly. That is not my intent. We have to agree to be kinder and loving. If you accept this, then I will try to be more cooperative.

I don't want you to talk to Mom and Dad about this. They have enough to worry about and there are separate issues between us. If I find out that you have talked to them I will never trust you again.

As previously stated, I hope this doesn't start any new issues, but I have lived with them too long and have grown wiser and more mature by going through these issues. My friends are precious to me and have supported us with health issues over the past 6 years. Not one of the family came when Ralph was in the hospital (3 months this last time) and several weeks in 2005). That spoke a lot to us. I guess Dad did come one time, but he kept telling me to go to work because Ralph was in a coma and wouldn't know if I was there or not. No empathy there.

This was a long letter, but I feel better getting it out. Please pray for our relationship.

Cheri

APPENDIX C

October 12, 2012

Dear Cheri,

Thank you for responding to my letter. I didn't quite know whether to respond back. If I didn't respond, you may again accuse me of being proud. If I did respond, you may become more defensive. I'm afraid no matter what I say or do it will be misunderstood and misinterpreted. And no, you didn't hurt my feelings by your comments. I have thicker skin than that. Please note that my tone throughout this letter is soft, gentle and non-threatening. I am not angry and am not trying to hurt you.

After much prayer, I've decided to respond, and make a suggestion. I recognize this is long, but I pray you will be willing to digest it. I would prefer not to continue discussing these issues through the mail. It is too easy to misread inflections and intonation on paper. However, if you reject my suggestion at the end of this letter, then perhaps corresponding will be our only avenue. These are my observations. My prayer is that you will consider my comments prayerfully and examine yourself honestly to see if these observations apply to you. Also note, it helped me to organize my thoughts by doing this in an outline form.

I. Responding to the issues you raised

I chose not to address any specific issues in my letter of apology, but since you did in your response, I'd like to respond to them. Cheri, there is a difference between intention and perception. I feel your perception of my intentions is inaccurate. You accuse me of "taking charge and controlling things" or saying or doing hurtful things. I'd like to respond to the situations you mentioned.

A. I have no idea what airplane ride you are referring to. When did I ever get you into an airplane? If I did, I had no idea you had a fear of flying. I didn't learn about your fear of flying until after you and Ralph went to Germany and you mentioned it to me then. So my actions (whatever and whenever they were) to get you into a plane were innocent. I feel you misinterpreted my intentions. I was not trying to be "tricky and sneaky."

B. About the mattress---please understand that it was not just me orchestrating that purchase. I wasn't "taking charge." Brent and I and our 4 children had all agreed to go together on this purchase. We thought you might want to be included so you wouldn't have to think of something to get them. We were trying to be considerate of you. We also knew that if we didn't ask you to join us, you might get your feelings hurt. If you didn't want to participate, all you had to do was say so.

C. I don't remember saying anything about your deck. If I did, it was an innocent comment. It was not my intention to disparage what you had done. As for the carpet, I was trying to say that to me it looked more off-white than the white-white I had imagined. I wasn't saying it looked bad, just different than what I expected. I think it's lovely. You say you don't care what I think, and yet you must or you wouldn't have gotten your feelings hurt over it. No one can "stab" you with their opinion if you don't care what they think. Help me understand why a comment about the carpet was worth crying over.

D. Regarding mom and dad's silverware, Lenox china and goblets--- they asked me to take them to try to sell them on e-bay. I am not keeping them. I was operating at their request. They felt it would be unfair to all siblings if they gave the china to one of us. It was very expensive and they want to keep things as even as possible. I didn't "take charge" as you perceived. I was trying to respect our parent's wishes. The things you've seen in my house that were grma's were given to me by mom and dad. I let mom and dad decide who gets what. They gave you things, too--- sometimes things I was interested in—such as the bed and grma's wedding rings. It didn't offend me. We aren't working together behind your back,

Cheri. If you have an issue regarding family heirlooms, you need to take it up with mom and dad.

E. Can you give me an example of what I have said or done to give you the idea that I am arrogant about being a college professor? I rarely speak about my job because I believe you aren't interested. My friends tell me I am not arrogant, just confident. Because I have been in several positions of authority, I have learned to stand on my own two feet and get things done. I've learned to "take charge" in professional settings. I wouldn't be where I am today if I hadn't. And that is not pride speaking, just relief that I've been able to make it in life on my own. I have no husband to rely on for finances so I had to make my own way. I'm sorry if that comes across to you as arrogant. I simply think of it as being confident and wanting to get things done. I wonder if you are jealous of my success in life. I am happy for your success in life. Can't we be happy for each other?

F. I am unsure where you got the idea that I look down on people with "menial" jobs. Please give me an example. I learned a long time ago that secretaries and custodians really run the school and I have always valued their contributions. One of my good friends is a secretary. I have always felt that no matter what job we do, we should do it to the best of our ability and to the glory of God. Please clarify this point for me.

G. I feel your comment about me not having a husband to "corral" me was a cheap shot. I have worked very hard to build a rapport with close friends and encourage them to chide me if I do something out of line or inappropriate. Husbands are not the only source of accountability for our actions. As a single person, I've had to be strong, confident and hard working since I have no one else to rely on. Being single in a "married" society is not easy. I have tried to make the best of my single status. Please give me some credit for using my friends to hold me accountable.

H. Yes, this last year has been better when we talk because I decided to make a renewed effort (although I've been trying for 30 years!). It has nothing to do with me finally realizing you have feelings. I've always known you have feelings—very strong ones.

I. Yes, I was cool in my response to you when you walked in at Mom and Dad's a few weeks ago (I just smiled and said "hi" instead of moving to hug you, as I usually do). Until I knew what your response was going to be to my letter, I chose to be cautious, like you normally are. I am tired of always being the one to make the first move, Cheri. I would love it if you made the first move toward me sometimes.

J. This is not the first time you have mentioned that your children are better than mine or Brent's. I agree that your children have turned out well, but so have ours. All three of us have done well raising our children--we can all three be proud of our parenting. Just because we had different parenting challenges than you did, doesn't negate our parenting skills. Chad, Kara, and Abbi are well adjusted and successful. Yes, even Amanda, given the parameters of her mental condition, is functioning to the best of her ability. It is rare for someone with severe Borderline Personality Disorder to be a fully functioning, self-supporting adult. Considering her mental issues, she has come a long way. I feel God used me to get her to this point. He gave me an incredibly difficult job, but I am certain He selected me for it---knowing I would remain faithful under nearly impossible circumstances and would do my very best for her.

And what does "wasting money on elaborate trips" have to do with them "turning out well"? Abbi goes on trips with Steve in his work. Amanda got a free ticket to Mongolia. When we went around the world we saved for years to afford that fantastic experience. It feels like you are judging us for being world travelers because that is not how you choose to spend your time and money. It has nothing to do with how well they turned out. I recognize that not drinking alcohol is a mark (to you) of whether our children turned out well. I am not happy that my children drink on occasion, but our children, though carefully nurtured, have to make their own decisions in life. I suspect if I made having tattoos or stretching your earlobes as part of the definition of whether your kids turned out well, you would be offended.

I would never dream of telling you my children are better than yours. It comes across as pride, Cheri---the very thing you accuse me of. Help me understand why it is so important for you to prove your children are better than Brent's and mine. Even your sentence, "I'm glad I'm not like any of the rest of you" smacks of pride. You appear to be very proud of your husband, your children and your home. As long as we all listen to you talk about your family and home and show interest in your life, we get along, but you don't want to hear about our families. Brent, Nore and I have learned not to discuss our families with you.

K. Your comment that you forgive me because you "have to," rings hollow for me. Maybe you are sincere, but that comment makes me question it. I also note you do not ask for my forgiveness. Does that mean you believe you have nothing to be forgiven for? I would love for us to be able to forgive each other for past hurts and start a new, more positive chapter in our lives.

Cheri, I have prayed about whether to include the rest of this letter for fear you'd perceive it as negating my original apology, which I was sincere about. But since you opened the door by addressing issues, I felt it was time to raise the following thoughts. Again, please know that I am not trying to hurt you, but merely to make you aware of my observations.

II. Issues between us

I waited 30 years to apologize because your response back then appeared incredibly defensive and I believed further communication on the subject at that time would get us nowhere. I felt God leading me to just drop the issue back then. It had nothing to do with my pride. It had to do with my perception of your ability to handle my comments. I only contacted you now because I felt God leading me to do so. I have not felt that leading until now. My letter to you had nothing to do with the fact that mom and dad aren't going to be around much longer—I was merely following a prompting from God. Perhaps God feels the time is right for us to make things right between us? I want to get to the root of any and all issues between us.

A. Cheri, I feel we approach life from two very different perspectives. Please understand that I'm not saying my way is right and yours is wrong: we are just different. I tend to react to things practically and pragmatically, while you react emotionally. Perhaps that difference is the root of our disconnect? For example, a few weeks ago at mom and dad's house, I mentioned that I have my funeral completely planned and paid for, the obituary written and the grave stone in the ground. I was being pragmatic and practical so my children don't have to deal with those issues. Your reaction was that I've "given up" (an emotional response). We react to things so differently. Another example: when you got cancer, you cried for days and wouldn't even say the word "cancer." You called it the "c" word. When the doctor called me at work and told me I had cancer, I responded "Well, praise the Lord" and I went right back to work (remember Ralph's old "attitude check" from his youth ministry days?). I never cried about it. When the last chemo was over, I got a bit misty eyed from relief. My response was more practical and pragmatic.

B. I have difficulty understanding your reasoning or thought processes. When I attended a conference in Tennessee and visited Jason, Karen and Levi, your response to me indicated that you were not pleased. I believe in shared joy, and was hoping you would be pleased I visited them. Help me understand why you were upset by my visit. I would be delighted if you went to visit my grandchild. However, rarely do you show interest in my life, children or grandchild.

Another example of my difficulty understanding your thought processes: A few years ago you mailed me a book called "The Grace Awakening" with no explanation or letter attached. I assumed you were trying to say that I needed to extend grace to you. I didn't take offense (I read the book and found it helpful), but I couldn't help but wonder if you were willing to extend grace to me, too. However, I may be guilty of misinterpreting your intentions when you sent it to me. I have no way of knowing what your intentions were because you didn't indicate any!

C. Cheri, sometimes it feels like you have a very critical spirit and a very stilted view of what Christianity is all about.

i. I watched you be downright cruel to Diana Hegel. Isn't how we treat others part of our Christian walk?

ii. Do you remember the song *Amazing Grace* that made the hit charts several decades ago? I mentioned that it was such a beautiful song and meant so much to me. Your comment was "Yeah, and she was pregnant with some guy's baby when she recorded that. Not very Christian, was it?" I was dumbfounded that you had missed the whole point of the song.

iii. You have done some things that disturb me. For example, when you moved out of the rental house in Lancaster, you chose to take the landlord's coffee table because you said he had treated you unfairly. To me, that was stealing, no matter how badly he treated you.

iv. Your response to being hurt by "cautions" from your parents and grandma was to be defensive, prideful and to treat us all with contempt. Those responses did not show evidence, to me, of a Christ-like attitude.

v. It feels like you have chosen to punish the family for past hurts. Are you not willing to trust God to take care of things and mete out "punishment" if it is necessary? It appears you feel that "getting even" is a viable option for Christians.

D. Your claims that you have less money and are poorer than the rest of us don't seem valid. None of us built an expensive 6000 square foot home. I suspect you make more money than I do. Our job is to live within our means, no matter what God has blessed us with.

E. We tread so carefully around your feelings, Cheri, but it feels like you do not consider ours. For example, when you and Ralph decided to renew your wedding vows, you told mom the date it would probably be, never mentioned it again and then called her that afternoon asking her if she was coming (she was astonished it was still scheduled for that day since she had heard nothing further). You did not invite Brent and me at all. We try to remain friendly and caring. We still try to include you in the family, but you exclude us at every turn. It feels like all we get in return for our continued efforts to include you is a cold shoulder. Continually being greeted coldly in person, in cards, and on the phone (when I tell you it's me, you say "yeah?") is getting very old. Over the years, in cards you send and in your response letter to me last month, you did not sign "love, Cheri," but just "Cheri." That speaks volumes to me.

Are you aware how frustrated I was by something you did while I was still living in Lancaster? You told me repeatedly that you wanted me to "have" your old stereo cabinet. Then after I'd had it for a few weeks, you wrote and told me you wanted $50 for it. I was dumbfounded. I didn't have $50, but managed to scrape it together to keep the peace. Had you stated a price up front, I would have turned it down. After the fact, I was stuck. I felt you took advantage of me. But rather than stir up hard feelings, I chose to pay you and remain silent.

F. The family has never felt welcome in your home. Except for the family photo day, (which we all appreciated), you never invite us to your home. You bowed out of hosting family dinners years ago. We do not feel welcome to call you and do not feel welcome in your life in general. That feeling carried over to our response about coming to the hospital to visit Ralph. My perception (which may be incorrect) is that you set parameters for how much contact you want from us. I did what I could for you and Ralph within the parameters you appear to have set. I tried to show you and Ralph my love and support by showing interest in you and your family, bringing you dishes of food when you might need them, sending Ralph cards, praying for both of you, and stopping to see you when I was in the area. Because those actions evidently didn't meet your definition of caring and empathy, they were unacceptable. Mom (in a wheelchair) and Dad went to visit Ralph in Fort Wayne and Dad went up other times by himself. He spent several hours sitting with you during one of Ralph's surgeries, but all you remember is that he advised you to go home. He did so because he was concerned about YOUR health. That sounds like empathy to me. Brent called and asked if he could visit, but you told him no—had you forgotten that? Since I believed you didn't want too much contact from me, I kept up-to-date on Ralph's condition through Mom and Dad. They told me what information you had shared with them. None of those actions seem to have registered with you as empathy.

G. Help me understand why you can offer unsolicited advice, but I can't. When I met with you to tell you about Amanda (in Warsaw a few years ago), it was simply to clear up what I guessed you were incorrectly thinking about her (that she had gotten pregnant and I sent her away). I simply wanted to explain to you about all the years of hell we had gone through and help you understand her mental problems (which she inherited from her birth father). I was not asking for advice. I felt no empathy from you. Instead of saying, "Oh, Becky, I'm so sorry this has happened. Is there anything I can do?" (or something to that effect), you just told me all the things I had probably done wrong (which felt like you were saying her problems were my fault) and made suggestions about what I should do.

I never sought advice from you about what college I should attend, if I should marry Rob, if I should wear my hair long at age 30, if I was too loud, or making too much noise, but you and Ralph freely gave me your opinion on all those issues. When I got cancer, you didn't empathize; you just told me all the things I should do. You did have experience with that situation, and your comments were valuable, but your approach put me off. It appeared to me that you were "taking charge" and telling me what to do.

III. Larger Family Issues

A. I believe the issues between us are a reflection of the larger dynamics in the family. Years after the fact I learned that when you wanted to marry Ralph, Grma Faye (who adored you) and mom and dad, tried to caution you. They didn't say that if you married him, they would disown you or fail to support you in any way. It appears to me that you haven't forgiven Mom and Dad or Grma Faye for trying to caution you. Aren't parents supposed to offer advice and voice concerns to their children? But you seem to have taken those cautions very badly. Your statement that "there is no excuse for the way we were treated" seems very telling. Loved ones cautioned you, that is all. In other words, it seems that while mere cautions were given, you perceive that as "mistreatment." The family has treated you well and been accepting of your marriage. Is my perception accurate that you haven't been able to put that caution behind you? It seems like you are still resentful of their voiced concerns and are still trying to prove they were wrong to caution you.

B. Please hear this—we do not dislike Ralph. He has many wonderful qualities. We do not care for some of his actions and attitudes, however. I'll just mention one here. He never apologized for burning down grandpa's barn and let dad take full blame for it in the paper.

C. Mom and Dad have wanted peace in the family for years but don't quite know how to go about getting it. They have tried to talk to you about their concerns, Cheri, but your hurt feelings seem to have prompted a defensiveness that is hard to penetrate. You have hurt us deeply, too, but we try not to let that dictate how we respond to you. However, you let your hurts dictate how you respond to us.

D. You claim you have separate issues with mom and dad. But I suspect those issues have the same root. Our parents don't have a deceitful or mean bone in their bodies. They have been more than generous with you over the years, despite your mistreatment of them. It breaks my heart to see the way you choose to treat them. However, resolving your issues with them is a matter between you and them.

E. Mom spent months in the Wabash hospital. You work less than a mile from there, but chose not to stop and see her on a regular basis. Brent and I frequently drove four hours to spend time with her. It hurt mom and dad that you practically ignored them during that difficult time. You allowed them to sit at home alone last Thanksgiving (Mom wasn't physically able to make it to Indy), rather than invite them to your home. It appears to me the only time you pay any attention to them is when you want or need something. Otherwise you ignore them. That hurts me greatly. Brent and I make great efforts to call them frequently, visit them and show interest in their lives. You live the closest to them, but choose to ignore them the most. That hurts.

F. I'll make one more observation and then will move on. It seems you view this family situation as something that developed when you married Ralph. I view it differently. This has been a lifelong situation. The whole family learned to be cautious around you, even as a child and teenager, but we made the best of things to keep the peace. You had a wonderful, loving, supportive family. Before you were married, you even told Ralph that your family was "different" (implying "better") than his. It seems that after you were married for a few years, you adopted his view of family and developed a warped view of yours. You put up defensive walls and have never let them down. It seems to me it was your choice to disassociate from the family and treat us poorly to get even for your hurt. To justify your perceived hurt, you ignored Grma Faye during the last years of her life, when you were the only one who didn't have to call long distance to check on her living alone. She was crushed. You are ignoring your parents. Your children have seen this modeled. I sincerely hope they don't treat you the way you have treated your parents.

In a further effort to be open and honest with you, I want you to know that I told mom and dad you responded to my letter, but gave them no details. They had asked me frequently if you responded and I felt I had to at least tell them that much. I hope that honors your request.

IV. Suggestion

I'm mindful of the scriptural mandate from Matthew 18 for resolving differences. We have tried to sort this out between us, but now I'd like to take the next step. Because our relationship is important to me (and I hope it is to you, too), I'd like to make a suggestion. Could just the 2 of us go to counseling to talk things out with a neutral person? I know it won't be pleasant for either of us, but I'd like to address things openly so we can begin to accept and work productively with our differences and heal our relationship.

I went online and found a Christian counselor at the Wabash Friends Church that I would be comfortable with. I am willing to take a day off work, drive down there to meet with him and you and split the $100 fee for each session with you. My insurance will not cover this, so it would be out of pocket, but it would be worth to me if it could help restore our relationship. I'd hope you still value a relationship with me.

I hope and pray you will give my observations some consideration without taking offense. Your letter prompted me to do some soul searching to see if your comments about me have validity. I seek to grow and improve. I hope you do, too, and that my comments will prompt you to do some soul searching, too.

I do pray for our relationship, Cheri, and I pray for you and Ralph (I always have). I'd like to hear back from you whether or not you want to work with a counselor. If you choose to, I will be happy to make the arrangements. Please let me know.

Love (and yes, I do love you),

Becky

APPENDIX D

Christian Symbolism in the *Harry Potter* books
by Dr. Rebecca Wilson

BE WARNED—If you have not read all the books, this will give things away! Proceed at your own caution!

The Harry Potter books start out as children's books, but by the third or fourth book become adult novels.

Many of my observations are supported by John Granger. He is known as the "Dean of Harry Potter Scholars." Some observations are his alone (citation included). Some are mine alone.

Granger, J. (2006). *Looking for God in Harry Potter* (2nd Ed). USA: Tyndale House

Granger, J. (2008). *The Deathly Hallows Lecture* (2nd Ed.). Allentown, PA: Zossima Press.

Rowling, J.K. (1997–2007) *Harry Potter* Series. New York: Scholastic.

Wilson, R. (2015). Children's Literature class. Bethel College: Mishawaka, In.

Some background: John Granger is a conservative Christian. He and his wife home schooled all seven(?) of their children. He wouldn't let them read the Harry Potter books because he had heard about the witchcraft. But one day his daughter was given a H.P. book at a party. He told her he would read it first so he could explain to her why she couldn't read it. He fell in love with the books and became an outspoken authority on the books. His research makes him a world authority on them.

Note: To those Christians who object to the use of magic and witchcraft, John Granger (2006, p.4-7) points out that there are two kinds of magic:
1. <u>incantational</u> (meaning to "sing along with" or "to harmonize")

2. <u>invocational</u> (meaning to "call in" demonic participants or powers) There is NO invocational sorcery in the Harry Potter books. <u>Not once</u> do the characters call in evil spirits. "The magic in Harry Potter is exclusively incantational magic in conformity with both literary tradition and scriptural admonition." (Granger, p. 7)

The Harry Potter series is the story of Christ, complete with Biblical figures which represent a God figure, Mary and Joseph, Herod, Satan and his fallen angels, the snake, Judas, the Holy Spirit, disciples, Pharisees and Sadducees, the prodigal son, Christ's death and resurrection, Bible verses, blood sacrifice, and the mark of the beast!

While the H.P. movies are O.K., remember they were produced by Hollywood and therefore the Christian themes are subverted. The books have much more depth and better explanations. Read the books first! Author J.K. Rowling admitted on the TV interview with Meredith Vieira (after the last book was published) that there is a religious theme to the Potter series and claimed she is a person of faith. She kept quiet about the Christian theme in her books (until after the last book was published) because non-Christians would have stopped reading them.

Rowling did not name the characters in her books at random! She pulled names from Latin, literature and mythology to represent certain character attributes.

The names James and Lily have significance—Joseph, foster-father of Jesus in the Bible, was the father of JAMES; Virgin Mary is a LILY (White Flower symbol of unsullied purity; Western Christian Art and some Eastern Orthodox Icons depict the white lily in the Archangel Gabriel's hand when announcing that Mary would conceive a child, Jesus). (Granger, 2006)

Hermione's name is the feminine form for "Hermes", another name for "Mercury." Her initials Hg are the chemical sign for mercury. Her parents are dentists (who make fillings with mercury). Ron's middle name is "Bilious", a synonym for "choleric", or hot and dry. "Mercury is the feminine and intellectual pole, sulphur is the masculine, choleric aspect, and their catalytic work is antagonistic, hence their being called the 'quarreling couple.'" (Granger, 2008, p. 26).

Most of the spells Rowling created have a Latin based meaning. None are real spells used in witchcraft.

The claims that children are being drawn to witchcraft as a result of the H.P. books was touted by Wickens! It has not proven to be true.

The words used to summon a Patronus—"Expecto patronum"—are derived from Latin words meaning "I await a defender"—the role of the Holy Spirit. (Granger, 2006).

The books contain <u>strong</u> battles between right and wrong, good and evil.

One of the portals between the muggle world and the magical world is King's Cross station—the cross of the King—where heaven and earth, eternal life and eternal death meet.

Dumbledore is the God figure (wise, fatherly, all knowing, patient, calm, loving, letting Harry choose, just as God lets us choose). He devised the ultimate plan for defeating Voldemort (Satan)—sacrificing Harry, whom he loves—just as God devised the ultimate plan to defeat Satan by sacrificing his beloved Son. He let Jesus choose to participate in the plan, just as Dumbledore let Harry choose.

Harry Potter is the Christ figure, selected to fight evil—Voldemort—for the salvation of the wizarding world, just as Christ was selected to fight evil for the salvation of the human world. John Granger feels Harry is the "everyman" figure instead of the Christ figure.

Harry suffers mocking and ridicule from those in the wizarding community who don't understand Dumbledore's plan just as Christ suffered ridicule from those of his day who didn't understand God's plan.

Just like Christ, Harry has his faithful followers, even if they don't always understand what Harry is trying to do.

The name "Potter" smacks of Christ—He is the "potter," I am the clay.

Gryffindor's flag contains a lion—one of the symbols for Christ.

The *Harry Potter* books are sprinkled with symbols for Christ—the phoenix, the Gryffindor lion, the philosopher's stone, the white stag, the hippogriff, etc. (Granger, 2008).

The Phoenix is a symbol of Christ. An "order" is usually a religious group. Therefore, the Order of the Phoenix symbolizes a religious group.

Voldemort is the evil Satan figure, trying to win followers, trying to overcome the world, trying to master death, trying to be the sole power in the world.

Fawkes is the comforting Holy Spirit figure. His cry brings comfort and balm to those who hear it. His tears have healing powers. He comes when loyalty to Dumbledore is shown, just as our loyalty to God (accepting Him) brings us the presence of the Holy Spirit.

The Patronus is also symbolic of the Holy Spirit—interceding for us against evil, defending us against forces which can destroy.

Ron might represent the disciple Simon Peter. Both were impetuous, both denied their leader, and then both came back stronger and more passionate than before.

Hermione might represent the studious writer, Luke.

The theme of prejudice is prevalent in the Harry Potter books, just as in the Bible. Voldemort and his followers lead the prejudice against muggles, mudbloods (half -breeds) elves, goblins, house elves, and blood traitors, anyone who isn't "pure blood," That is comparable to the prejudice against Jews, Samaritans, women, and others who are believed to be second class citizens in the Bible. Christ came to set us free from such prejudice, just as Harry and his followers are trying to rid the wizarding world of such prejudice.

Just as Herod and Satan sought to kill the infant Christ, whose victory over evil and gaining of the rod of power was prophesied, so Voldemort sought to kill the infant Harry because it was prophesied that Harry would be his downfall.

Several times in the *Harry Potter* books we see a character throw his arms wide, like Christ on the cross, when they are protecting someone or sacrificing themselves for another…Lily Potter, Xeno Lovegood, and Remus Lupin.

Voldemort was originally a part of the "normal" wizarding world (just as Satan was part of heaven), but he chose to separate himself from that just as Satan chose to separate himself from God. Voldemort became the epitome of evil (like Satan) and gathered his followers (Death Eaters) to do his bidding, like Satan gathered his fallen angels around him.

Harry was born a wizard, and at the age of 11, stepped into the wizarding world to begin his true calling in life. Christ was born a human and about the age of accountability (11 or so?) stepped out into the world to begin his true calling on earth.

Harry's ability to "Love" is what distinguishes him from Voldemort, and ultimately saves him, just as Christ's ability to love saved us.

Professor Quirell (being possessed by Voldemort) couldn't touch Harry (without damage) because of the love that was in Harry's skin, just as the love of Christ abides in us.

Voldemort (evil) doesn't understand love and underestimates its power. What he does not understand, he does not value, just as Satan does not understand or value the power of love.

Harry's connection to Voldemort (his ability to know what evil is thinking and feeling) is like our conscience and our constant inner struggle between good and evil.

Dumbledore implies there is an afterlife when he says, "To the well organized mind, death is merely the next big adventure." (Rowling).

The use of the snake, Nagini, to represent evil, smacks of the serpent in the Garden of Eden. Nagini is Voldemort's closest friend and contains one of the fragments of his soul. The serpent in the Garden was Satan.

The Ministry of Magic represents the Pharisees and Sadducees—they are more concerned with appearances than true actions which will help others. They are more concerned about how others will view them than they are in solving problems. They refuse to believe evil is active in the world (Voldemort's return). They just want to keep up appearances.

The Order of the Phoenix represents the Disciples/Apostles. Many of the Order of the Phoenix members die in their fight against Voldemort. Most of the disciples died in their fight to establish God's kingdom on earth.

George having his ear cut off smacks of the soldier in Gethsemane having his ear cut off by Peter.

Harry's frustrations with Dumbledore (feeling abandoned by him in the last book) are like Christ feeling abandoned by his Father during the crucifixion.

We are protected by Christ's blood sacrifice as Harry's mother's blood sacrifice protected him, and Harry's sacrifice then protected the other followers (Voldemort's spells did not "stick" after Harry's death).

Harry is referred to as "the chosen one"—It is his task alone to battle Voldemort, just as Christ was our "Chosen One." Harry recognized that it had to be him who struck down evil—no one else. The Old Testament prophecies identify Christ as the one who will overcome Satan, just as the prophecy by Professor Trelawney identified one who would overcome Voldemort.

After one discussion with Dumbledore, Harry realizes he is not being forced to fight Voldemort, but that he has made the <u>choice</u> to fight him. For Harry, that makes all the difference. It is his choice—just as Christ made the choice to fight evil for us.

After Ron abandons Harry and Hermione, he tries to return to them, but is unable to do so. He only manages it after the light from the deluminator enters him and leads him back—representative of the light of Christ leading us to God?

Snape is probably the most confusing and complicated figure in the *Harry Potter* books. He acts much like Judas. Judas worked to assure that Christ would be sacrificed; Snape helped keep Harry safe until it was time to be sacrificed. However, Snape is also the antithesis of Judas. Judas pretended to be good while working towards the evil. Snape pretended to be evil while working towards the good. Judas betrayed Christ (whom Harry represents), Snape betrayed Voldemort (the Satan figure). Judas's death was without redemption, he had remorse but no redemption. Snape's death was full of redemption, as was his life.

Snape was as much "Dumbledore's man" as Harry was. Harry represents the beloved son, while Snape represents the faithful agent. Snape was, in many ways, the figure of Michael the archangel (Jude 9) battling behind the scenes directly with Satan/Voldemort. Snape was a death eater and much like Voldemort, so much so that he could pass as a high agent of Voldemort. Michael and Satan are both angelic in nature, but their choices placed them on opposite sides in the battle between good and evil.

Snape, while seemingly evil and full of anger, made a choice for love, but did not want anyone to know. He chose to work behind the scenes to help Dumbledore and Harry because of his love for Lily. His story is one of sin, remorse, repentance and in the end, redemption.

While external similarities exist between them, Harry is totally different in nature than Voldemort. Christ is totally different in nature than Satan.

The number seven comes up repeatedly---there are seven members on a Quidditch team, Voldemort made seven Horcruxes, there are seven years in magical education, they made seven Harry clones to escape Privet Drive, there were seven books in the series, Harry symbolically "dies" seven times, etc.

Harry dies a figurative death in every book. He went "underground" in each book (representing death) and rose again each time—jumping down the bathroom opening to find the Sorcerer's Stone, sliding down the tunnel to the Chamber of Secrets, digging Dobby's grave, going down the secret tunnel under the Whomping Willow, locked in the basement at Malfoy Manor, in the graveyard during the Tri-Wizard's tournament, visiting the lowest level in the Ministry of Magic to fight the Death Eaters, subterranean cave and lake, and dying at Voldemort's hand. (Granger, 2008).

A cycle (ten steps) is repeated in each book—starts at Privet Drive, then magical escape, mystery, crisis, underground, battle, loss and death, resurrection, Dumbledore denouement, King's Cross. (Granger, 2008). Symbolic of the Christian life?

Godric's Hollow has a statue of James, Lily and baby Harry, which Harry and Hermione find on Christmas Eve. Does it represent the nativity scene?

The inscription on the graves of James and Lily Potter is symbolic of the way Christians have victory over death. "The last enemy that shall be destroyed is death"—straight from I Corinthians 15:26.

The inscription on the graves of Dumbledore's mother and sister is "For where your treasure is there will your heart be also,"—straight from Matthew 6:21.

Jesus (Harry) is the "THE BOY WHO LIVED"—the Baby that Herod/Voldemort was trying to kill, but "who lived."

There is a definite similarity to the Grail-type quest in the search for the Hallows.

The imagery of the Trinity is unmistakable (Undefeatable, all powerful wand = God; Invisibility Cloak = Holy Spirit which gives you power to defeat things you couldn't alone; stone = Christ, the stone that the builders rejected)

Whoever possesses the three Hallows will be the "Master of Death." What Harry learned is that being Master of Death doesn't mean you won't die; it just means the power of death has no hold on you. There are worse things than dying.

For a while, Harry is sorely tempted to pursue the Hallows instead of following orders to find the Horcruxes, much like Christ was tempted by Satan to pursue earthly riches and fame instead of fighting evil.

Harry made a conscious decision not to pursue the Hallows, and to follow Dumbledore's plan, like Christ made a conscious decision to follow God's plan. It was a struggle of faith—a struggle we all face.

The Weasley family's struggle with Percy's desertion and then being reunited with him resembles the story of the Prodigal Son. The change in the character Kreacher is symbolic of the transforming love of God.

Harry is a very forgiving character (even though he has a temper!). He doesn't give up on people. He constantly gives people second chances, even those he hates—he welcomed Ron back after he deserted Harry and Hermione, he rescued Griphook even though he was untrustworthy, he rescued Draco and Goyle in the Room of Requirement and then saved Draco's life again a few minutes later, and he even gave Voldemort a chance to repent in the final battle. Christ constantly gives us chances to repent.

Even though Harry was angry with and hated some people, he never wanted them to be harmed. He wanted to kill Sirius Black (before he knew who he was), but couldn't carry it out. He tried to kill Wormtail, but was unable to do so because of his conscience. He wanted to punish Bellatrix LaStrange for killing Sirius, but didn't have enough hatred to make the cruciatus curse work. He felt terrible when he accidently injured Draco Malfoy with the Sectumsempra curse. When he was pursued by Death Eaters he used a disarming curse, never a killing curse—"I won't blast someone out of my way just because I can! That's Voldemort's job." These are all examples of a loving spirit that can't carry out evil.

Hermione claimed that Harry had a "saving people thing." So did Jesus!!! And aren't we glad He did!

Harry was constantly alert to ways to solve problems, save those in danger and help those less fortunate—certainly a characteristic Christ displayed.

The Death Eaters were branded with Voldemort's symbol (a snake), much like the Bible tells us the "mark of the beast" will signify those who follow evil.

Dumbledore's grave was broken open, just like Christ's was.

Harry's emotional walk into the woods represents Christ's emotional struggle in Gethsemane.

Harry willingly walked into the woods to give up his life to Voldemort without resistance, as Christ willingly gave up his life for us without resistance.

As Harry walks into the woods to meet Voldemort and his own death, he is surrounded by his deceased loved ones in spirit, much as we are surrounded by a "cloud of witnesses." He talked to his loved ones just as Christ talked to his Father. Christ knew Father God would walk with him up until he was nailed to the cross, just like Harry's loved ones walked with him until his death.

Harry asked his loved ones if they would stay with him and they said they would until the end, just like Christ promised, "I will be with you always, even to the end of the age."

References to God and heaven are sprinkled throughout but never addressed overtly. Even in the last battle, Harry and Voldemort direct their best spells "to the heavens" in the hopes that they will be effective.

Harry is mocked by the Death Eaters and Voldemort before he dies—they call him the "Boy Who Lived," just like Christ was mocked before his death and called the "King of the Jews."

After Voldemort "kills" Harry, the connection between Harry and Voldemort is broken, much like our connection to Satan is broken because of Christ's death for us. Voldemort no longer has a hold over Harry, just like Christ's death frees us of the hold Satan has over us.

When Harry "dies" he goes to "King's Cross" station! The "Cross of the King"—what a wonderful analogy!

In King's Cross station, "time" does not seem to exist, just like it won't for us in heaven.

In King's Cross station, Harry was naked, much like we will transition into the next life with nothing by our character.

The whimpering figure under the chair in King's Cross station is the splintered portion of Voldemort's maimed soul. Harry has finally had that portion of Voldemort removed from him just as our souls are cleansed from any claim Satan has on our souls by Christ's death. The connection to Satan is broken.

Dumbledore tells Harry there is no longer anything that can be done to help Voldemort's whimpering soul—just like once we die, the choices we made in life will no longer be reversible.

In King's Cross station, Harry and Dumbledore discuss Harry's options of "going on" (implying there is life after death) or returning to life.

Harry chooses to return to life, to finish the job of conquering Voldemort, just like Christ returned to life to destroy eternal death for us. This is the resurrection story!!!!!

Dumbledore reinforces that there is a non-physical (spiritual) realm when he says, "Just because it's happening in your head doesn't mean it isn't real."

The first person to encounter Harry after he returns to life is Narcissa Malfoy---one of his former enemies. The first person to encounter Christ after his resurrection was Mary Magdalene—a former enemy in that she was a "house" for seven demons, which Christ cast from her. Voldemort had split his soul into seven parts.

When Narcissa checks Harry for a heartbeat, her nails pierce Harry—symbolic of the nails that pierced Christ.

Harry's body is subjected to jeering and physical abuse, like Christ suffered beatings, torture and humiliation.

After Harry's return to life, Voldemort's spells have minimal effect on the crowd at Hogwarts. He no longer has the power over the masses because they are covered by Harry's sacrifice.

After Harry pretended to still be dead (in Hagrid's arms), he finally covers himself with the cloak and "disappears" for a while until it is time to reveal himself again in the Great Hall, symbolic of the time Christ disappeared from the tomb until he was seen again.

When Harry came out from under the cloak, the crowd cried, "He's alive!" much like Christ's followers cried, "He's alive," after Christ rose again.

Remorse (repentance) is the only thing that could help Voldemort turn from his evil ways –just like for us, having remorse for our sins is the only thing that will save us and the beginning of salvation. No one is beyond the hope of salvation through repentance. Snape, Percy, Grindelwald and Scrimgeour all took advantage of that repentance, but Voldemort didn't—he failed to take advantage of the hope held out to him.

After Voldemort's death, in the Great Hall, house tables are no longer used to separate the groups. Everyone sits mixed together—pure blood and mudbloods alike. "For you are all sons of God through faith in Christ Jesus. For all of you who were baptized into Christ have clothed yourselves with Christ. There is neither Jew nor Greek, there is neither slave nor free man, there is neither male nor female; for you are all one in Christ Jesus." Galatians 3:26-28

When the battle is won, Harry needs to retreat under the cloak for some peace and quiet, and invites Ron and Hermione to join him, as Christ did frequently with his beloved disciples—he felt a need to retreat from the masses.

Harry never uses a killing curse on Voldemort (in the graveyard or in the final battle), but lets him die at his own hand (killing curse rebounding on himself) just as Christ did not seek to destroy those who wanted him dead. Harry is referred to as everyone's "savior" after he battles Voldemort, just as Christ is our Savior for battling Satan.

Satan may be powerful, but he is clueless what love can do and we are snatched from his grip by love, something he cannot understand.

The blood sacrifice of God's loved one, Jesus, saves us from eternal death. The blood sacrifice of Harry's mother saved him from death. Harry's sacrifice saved the wizarding world from death.

Love is the ultimate victor over evil! What a message!

Joanne Rowling created a magical parallel world as an engaging and entertaining way to convey a profoundly Christian message. It helps us see the Christ story afresh with new eyes.

How tragic that the very one who played Harry Potter, the Christ figure (Daniel Radcliffe), doesn't believe in God and sees no value in faith/religion. There are none so blind as those who will not see!